BEST SEAT IN THE HOUSE

John Beland

DEDICATION

This book is dedicated to my brothers Bob, Jim, Tom and Joe, as well as to my children Sarah, Jessie, Jennifer, Tyler and Chris and to my parents Clib and Celine Beland who allowed me the freedom to pursue my dream against the advice and warnings of everyone around them.

Also, this is for my dear sister Susan, who was always there for me rain or shine, throughout all the years all the hills and valleys of my crazy career. And finally, to my muse, Lois Fletcher who plucked me out of the dark Troubadour stairwell in 1967 and gave me a career. I hope I made them proud. That's all I really ever wanted to do in the first place. They inspired me then as they inspire me now.

But most of all for my Pauline

John Beland

CONTENTS

John Beland

ACKNOWLEDGMENTS

So many people are responsible for my career. I could boast and brag that I achieved success solely by the sheer weight of the talent I possessed, but that would be a gross fabrication. The truth is that many factors played into my journey: luck, guardian angels, and the times. But at the forefront of it all were friends who took me under their wings, guided me, taught me, took a chance on me and gave me the important breaks I badly needed. Because I followed their advice and faithfully listened to their words of wisdom the planets and the stars aligned perfectly, providing an easy road map for me to follow as I navigated my way through a forty-plus year career. Thank you, Universe. To those who helped me along the way I am forever grateful. Some names will forever stand out in my heart such as Carmen James, Gregory Peters, Dexter Coughlin, Charlotte Irons, Robert DeMars, Lois Fletcher, Dan Dalton, Gib Guilbeau, Jimmy Bowen, Johnny Tillotson, Larry Murray, Ken Mansfield, Dewayne Blackwell and many others. I also must thank the many artists who allowed me to play a part in their amazing careers, whether it be in the recording studio or on tour: Stars like Linda Ronstadt, Arlo Guthrie, Johnny Tillotson, Kris Kristofferson, The Bellamy Brothers, Kim Carnes, Mac Davis, Dolly Parton, Ricky Nelson, The Flying Burrito Brothers, Bobby Bare and many more. To all these talented folks I'm humbly grateful.

INTRODUCTION

Ever since I can remember, all I ever wanted to do was to play the guitar. I don't know what it was about the instrument that reached out and grabbed me at such a young age. But I can still remember being no more than five or six and stopping whatever I was doing and turn my attention to the TV every time an act with a guitar appeared on the screen. Les Paul and Mary Ford, Homer & Jethro, George Gobel and of course Elvis. And when the Everly Brothers exploded it was all over for me. I started cutting pictures of guitars out of the Sears catalog and stuffing them safely away in my jean pockets, much to the frustration of my mother and father. Every time mom did the laundry she would find crumpled up pictures of guitars in my jean pockets. It had become an obsession, an affliction (of sorts) and a pipe dream all rolled up into one incredible fantasy.

But it didn't take long before the fantasy became something of a reality to me. A calling of sorts. I hadn't a clue that I would wind up where I did. I never dreamed that I would ever leave the confines of my little town and wind up at the corner of Hollywood & Vine thousands of miles away. The idea of becoming a world-famous musician was as farfetched as traveling to the moon or the Cubs winning the World Series. After all, name one famous musician who has ever come from my neck of the woods. Hometown, Illinois wasn't exactly the music mecca of the entertainment industry.

I was just another tiny fish in a sea of wannabe guitar players from New York to Los Angeles all dreaming of fame, fortune and glory. What made me think that I was any better than them? Hell, my own high school music teacher, Mr. Pettibone, made it crystal clear that I was just another ignorant student with no desire but to sit in his class and count the minutes for the bell to ring. Some motivation.

What chance did I possibly have to break out of the little town I lived in and actually sit myself down, front row center, on an actual real-life recording date in Hollywood? About as much chance as following Christ's walk on the water. But it happened.

I really don't know how I ever landed where I did. All I remember is that in 1962 I was shuffling down the street I lived on back in Hometown, Illinois, headed home for dinner when a giant musical Tsunami came from out of nowhere and swept me away into a life I could never have imagined. Here's how it all began for me

1 MY LITTLE TOWN

Blink and you'll miss it. And in most cases, you'll barely find it on maps of the city of Chicago---but it's there. Sandwiched between the south suburban townships of Evergreen Park and Oak Lawn lies the tiny berg of Hometown, Illinois where I was raised. Back in 1951 my parents and I were one of the first families to settle into this lower middle class suburban town of cute little pastel duplex houses. Developer J.E Marion had built this small hamlet in 1950 primarily for returning G.I's who, with the help of the G.I Bill, could afford very reasonable housing with the help of Uncle Sam. Today Hometown has a population of around 5,000 but when we first arrived there were only a few hundred --- all white of Irish, Polish and Italian decent, and mostly Roman Catholic.

When we first moved into our house at 4152 West 90th Place, the Korean War was raging. Harry Truman was president. A loaf of bread was 16 cents. Gas was 19 cents a gallon. The Yankees beat the Giants in the World Series. A new TV show called "I Love Lucy" premiered. Valdimir Putin, Mr.T, George Strait and Liam Neeson were born. The top book was J.D Salinger's "Catcher in the Rye" and a radio disc jockey named Alan Freed first coined the term "Rock & Roll" in an effort to introduce black rhythm and blues to a broader, whiter audience. The top country music artist in America was Hank Williams.

People Are Moving Into . . .

Hometown U.S.A.

Charming New Community by Merrion

400 ADDITIONAL UNITS ARE NOW UNDER CONSTRUCTION

PRICED FROM **$8,850** VETS $250 DOWN

5 and 6-rm. ranch houses featuring— forced air and radiant heat —fully insulated. Living room, dining room combination—and complete landscaping. Model at 90th Place and Crawford. James P. Meade, Sales Agent. Phone SA 1-6777 or Oak Lawn 345.

J. E. MERRION & CO. (Not Inc.)
Developers of Prize-Winning Merrionette Manor

Ad for hometown illinois

9

My father's name was Clarence, but everybody called him "Clib" a nickname he picked up in the Navy while serving aboard the USS New Jersey during World War 2. We never figured out what the hell "Clib" meant but for the rest of his life that's what his closest friends and family called him. He was strikingly handsome, slim with a mop of black hair and an adoring smile. Besides cartooning, his other passion was dancing. He was a jitterbug expert and could really "cut a rug." Kind, funny and extremely talented, I adored him. Everybody did. Dad was a plumber who worked alongside of my uncle Wally and Grandpa Beland in the family business Beland Plumbing on Kedzie Avenue on the south side. He was also an amazing artist whose dream it was to become a professional commercial cartoonist one day, a dream that never materialized. Instead he opted for a steady pay check, crawling through other people's filth in the harsh Chicago elements in order to put food on the table for mom and me. A "real job" as my Grandma Foley would say. I still can remember finding little scraps of crumpled paper around the house, each filled with his doodling, his cartoons, remnants of a dream that faded with every year.

Dad

My mother's name was Celine, one of 6 kids born to my widowed grandmother Florence Foley. When mom was just about to make her first holy Communion, she was hit by a car and dragged down the street. The doctors at the hospital wanted to amputate her arm but my grandmother stood over my mom and kept them at bay until she could get a second opinion, which she did. My mother's arm was saved. She made her first Holy Communion from her hospital bed. Mom had the looks of a movie star. I'm not just saying that because she's my mom. She was a knockout! And she had a personality to match. She could do just about anything. Everyone loved her but no one as much as my old man. They were married in 1947. I was born July 24th, 1949, their first child. They named me John Edward, but as I grew everyone called me Jackie.

Mom

My life was always surrounded by music. The little kitchen radio in our house was always turned on until the evenings when my dad would switch on the tiny Motorola television housed in the big oak cabinet. My folks loved shows like Milton Berle, Your Show of Shows, Arthur Murray's Dance Party, Perry Como Show, just about anything that had music in it. Like I said earlier, my dad loved to dance. And even if he couldn't play a single instrument he could tear it up every bit as good as Fred Astaire or Gene Kelly, at least in my eyes. I can still remember him and my Aunt Collette jitterbugging on the sawdust floor of the beach side road house in Cedar Lake, Indiana where our family had a small cottage. The jukebox would blast out Fats Domino, Bill Haley, Johnny Ray, The Four Lads and Connie Francis as my dad would toss my aunt Collette around as if she was made of feathers. What a sight to see! And there I would be, my hands and face pressed up against the glass of the colorful Wurlitzer Jukebox watching the pancake discs changing from one song to another. Brenda Lee, Eddy Arnold, Les Paul and Mary Ford all filling up the room with magic that echoed across the lake like stones skimming across water. The neon lights of the big Wurlitzer flashed its colors like 4th of July fireworks as I stood right next to it mesmerized by the music, tapping my foot on the sawdust floor while mom and dad slow danced to Fats Domino's "Blueberry Hill." These were the golden days and all those musical seeds were being carefully planted and nurtured inside of me.

Like most kids in the early Fifties, I grew up with a Davy Crockett coon skin cap on my head, a Lone Ranger mask on my face, a pair of Mattell Fanner 50 cap pistols strapped around my waist with an endless supply of Saturday morning TV westerns to lose myself in. If it wasn't cowboys and Indians it was baseball, namely the Chicago White Sox. Aparicio, Fox, Landis, Miñoso, Lollar – the "Go-Go White Sox". Baseball cards littered my room and every room in the house. There were always plenty of things to keep a kid with a vivid imagination like mine occupied. If I wasn't knocking in the winning run for the White Sox, I was riding my bike through the nearby prairie chasing down the notorious Cavendish gang, cap pistols blazing away while humming the William Tell Overture.

Reach for the sky 1955

One Christmas, when I was six years old, I received a gift from my Aunt Delphine and Uncle Tony, a gift of profound significance. It was a cream-colored Davy Crockett guitar, and it wasn't a toy. It was a real guitar with six strings and a lariat red rope for a strap. I couldn't believe it! A real guitar! I remember walking around the house all night strumming it, nonstop, driving everybody berserk. Tactfully, my mom suggested that I play it out in the backyard where it would "probably sound much better." That night I slept with it. Opening my eyes throughout the night to make sure it was still there. How I loved that guitar. I kept it for the next few years never having a clue as to how to play it. Every time I tried my fingers would blister and it hurt like hell. Undaunted, I continued to play through the pain until my fingers started getting callouses allowing me to play for hours without the hint of pain. Holding the guitar in the proper position came as natural as learning how to walk. It felt natural, as if I was born with it. That guitar and I made an instant connection that affected my very soul.

Receiving my 1st guitar for Christmas

The years passed. By the start of the sixties we were now an expanded family. One by one it grew and grew, first my brother Bob, then my brother Jim, my sister Sue, brothers Tom and Joe. As for me, I was now a pre-teen and running with my pals and trying not to get into any serious trouble.

One of those friends was a curly headed brown eyed Italian kid from the other side of the railroad tracks where the trains used to roar through town a half a dozen times a day. His name was Carmen Auriemma. Carmen and I shared a mutual love for guitars. Though the other kids our age were into cars and girls, Carmen and I were hooked on Gibson guitars and Fender amps. We would hang out at Rossi's Music Store in the next town for hours, taking all the guitars down off the wall and playing them, all the while pretending that we were actually going to purchase one. Carmen and I would stand there drooling all day at the beautiful expensive Fender, Gibson and Gretsch guitars displayed in the store window, day dreaming about what it would feel like to own one of these gems. Yet, without a penny between us, the closest we could get to one of these beauties was to stand outside the music store and stare at all of them through the window. Then one-day fortune smiled in the form of thirty-five dollars. Carmen had badgered his parents daily to give him the money for a cheap Japanese Kingston Electric guitar he had seen at the music store. Finally, they caved in and gave him the money. He also found a cheap little amplifier to borrow and together we started learning how to play.

About a year earlier I had talked my dad into paying for a trial course on the guitar that Rossi Music was offering as a promotion. Lessons were only a dollar each for six weeks. The store also supplied you with a professional arch top Kay guitar. My dad thought it was just another "phase" but reluctantly agreed to forking over the six bucks thinking that by the sixth week I would have moved on to the next 'big thing." Wrong. I worshiped that Kay guitar the store loaned me. It was Sunburst and you could see yourself on the body if you turned it around. I used to drag that guitar with me across the prairie on my way home from the lessons, stopping every few yards to open up the case and just stare at it. Sometimes I'd sit alone by the creek and strum chords and pretend I was some famous rock and roll star like Ricky Nelson. I would sing to myself and strum away for hours at that prairie creek secure in knowing that not a soul could hear me, except the birds.

At the end of the six-week trial course my dad met with the owner of the music store, Mr. Rossi. To dad's shock Rossi said;

"Mr. Beland, your son shows a natural ability on the guitar and has excelled as a student. I strongly suggest you allow him to continue with his lessons." Dad was frozen still but looking at me through the corner of his eye.

"How much are these lessons going to cost me"? He suspiciously asked.
"The lessons are only $2.50, Mr. Beland. They're very affordable" answered Mr. Rossi with a big smile on his face.

My dad agreed to let me continue with the lessons, especially since the price was reasonable.

"However," said Mr. Rossi as he cleared his throat. "We do expect our students to provide their own guitars from this point forward. I personally feel John would excel on one of our Gibson models up on the wall."

My dad stepped closer to Mr. Rossi and very slowly said "How much is that going to cost me?"

"Well, Mr. Beland, that particular model sells for $400.00, and….."

"Four hundred dollars?" my dad yelled out for the whole store to hear. "What kind of racket is this?"

And with that my father grabbed my arm and dragged me out of the music store. As we pulled away in the family car I sat in the back seat looking out the rear-view window at the Mr. Rossi's shop as it shrank smaller and smaller and finally out of sight. "What kind of idiot does that guy take me for?" mumbled my dad as we headed back to Hometown. So much for my career as a famous guitarist, I thought.

But now Carmen and I had a real electric guitar to practice on and though it was a cheap $35.00 Kingston Japanese model, to us it was priceless. We spent nearly every free minute of the day and night huddled together in a friend's garage, passing the guitar back and forth to each other, working up new chords and trying to figure out how to play the songs we heard on the radio. Sometimes the temperature would drop below zero and we would only have a little space heater to keep us from freezing, but regardless of the brutal Chicago winter we persisted. Through the frigid winters and the scorching summers, we practiced day and night on that one little cheap Kingston guitar.

As the months rolled by I started to borrow guitars from

wherever I could find them. In some cases, I befriended other kids for the sole reason of borrowing their guitars. And in most cases I failed to return them when I promised leading to more than one confrontation. Carmen and I would attend all the Saturday night dances at the neighborhood teen canteen. That's when the local bands would play, bands like the Corvettes, Rudy and the Del Tones, the Contours etc. Carmen and I would stand right in front of the guitar players for the entire night, studying their fingers and pretty much intimidating and annoying the hell out of the poor guys who were playing guitar. The next day Carmen and I would share what we remembered from the night before, me with my borrowed guitars and Carmen with his cheapo Japanese Kingston. Soon we were getting pretty good, good enough for us not to have to rely on watching other guitar players at the teen dances.

But still I didn't own one; my folks just didn't have the money for something so silly. They had five other kids to support and times were starting to get a bit tough for my dad. In desperation, Carmen and I would recruit kids from around the neighborhood who owned guitars to join our fictional band. We would talk the kid into rehearsing in the garage with us and at the end of the night convince him to leave his guitar with us, instead of dragging it all the way home. Once our victim left the premises, Carmen and I would get to work on some serious rehearsing with two guitars instead of just one. Eventually the kids who owned the guitars would get wise and quit our make-belief group and we would start the scam all over again with a brand-new victim. We were pretty cruel.

The music scene was changing dramatically in 1963 and Chicago suddenly became ravenous for the new wave of rock and roll pouring in from England. Gone were the teen crooners so dominant on the radio for the past 5 years. The Bobby Vinton's, Bobby Rydell's and Frankie Avalon's were knocked right off the charts. Even my idols, The Everly Brothers and Ricky Nelson were swallowed up by the new British Invasion. And it all started with four long haired musicians from Liverpool, England called The Beatles. The Beatles? Really? I remember the night I first saw them on TV. They were part of a five-minute home movie that talk show host Jack Parr had made during a recent vacation to England. He featured a very rough clip of the Beatles with the segment intended as a comedy bit.

But as Parr joked away about their long hair and funny name I was mesmerized, frozen to the TV along with millions of other kids. It was a quick segment but long enough to affect a lot of young would be musicians such as myself who had never seen or heard anything like this band. Everything about them was impressionable, from their collarless grey suits, long hair and cool boots to their unique Gretsch, Rickenbacker and Hofner guitars. And unlike most pop acts of the day, the Beatles were a self-contained band with three lead vocalists. They were like a bolt from the blue. Until the Beatles appeared I listened to the radio like any other normal teenager, nice beat and catchy song. But when the Fab Four hit the airways I started listening to pop music in a whole different way. "That's what I want to do" I thought. "I want to do what the Beatles are doing."

"Someday I'm going to make a record" I would say to myself. But as I dragged my latest borrowed guitar home in the cold winter's snow, stopping at the railroad tracks that split Hometown right down the middle. I'd look down the line as far as I could see, imagining those rails taking me to faraway places like Hollywood or Nashville, where all the incredible music came from. I'd stare and wonder until my thoughts were suddenly shattered by a passing train ripping by, leaving me in its loud wake of wind and snow. "Yeah" I lamented "Just another fast train that never stops in Hometown --- Hell, it didn't even slow down. I'd shake off the snow as the train faded into the distance, pick up my guitar and shuffle off on my way home thinking, "Hollywood...fat chance. Nobody ever gets out of this nowhere town.

Discovering new chords

As the months flew by my passion for the guitar only grew, as my school grades plunged. I was failing everything, except for Art Class. In that I excelled. In fact, other than music my next passion was art, namely cartooning. I considered a career in it until the guitar came along and knocked that notion to the number two slot. My father had high hopes for my future as a cartoonist. No doubt because of his one dream in life of becoming a successful cartoonist himself. I had my own strip running in a local paper and my art teacher, Bob Dominiak, even approached my parents about helping me land my cartoons in high profile newspapers around Chicago. But it wasn't meant to be. With every day I picked up and played the guitar the desire of becoming a commercial cartoonist diminished, overtaken by my obsession for music.

Around this time, I also became interested in playing the Hammond B3 Organ, namely the one sitting in the choir loft in the back of our little church. I loved listening to the sound of it every Sunday at mass. It was so majestic and powerful. I just had to find out how it felt to actually sit behind one and play it. It just so happened that there was a window always left open in church when the priests closed down for the night, just big enough for me to crawl through. It was a bit scary climbing into a dark church where the only light came from the flickering candles at the altar.

Undaunted, I slipped through the window and made my way up the darkened isle, past the seemingly observing statues of the Virgin Mary and the saints till I got the choir loft. There it stood, the mighty Hammond B3 Organ with its mahogany, oak casing and ivory white keys with rows of huge wooden foot pedals beneath. I took a look around me, to see if the coast was clear. The priests and the nuns had all gone home leaving me there, in the back of the darkened house of the Lord perched behind the giant organ like the Phantom of the Opera. I held my breath as I reached over and switched on the start button. Suddenly the whole organ started shaking and a loud rumble of the motor started to reverberate around the building. I was panicked and expected the entire Hometown Police department to come bursting through the doors any second. But then the rumble and the roar finally settled down to a low hum and I was ready to start experimenting with the strange new instrument. I loved the sounds and the effects and power behind each key. I was determined to learn how to play it as much as I was determined to play the guitar.

After a few hours I left the way I came, slipping out the window into the night and on my way back home. Five times a week I repeated the same scenario, stealing away inside the church through the open window without the slightest interference from anyone. Soon I was playing songs on the organ and feeling at ease on it. I couldn't help but snicker knowing I was pulling a fast one on the priests whom I suspected would have excommunicated me for breaking into church and playing "Green Onions" on their revered instrument.

Many years later when my father was gravely ill he received a call from our old parish priest, Father Pat. With words of faith and support he brought comfort and peace to my ailing dad. At the end of the conversation however, he said this to my pop.

"Clib, we're all proud of young John's achievements in the music business. I know you and Celine are very proud of him. Please give him this message from me when you next speak with him. Tell young John that he wasn't fooling anybody by sneaking into the church and playing the organ. Father John and I purposely left the window open each night and quietly hid in the back room until he was finished with his playing. As Father John put it, "We preferred John sneaking into church to play the organ than stealing into someone else's car, like the other boys were doing." You can't get one past God.

By 1965 I was playing in a band with a few high school classmates of mine from the nearby town of Bridgeview. It was a good little band with a terrific singing drummer named Johnny Livigni. John was a great musician with an equally great voice and our band, called the Mods, was fairly popular at school. I was still borrowing guitars but lately I had acquired a big orange 4 pickup Japanese electric guitar on loan to me from one of our friends who had been drafted and was on his way to the Army. I promised to take good care of it until he came back. Until that day the guitar was all mine.

My big orange Japanese electric guitar.

The Mods played teen dances and private parties as well as bars in and around the Cicero Avenue area of Chicago. Al Capone's old stomping grounds. The pay was minimal and we usually played 4 sets a night of rock and roll and r&b material but it was a great way to develop yourself as a player. And it wasn't too bad having a few bucks in your pocket at the end of the night either.

One Friday I came home from school to find my mother waiting at the door for me. In her hand was an envelope containing five failure notices from school. She was livid.

"Wait until your father gets home young man" she scolded. "Get to your room and you can forget playing with that damned band of yours!"

I was panicked. Saturday was going to be a huge gig for us at the local YMCA Teen Dance just across the prairie from our house. Every kid in the area would be there. Not only that, but we had a gig this very Friday night at a local bar. I "had" to be there! I begged my mom but to no avail and headed to my room like a man headed for the gallows. I couldn't let the guys down. I had to be there that night or the band would lose the gig, money and all! I decided to make a jailbreak and slowly and quietly climbed out my bedroom window with my guitar, only to be met at the bottom by who else? My mother.

"Where in the hell do you think you're going?" she slowly said.

"Mom, I have to go to the gig. If I don't the guys will lose their money be in serious trouble! I have to go, please!"

My mom stood there silently thinking it over, all the while shaking her head back and forth.

"OK, you can go. But hear me and hear me good. You be sure to be back in this house by 10pm! Do you hear me?"

At that stage I would have agreed to French kissing Boris Karloff in order to make it to the gig.

"Thanks mom" as I gave her a big hug. "I promise I'll be back by ten!" and off I ran down the street to catch up with the guys.

Well, as it was, the last set the band played ended at 2am. By the time we packed up and got paid it was nearly four in the morning. It was around 4:30 when I was shuffling my way home down the street we lived on, dragging my guitar in tow. A cop car pulled alongside of me and shined a light in my face.

"Hey kid" said the officer, "where ya headed for this time in the morning?"

"I'm headed home. My band played a late gig tonight" I answered. The cop leaned out the window of his squad car and said "Are you Jack Beland?"

"Yeah, why?" I curiously answered

The cop smiled and started to pull away.

"I thought so" he said with a chuckle. "Good luck, kid"

I wondered why he was smiling. What was so funny anyway?"

I got to the front door of our house and took my shoes off so that I wouldn't waken anyone up, namely my parents. I opened the door slowly and as quiet as a church mouse I snuck inside, in one hand my guitar and in the other I held my shoes. Then, as I turned to close the door the lights suddenly came on. I dropped my guitar and shoes to see my mom and dad with their arms crossed waiting in the living room for me.

"Where in the hell have you been?" my dad bellowed out. "Your mother has been worried sick over you!"

"I was playing with the band and the last set wasn't until..."

"I don't want to hear it!" he roared. "Get yourself to bed and while you're at it, you can kiss that damned guitar of yours goodbye. You're finished with all this guitar crap. And I can guarantee it'll be a cold day in hell before you pick up another one!"

Well, my parents bark was always worse than their bite and the next day I was back playing with my band across the prairie at the YMCA. And what happened next was an image that remains in my heart today, one I carried with me through the years to the Hollywood Bowl, the Grand Ol' Opry and Carnegie Hall. As I stood under the stars playing my big orange guitar on the flatbed truck stage with my little band, I glanced over by the bushes and there I saw my mother and father peering out, watching their son perform. They never knew that I had spotted them. It was a secret I have kept in my heart to this day.

2 CALIFORNIA DREAMING

All the leaves are brown and the sky is grey
I went for a walk on a winter's day
I'd be safe and warm if I was in L.A
California dreaming on such a winter's day.

B y now I had a band and a girlfriend, Mary Hyland. It was all so innocent like Mickey Rooney and Judy Garland in the Andy Hardy movies. We went to concerts and local dances together, most of the times my dad drove us. The Chicago music scene was exploding all over the windy City and Mary and I were right in the thick of it, following the local bands as well as the Beatles, Stones, Dave Clark Five and the rest of the British invasion. When we would go to concerts and see big groups like the Yardbirds, I would stare at the band all night imagining what it would be like to be on tour with a famous group like that. Still imagining. Still wondering.

It was Christmas 1966 when my dad made an announcement at the table that would change all our lives. Without any warning, he simply said "By the way, mom and I have some exciting news." I thought it was going to be another "baby on the way" announcement. I continued eating dinner barely listening to dad's big news.

"We're going to be moving to California."

What? Did I just hear right?

Mom chimed in "Your Uncle John in California just offered dad a great job as an executive in his company! Isn't that exciting?"

The other kids were too little to grasp the news, but I did. Boy did I grasp it!

"I don't want to move!" I spoke up. "I have a band, and Mary and friends. I can't leave. We just can't leave Hometown!"

Dad and mom were fumbling for the right words, but I kept on, my voice filling with panic, fear and defiance.

"I won't go!" I shouted. "You can't make me leave everything and everyone just because of a new job! I won't go!" and I stormed off to my room and slammed the door. What was going to happen? Everything in my world would soon be a memory, friends, the band, Mary. This couldn't be happening!

My dad had reached wits end. Supporting six kids and a wife on meager paychecks from two back breaking jobs had put him up against the wall. It seemed that the only work available to him consisted of busting his ass. Surely there was a better way to provide. The answer came in the form of a phone call from my Uncle John, who was married to my mom's sister Aunt Elaine. They lived in sunny California where my uncle owned an office supply company south of Los Angeles. In a way, they were celebrities in the eyes of my mother's side of the family. Once a year they would blow into Chicago with their California tans and Hawaiian shirts and expensive clothes, throwing their money around on fancy restaurants and filling everyone up with tales of life in the Golden State where the streets are paved with gold. Mom's family ate it all up and I guess dad was envious as well shouldering a sense of inferiority. I couldn't stand them. They seemed nothing but blowhard phonies to me, but I kept my feelings to myself. Now, my uncle had offered my dad a job as an executive in his company. The pay was much higher than what he had been earning toiling away at two jobs. This was a chance for him to rise above being a manual laborer and work at a job where you didn't have to crawl through the mud and filth of others. It was a chance to make mom proud, which was ridiculous because she worshipped my father. But he had his pride and when my uncle called, dad jumped at the chance.

We were moving and that was that. After all those years of staring down the railroad tracks that split my little town in half and wishing I could live out where the music I loved was being made I suddenly changed my mind and started back peddling. I wanted no part of it. Hometown was my universe. I was born and raised there and had friends, a band and a girlfriend. Now that would all be behind me. I felt miserable. Sadly, I informed the guys in the band that I was moving. I told my girlfriend goodbye and that I would write to her every day. I joked and told everyone that maybe I would go to Hollywood and become a famous guitar player and have hit records and be on TV. Everyone laughed, of course. Everyone but me.

Nearly everybody in Hometown came to see us off at the train station that cold, snowy winter's day in 1967. Mom hugged her best friend Joan Johnson while dad tried to hold his own emotions as he said goodbye to his close friends Mr. Davies and Mr. Casey. "Don't worry Clib" Mr. Davies shouted out as we boarded the Super Chief. "I hear the streets are paved with gold out there! Good luck!"

We took our seats in the coach section as the train slowly pulled out of the station. My mom burst out crying as she cradled my baby brother Joe in her lap. My face pressed against the window, watching our friends and family slowly fade into the distance as we slowly pulled out of the train station. What was ahead? It was a haunting thought that I couldn't get out of my head. Soon, we were well on our way. Hometown was now a memory. Ahead was the unknown. I glanced back at my mom and dad embracing each other and knew that they were scared too.

So began our three day journey to California. For most of the trip I would stare out the window at the ever-changing landscape. I had never been out of Illinois except for our summer visits to the family cottage in Cedar Lake, Indiana. Now we were headed for the Golden State, the very place I had wished to see back when I stood on the train tracks back in Hometown. Now my wish had come true and we would soon arrive at the place I had imagined so many times.

After three days of rolling across farmlands, open plains and mountains we arrived at Union Station in Los Angeles where we were met by my Aunt Elaine and Uncle John and their family. They were a sight to see in their summer attire and tanned skin especially considering that we had left Chicago in the dead of winter. We all crammed into their station wagon for the hour drive to our new home in La Puente. I was surprised to see actual mountains topped with snow in the distance, and trees bearing real oranges. I thought "We're certainly not in Hometown, Toto."

We first stopped at my Aunt and Uncle's fancy house in the upper-class neighborhood of Hacienda Heights, not far from where our new house was. All the way there my uncle went on and on about southern California and all the economic opportunities that were everywhere. My aunt chatted non-stop with my mother like a skipping phonograph record. I was crammed into the back seat with these strange younger new cousins I had never met, silent and sulking and hating everything and everyone around me all the while wishing we were on our way back to Hometown. It didn't take long to find out that things weren't as bright and rosy as my relatives had led us to believe.

Although my uncle's family lived in a big expensive home in Hacienda Heights, we were going to be living in the next town over, the lower income community of La Puente. In fact, the house chosen by my aunt and uncle was little more than a small tract house on a crowded street just above the freeway. Something felt strange to me. "Why weren't we living in the same neighborhood my uncle and aunt lived in?" If dad was going to be an executive surely, we could afford it. Why were we living in this crappy town on this crappy street?

Our worst fears were realized when we found out that the "executive" job my dad had been led to believe was, in fact, that of a delivery boy. There was no executive position waiting for him in my uncle's company. Where in the world had that concept come from? The roof had caved in on us and we were virtually alone and on our own in a part of the country we knew nothing about. It was a desperate time. Many nights I would hear my dad crying in the other room, calling himself a failure to my mom. In her broken voice, she would try and console him, but the truth was they were both scared and broken, with six kids in tow. It tore my heart out to hear them. I was scared too.

To make matters worse, I had tried to run away from home back to Hometown. Each time my father would catch me and drive me back. I couldn't stand living in the crappy little house my aunt and uncle had dumped on us. I was lonely for my friends and girlfriend back in Hometown. The only escape outlet I had was a cheap little acoustic guitar I had brought with me from Hometown. I started writing songs about the depressing situation I was in. Not realizing it, my songwriting started to improve as the months went by. They certainly weren't potential hits, but the songs weren't half bad, and I kept it up daily, writing it all down on a legal pad. As rough and as terrible as these first songs were I found songwriting to be a catharsis for all the turmoil I was feeling during these hard times. It became a way for me to let off steam by putting my deepest thoughts on paper, and then to music instead of carrying them all around, festering inside my gut. Finally, I decided to act, to change direction and see if I could hitch a ride to Hollywood, about an hour and a half away. My plan was to leave in the morning when I would normally leave for high school and return by 4pm so my parents would think I was coming home from school. And that's just what I did.

I found a freeway on-ramp not far from my school. Stuck out my thumb and hitched a ride straight to Hollywood. It was simple. I knew nothing about Hollywood except for what I read in the magazines or saw on TV. But I remember how excited I was as I landed at the corner of Gower and Sunset and saw the iconic towering Hollywood sign towering above in the nearby hills.

There I was, standing directly in front of the famed Paramount Movie Studios main gate watching the people flooding in for work, each one receiving a nod of approval from the security guard. Dozens of actors, actresses, limos, trucks, cameramen and soundmen all headed inside the lot for another day of making motion pictures. I stood there in awe, wanting to get inside and catch the action and see how movies were made. Concealing myself, I simply pulled up my shirt and fell into the wave of workers parading in. The security guard had hardly looked up from his magazine, just waving anyone and everyone through. So, holding my breath I simply strolled right by him without detection. I was in! I walked around checking out the sets and the props and smiling at the actors passing by, some in full costume, Indians, German soldiers, cowboys, pirates, you name it. Like some make-belief city it buzzed with activity.

I noticed a big, windowless building with a metal door, and a big light above it. It looked a bit military, like a warehouse for jeeps and tanks. I looked to make sure the coast was clear and then opened the heavy door, slipping quickly inside. It was pitch-dark and as silent as a tomb, but I kept walking very cautiously, trying my best to not fall over anything in the dark. In the distance, I saw light and heard people shouting orders to each other. Moving closer, I saw a soundstage where they were preparing to shoot a scene. There were all these gorgeous dancers on a big white stairway, and in the middle, was someone I recognized. It was *Barbara Streisand* herself! She was in a wedding gown and pregnant, or at least she appeared that way. Someone yelled *quiet!* A loud clanging bell quickly rang, followed by music. Streisand walked down the stairs singing, flanked by dancers as the cameras moved all around and over her. It was an incredible sight to see! I would find out later that they were shooting the famous bride scene for the film Funny Girl.

I stayed in the shadows for hours watching take after take until I decided I had better keep watch on the clock in order to make it back home. I would need to be on time, appearing to be returning from just another day at school. What a day it had been! It wasn't just watching movies being shot that was exciting; just being in Hollywood felt right, as if *I belonged* there. Something was calling me, and I wasn't about to turn away.

For the next seventeen days, I followed the same routine, hitchhiking to Hollywood and then back. My folks hadn't a clue where I really was. Neither did the school. But all I knew was that I was feeling a sense of freedom and adventure, miles away from the grim realities of La Puente. I was in the town where dreams come true; where stars walked the streets, and rock and roll records were made. It was the epicenter of the universe.

Besides hanging all day at the Paramount lot, I also checked out other parts of town until I had a general idea of where I was at all times. Managing to locate some of the big record companies, I spent a lot of time in their lobbies, pretending I was waiting for someone or had an appointment. I'd stare at the framed album covers on the walls and wonder what it must have been like to be there when these records were recorded. At CBS Records I walked around staring at the framed albums of some of my favorite acts, like The Byrds, Bob Dylan, Paul Revere & The Raiders, and many, many, more.

Just down the street from CBS, at the corner of Vine Street & Sunset Boulevard, stood the biggest music store in town. At *Wallich's Music City* you could not only browse through all the latest releases, but also listen to them in one of their soundproof booths, each one with a turntable, and a set of headphones. *(Needless to say, a lot more than playing records went on in those booths.)* I'd spend hours thumbing through the record bins and listening to the latest releases from acts like The Grassroots, The Left Banke, the Bobby Fuller Four, The Monkees, the Turtles and of course the Beatles. But, for me, the most interesting part of Wallach's was the musical instrument department, a tiny little room with barely enough room to walk around. The counter took up half the space, filled with all high-end gear. All the top brand-name guitars would be hanging high on the wall behind the counter: Gibson, Fender, Gretsch, and others. I would stand in the corner and watch the local studio musicians bring their guitars into Wallach's for repair work. The repairman was a crusty old character named *Milt*. He never smiled, and would always say the same thing when first eying any musician's guitar, "... Oh, one of *these* things." Eavesdropping, I learned who some of the session guitarists were who came into Wallach's: Howard Roberts, Barney Kessel, Glen Campbell, and my own guitar hero, James Burton. I never spoke a word when they walked in, but paid strict attention to their guitars, as well as the way they handled themselves: cool and big time. They were a different breed of musicians from the bands I saw on TV. Studio musicians wore sport shirts, expensive slacks, loafers, short hair and over all very straight. I mean these were the guys on most of the hits that played on the radio yet they all looked like undercover police detectives or guys on a golf course. But they all carried in the best, most expensive guitars imaginable. And they had a way about them, cool and confident. Big bucks, top of the heap. Yeah. *That's* the gig for me.

With every trip to Hollywood, it became harder to leave, especially knowing that I was headed back to the grim realities of La Puente. I hated everything about the fucking place, blaming the town for all our troubles. I especially despised high school, not that I attended it much. The only good thing I ever took home with me from high school was a borrowed tape recorder I got from the audio-visual room. Actually, I didn't *borrow* it. I'd set it up in the bathroom sink of our house and laid down about a dozen songs, just me and my rough little Spanish guitar. The echo in the bathroom was perfect for recording, however, the noise of my brothers and sister screaming and fighting in the background didn't help at all.

One day, I came home "from school" as usual, but, this time, something was different. My dad and mom were waiting for me. Mom was crying as dad scowled. "How was school today, Jack?" He asked. He had never asked me that question in the past.

"Uh, fine ... just fine," I answered nervously as he walked right up to me.

"Yeah? Well, I'm glad you think so, because the school called. They haven't seen you for seventeen days!" I froze. ... *Busted.*

"So, where in the hell have you been for 17 days," he shouted. After a few seconds of silence, I decided to come clean, no longer caring what happened to me. "I've been hitchhiking to Hollywood and

hanging out there," I blurted out.

My folks stood before me stunned. *"Hollywood?"* they shouted in unison. Mom became hysterical, while my dad kept repeating the word *Hollywood* over and over again. He then informed me that I was to be expelled from high school and sent to what they called, a *continuation school* until I was 18. Furthermore, we had an appointment the very next morning to see the Dean at my high school, something I dreaded. I felt terribly guilty about hurting my parents, who already had enough trouble in their lives. Now, I had just brought more down upon them.

The next morning, dad and I stood before the Dean of La Puente High School. He sat behind his big oak desk as dad and I took our seats in front of him. An arrogant wind bag, he asked, "John, I see you have been running away to Hollywood. Is that correct?" I wanted to tell him to get screwed, but I simply nodded. My dad sat beside me with his eyes closed nodding his head in disgust. "John, what do plan to do with your life?" he then asked. "I want to be a professional musician in Hollywood" I shot back. Then came the words I'll never forget; words that have forever stayed in my head. Leaning back on his chair with a smirk on his face, he said, "John, do you know how many kids like you come out to California each year, all hoping to make it big in show business, only to end up with broken hearts?"

I almost burst out laughing, but remained silent. He then went on to officially inform me that I would be transferred to a *continuation school*, where troubled kids like me are sent to finish high school. Then, wishing me luck, he escorted us out of the office. I wanted to tell that pompous, boring asshole he didn't have a clue about anything in show business, but I just left with my head down and my dad looking defeated. On the ride home the silence in the car was almost unbearable. I knew I had let him down and only compounded the mountain of hardship he was already enduring. I had to do something. But what? What options did I have? Only one.

When the morning came to go to the continuation school, I was prepared. I swiped $20.00 from my dad's wallet while he was in the shower, then tucked the little tape recording I'd made in our bathroom, inside my shirt. Dad drove me to the school and kept saying, "Jack, do the best you can. When you turn seventeen, we can get you into the Navy to learn a trade. So, just make the best of it, for your mother's sake."

The car stopped outside the front entrance of the school. Through the chain link fence I could see some pretty rough characters peering out at me. It looked more like the holding tank at the County Jail, than any high school I had been to. I said goodbye to my father and stood there motionless as I watched his car drive away and out of sight. Once he was gone, I turned around and looked at the kids behind the fence, shot another look at the front door of the school, then ran as fast as I could to the nearest freeway on-ramp. I was headed back to Hollywood, and this time there would be no coming back.

3 HOLLYWOOD 1967

"The images still linger
And the ghosts still stand their guard
Saying come on in and find your place
On Sunset Blvd"

"Sunset Blvd" Flying Burrito Brothers

As scared as I was, I felt an almost euphoric sense of freedom I had never experienced before as I stuck out my thumb hoping for a ride. Eventually, someone gave me a lift, but only as far as downtown Los Angeles. The last time I had been there was when we first arrived at the train station from Illinois. Then, the sky was blue, and the mountains looked majestic in the distance like a picture postcard. But now it was nearly 11pm and there I was, walking alone in one of the most scariest parts of LA, the Mission Row District, home for all the wino's, whores, gangs and deadbeats you could count. Nearly everyone I passed on the street looked as if they wanted to slit my throat. And every time a cop car passed by I turned my head away in case they may be looking for me, knowing full well my folks had called the police and reported me a runaway when I didn't show up at the house after school. I had to get out of this area quick. After grabbing a hamburger along the way, my nest egg had depleted down to $15.00. So, when I spotted a city bus that said Hollywood, I jumped on as fast as I could.

It was a long, slow moving, rattling ride from downtown LA to Hollywood, but that was ok with me. For once I could sit down and rest instead of being stuck in a bad part of town. I took a seat near the driver and stared out the window, a million thoughts racing through my mind. I wondered how my folks were taking it. Surely, they felt responsible for my leaving. I felt bad about what I was putting them through, but I was determined to never go back to that life again. I was free, and I knew in my heart there was something waiting for me in this town.

After what seemed to be a million stops along the way, I finally arrived in Hollywood at the corner of Franklin and Vine. It was 3am and the streets were nearly empty. All my previous time in Hollywood was spent during the daylight hours, but at this hour of the morning it took on an eerie quality. The first thing I noticed was the Capital Records Tower just down the street, so I headed there. It was impossible not to notice the funny looking building that was originally built to resemble a stack of records. On top of the roof a beacon flashed from a small radio tower. I was dead tired and needed to find some place to rest. If I stayed on the streets there was a good chance the cops, always on the lookout for runaway kids, would have picked me up. I walked around to the back of Capital Records' parking lot where I spotted a big trash dumpster. I sat down, leaned up against it, and fell into a much-needed deep sleep.

I woke up to the sound of a big tour bus pulling into the Capital parking lot. Wiping the sleep from my eyes I could see the words on the side of the bus that read BUCK OWENS & THE BUCKAROOS. I'd heard of him, that guy Buck Owens. I remember seeing his albums at the Hometown Drug Store as well as his appearances on the Jimmy Dean Show. I got up and walked over by the bus as members of his band, in full stage attire they stepped out single file and headed to the back door of Capital. Finally, the last one to leave the bus was none other than Buck himself.

"Hi Buck!" I shouted. He turned around and smiled and waved a hello to me and then disappeared into the building with the rest of the band.

"I'll be damned, the first real star I've seen since arriving in Hollywood. Little did I ever dream that decades later I would actually produce Buck at his studio in Bakersfield and tell him this exact story. But more on that later.

Since I was at Capital Records, I thought I would take a chance, like I did at Paramount, simply walk in and see how far I could go before being thrown out. I took a deep breath and walked around to the front entrance and simply fell into the crowd of people heading towards the elevator. I blew right past the receptionist who never noticed me. Before I knew it, I was on an elevator head to the top floor. Now I was nervous. What the hell was I doing here? Finally, the elevator stopped on the top floor. The doors opened, and I slowly stepped out. The hallways at Capital were circular and it felt like I was walking inside a space ship. It was still early in the morning and most of the office staff hadn't arrived. I walked along the hallway staring at the gold albums on the wall, the Beatles, the Beach Boys, The Lettermen, Al Martino and other top Capital artists. Solid gold albums covering the walls around me. Suddenly, a voice from behind me said "Can I help you"? I turned around in panic and there stood a young guy in a suit with his arm extended out to shake my hand. "My name's Abe Hoch, is there something I can help you with"?

I shook his hand and in a trembling voice said "My name is John Beland and I'm a singer. I have this tape and…"

"Hi John, come on in and let's have a listen."

I couldn't believe it! I thought he was about to call security on me but instead, he escorted me to his office to play my tape. His office was filled with autographed photos of all the Capital acts and behind his desk was a state of the art sound system. I sank into a big leather chair and Abe threaded my tape thru his big professional tape recorder.

"Tell me about yourself, John." he asked.

I tried not to reveal how nervous I was and answered, "I write songs and sing and I play guitar, too" I replied.

Abe smiled and said "Great. Let's have a listen."

And with that he hit the play button. Instantly, the first thing that came across his big speakers was my brothers and sister yelling in the background. I was mortified, to say the least. Hell, how did I know that my tape would be played by a Capital A&R man?

I felt like I was at the dentist getting a tooth pulled as Abe listened to about 4 songs. The worst moment came when, in the middle of one song, you could hear a banging on the bathroom door and my dad yelling "Jack, get the hell out of the bathroom"!

I wanted to throw up from embarrassment. Abe was a cool as could be. He stopped the tape and put it back in the box and handed it back to me. He smiled and told me that I had a "unique" style. And then he gave me some solid advice, telling me about this club down towards Beverly Hills called "Doug Weston's Troubadour ". He explained that on Monday night's the club featured, what they called, "Hoot Night." This meant that if you got there early enough and waited in line, the first 10 acts could get 15 minutes on stage He went on to say that many record people, booking agents and personal managers attended these Hoot Night's regularly and that quite a few singer/songwriters and bands that performed at the Monday night Hoots landed record deals. Major stars were discovered on that very stage, groups like the Association and the Byrds. He also told me that the Troubadour was a great place to learn the craft of songwriting, playing and performing simply by watching all the other acts onstage. Abe walked me back to the elevator, patted me on the back and wished me luck. I believe that he knew all along I was a runaway. But he took the time to listen to my music when he could have very well called security and be done with me. I never forgot him and the kindness he showed me. I'm proud to say that we remain friends today.

Outside of Capital I was back on the streets, my eyes still stinging from the bright morning sun and so little sleep. The first thing I did was to call my mom and dad and tell them I was alright. There was a pay phone directly across the street from Capital, so I took a deep breath and dialed the number. My folks were ecstatic to hear from me, to say the least and they begged me to come back home. My dad even promised to move us back to Hometown if I returned. But this time there would be no concessions on my part. I had made my decision and I was sticking to it. I wanted to see if I could make it in Hollywood and I wasn't about to sacrifice my dreams like my father had done so many years ago. I could hear my mom crying in the background and feel the sadness in my father's voice. I told them I would be alright and would call them whenever possible. They continued to beg me to come back, so I just hung up the phone, fell on the ground and cried like a baby as the morning sun beat down on me and traffic whizzed by. I knew I had hurt them deeply and it was almost too much for me to handle.

I made my way up Hollywood Blvd staring at the shop windows and looking at the names of the stars engraved on the sidewalk, some I recognized and some I never heard of. Suddenly, bang! I was knocked down on the ground from out of nowhere. Next thing I knew a man was reaching down to help me up. "Are you ok, kid" he asked?

I dusted myself off and said "Yes, sir. Thank you" and looked up. There before me stood the one and only Larry Fine, of the Three Stooges. He was dressed in a blue pin stripe suit and was coming out of the Bank of America when he ran into me.

"Are you Larry of the Three Stooges" I asked?

"I sure am son. Listen, you got to be careful when walking down this street. Lots of people here. So look out." And he walked away. I couldn't believe I just met one of the Three Stooges. Only in Hollywood!

From Hollywood Blvd I crossed over to Sunset Strip. It was quite a scene and the closer I got to the center of the action, the crazier it got. I spent most of the day in Wallich's Music City playing records and checking out the musical instrument department well into the dinner hours. Then, following Abe's directions, made my way slowly up the strip towards Beverly Hills. When I reached the famed *Whiskey-A-Go-Go,* the sidewalks were jammed with people of all sizes, shapes and colors. Music was blasting, kids were dancing, anti-war protesters were protesting, and cars were slowing down to a crawl to witness the madness.

Finally, I made my way down to Santa Monica Blvd and Doheny Avenue and there it stood, the legendary Troubadour. It looked a little like a Swiss Chalet and there were all sorts of people milling around outside. I squeezed my way through the crowd and managed to slip inside where the bar area was. I had now become an expert at "slipping inside." The place was packed with all sorts of people from all walks of the entertainment industry, musicians, actors, record people. All loud and roaring drunk. Next to the bar there was a main doorway that led to the showroom where, on this particular night, songwriter Hoyt Axton was performing. Axton had written a few major folk hits and was very popular at the Troubadour. One of his better-known compositions was for the Kingston Trio called "Greenback Dollar" and the following year would write the massive pop hit for the group Three Dog Night called "Joy To The World."

I snuck past the security guard and slipped into the showroom, making my way up the stairs to the balcony section. I leaned over the railing and watched Hoyt perform to a rousing reception. I mean this was amazing. The crowd kept quiet as he spoke and truly listened to his songs as he played. I had never been in a club with an audience like that! But as impressed as I was watching Axton perform, I was more taken with the Troubadour itself. There was a certain feel to the club, not as intense and manic as the other rooms up on the Strip. Here, the audience *listened* through a close connection between them and the performer. There was no talking, or dancing going on while the acts performed. It was total music *immersion*; strictly listening, where you could take in the total talent of the acts onstage; their sharp energies. Performers radiated to a crowd of mellow, laid-back, diehard folk-music enthusiasts. There was a much higher regard for the artists and their music by the crowd at the Troubadour than the wild, loud, drunken crowds up on The Strip. I had fallen instantly in love with this serious and wonderful place filled with true music appreciators.

The folk scene at Doug Weston's club appealed to me instantly. It was intelligent and respectful, with high emphasis on the music. Up on Sunset Strip it was bands like *Hendrix, The Who,* and *The Doors* blasting out of stacks of screaming amplifiers to packed rooms of stoned, whacked-out kids, oblivious to what was happening right in front of them.

At the Troubadour, it was all about artistry; the songwriters, players, and singers. Artists. It was Martin acoustic guitars, banjos, and mandolins. Here, it was about reverence for the lyrics and their heartfelt meanings. Some years earlier, Doug Weston's Troubadour had started as a grass-roots folk scene, featuring the biggest names in folk music: Phil Ochs, Odetta, Ian & Sylvia, Gordon Lightfoot, and many others. By the time I arrived on the scene, the changes had begun and coming very quickly. Many of the diehard folk artists were now adding electric bass guitars and drums to their stage acts. A lot of folk musicians were now moving to a more pop direction; some of them reappearing in new bands like *The Sunshine Company, The Hearts & Flowers, The Nitty-Gritty Dirt Band, the Byrds,* and a new trio called the *Stone Ponies,* featuring a young, attractive lead-vocalist named *Linda Ronstadt.* This was the scene as I first walked into the Troubadour. But that first night, I stayed in the shadows of the main room, watching Axton perform until closing-time. Then I made my way down the street to a little park at the corner of *Santa Monica* and *Doheny.* A bunch of kids my age were all gathered around the big fountain, playing guitars and beating tambourines. I was exhausted, and it looked to be a peaceful scene; a safe place for me to rest after a tiring adventurous day.

I found a place on the grass and sat down to rest and watch the musicians, trying to keep the realities of my situation out of my mind, at least for the night. The thought of what my parents must have been going through still haunted me. As I sat amongst this group of kids, I listened to the music going on all around me, trying to block out the guilt I was feeling. A smiling, girl sat down beside me. She took a deep hit from a joint, and then offered it to me. The last thing I wanted to do was disappoint this incredibly beautiful young girl, but I passed, having never in my life even smoked a cigarette, let alone a joint. The lingering smell of pot and the sound of guitars and singing continued to fill my head. As the clock slid past three a.m., I lay back in the grass and looked straight up at the stars, trying to relax. How had I ever gotten here? It seemed that one minute I was in Hometown listening to records with old friends and the next sleeping in a Hollywood Park with a pack of rock-and-roll gypsies.

I drifted off into a deep sleep as the guitars and tambourines played away through the early morning hours, awakening immediately to the loud Police bullhorn. *"Everyone* out of the park, *now!"* It screamed at six a.m. when the Cops arrived to routinely clear all the hippies from the park. We all scattered frantically, like a flock of geese, with no one getting caught. I was disoriented, running as fast as I could as I wiped the sleep from my eyes. The LA cops were always at odds with the kids up on The Strip and anywhere in the vicinity. The famous *Sunset Strip Riots* had exploded between the kids and the LA Police Department just the year before. Since then, tempers hadn't cooled in the slightest, and the LAPD were still on the prowl, looking for any excuse to bust anyone under twenty-one with long hair. This is what the *Buffalo Springfield* sang about in *For What It's Worth:*

> "Something's happening here.
> What it is ain't exactly clear.
> There's a man with a gun over there,
> telling me I got to beware.
> Think it's time we stop, hey!
> What's that sound?
> Everybody—look what's going down!"

For the next few days, I repeated the same routine, sleeping in various local parks along with kids like me, on the run. During the day, I would hang out at Wallich's, looking through the latest records, and then follow all the kids up to The Hamburger Hamlet, where we'd hit the tourists up for their spare change, and make a few dollars. They all seemed to enjoy *tipping the hippies*. At the end of the day I'd return to Troubadour and then make my way to the balcony to watch the shows.

By now, things were beginning to get desperate as I lived on spare change, walking around in the same clothes I'd left home in. I had no plans for the future. Existing hand-to-mouth, I didn't know how long I could continue to slide slowly from bad to worse as I evaded capture and reprocessing by the LAPD. Days later, I hitched a ride down on Melrose Avenue. A shiny, new Ford pulled over to the side as its driver waved me in.

"Where you headed?" he asked.

"Just ... up to Sunset," I answered. He was a funny looking character that reminded me of the late comedian, *Rip Taylor*, with his handlebar mustache and funny voice. "My name's *Dexter Coughlin*," he said as we pulled out into traffic, "... and, yours?"

"John Beland." I replied, for some reason deciding to use my given name. *Why?* I wondered. I had no idea. *Jack* had always sounded very unimportant, I reasoned. I also thought that if I became successful, my teachers back in Chicago and La Puente might better remember me as the student whose success they had discouraged. Dexter smiled as he drove along.

"So, what are you doing in Hollywood, John Beland? "He asked. I told him that I was a guitarist, although I didn't even own a guitar, and a songwriter as well, trying to get into the business. I'm certain he had a chuckle at my dirty dishevelment, clearly knowing I was a runaway, and broke.

"Are you hungry, John?"

I was beyond hungry. I was starving, weak even, with about ten cents to my name. Before I could answer, he interrupted tactfully. "Tell ya what" he said, "*I'm starved!* Let's get a burger, yeah? My treat!" I had nothing to lose; never in my life had I ever known hunger, and was now being sucked down by it, weaker than I had ever been. I knew this guy was O. K. *"Sure!"* I shot back. *"Thanks a lot!"*

Dexter took us to a Hollywood landmark called *TAIL OF THE PUP*, the most popular hot dog/hamburger-stand in LA. We sat outside, and I'm sure he knew by the absence of any table manners that I hadn't eaten in quite a while.

"Have you ever been to Hollywood before, John?" He asked. With my mouth full, I answered him. "No, I haven't. I just got here a week ago. I have this tape I made at my house ... with a bunch of my songs on it. I recorded them in the bathroom. I was hoping someone might listen to them and ... well ... give me a *record deal.*" Dexter smiled and took the tape gently from my hand. He looked it over, wrapping it securely. "Hey—be right back," he said, heading to the car as I devoured my hamburger and large order of fries. Even the catsup was a delicacy.

He returned just as I was thinking of ordering another. "... You know John," he said finally, "I have a friend up in Bel-Air who's really into music. He knows a lot of people. He might be interested in hearing this," he laughed. "In fact, he's been telling me that he was thinking of getting into music management. Want to drive up and meet him? ... His name is *Rob Demars.*"

Now, let me tell you without any exaggeration that I had learned very quickly how dangerous life on the streets could be, constantly fighting off some big, nasty perverts cruising for young boys. Many times, hitchhiking, I demanded to get out of the car after being approached or offered money for sex. So, when Dexter offered to drive me to Bel-Air, I was hesitant for a moment, not wanting to get myself into any weird situation I couldn't get out of. But I had a good feeling about him; he seemed sincere and kind, without a hidden agenda. He genuinely seemed to want to help me out, but I could still kick his ass, even in my weakened condition. He *obviously* gay by the way he spoke and acted, but he made no advances on me so I decided to take a chance, and agreed to go with him. We drove through the big white gates of Bel-Air, where the top names in show business lived. It was a long, winding drive through hill after hill of their huge mansions and perfectly-kept yards. I felt like we were driving up to the house of some royalty. Dexter talked all the way up the hill, but, stunned by the incredible real estate we were passing, I didn't pay much attention to him.

Finally, we arrived at the home of Rob DeMars, high above Bel-Air on Stradella Road. His house was smaller than the giant mansions I had seen on the way up, more of an expensive ranch style house. Dexter knocked on the door. It was answered by a young, clean-cut guy about 25 years old.

"Hi, Rob," Dexter greeted him, "and, this is the young man I spoke to you about." It appeared Dexter had called Rob and filled him in on me while I was attacking lunch.

"John, this is Rob DeMars."

The guy who shook my hand was a sharp, good looking and very friendly fellow, not anything like the rich snob I was expecting to meet. He looked Ivy-League, far different than any music manager I had ever seen. As we walked inside, I could tell that DeMars was well-off, his home filled with the finest furniture, carpets and artwork. Rob's house was anything but an ordinary ranch house; the entire building hung right over a cliff, with a breathtaking view. Suddenly, I looked and felt like Chaplin's *"Little Tramp";* an embarrassing mess. Rob brought me a Coke and asked Dexter and I to join him in his music room. It wasn't a very big room, but it was loaded with the latest stereo equipment, tape recorders, drums, a bass guitar and an old Martin acoustic. He also had a multi-walled record collection that rivaled any radio station in LA. He asked to hear my tape. I reached into my shirt and handed over the beat-up Scotch Tape box. Rob threaded it into his recorder and hit the play button. Once again came the amplified sound of my brothers and sister, as well as my dad banging on the bathroom door. Again, the embarrassment. But he listened to every one of my songs.

"Did you write these songs yourself?" he asked, his tone serious, and exploratory.

"...Yes."

"And these are *all* yours?"

"Yes, they are."

"This stuff isn't bad at all. Do you play any other instruments?"

I told him I played drums, bass, a little piano, harmonica and organ. He sat down and looked at Dexter, who smiled back. "So, tell me how you got here, John. ... Do you have a home ... a place to live? I told him everything, and he listened intently; how I'd run away, and was living on the street with no money. All I had was a tape recording. Rob thought for a while as he looked out a broad, spacious window. Then he took Dexter into the other room, leaving me to sit alone in his impressive music room amidst the expensive recording equipment and vast record collection. I plucked the strings on his Hofner Beatle-bass guitar in the corner, and then lightly hit a couple keys on the piano as Rob and Dexter returned.

"Listen, John," Rob began, "I think you have a tremendous talent, and a lot of potential, but nobody to represent it. Now, I can't promise anything, but I'll try to help you as a manager, if you're interested. You can stay here, in one of the guest rooms with a private bath. Help yourself to anything in the kitchen. Oh, and, I have some extra clothes that should fit you, for now." He paused for a moment, and then turned back to me. "... Tell me, would you be interested in my managing you and publishing your songs?"

Had I died of hunger somewhere along the way, and was I now preparing to enter *Heaven?* No, I realized, I was still alive. Relieved, I tried to be calm, and told Rob I was very interested. We shook hands, and it became a deal. I thanked Dexter for his kindness. He just smiled and said, "Don't forget—you owe me lunch!" And, with that, he left.

I began my first internship as an artist under the watchful eyes and ears of Rob DeMars. I now had a manager, a roof over my head, and all the food I could want. And it would all come from my music. At last, things seemed to be turning around for me.

Taken when I first arrived in Hollywood

4 THE SAD CAFÉ

"We thought we could change the world
With words like *love* and *freedom*
We were part of the lonely crowd
Inside the Sad Café"

The Troubadour 1967

In the weeks following my move to Rob's house in Bel-Air I went to work refining my skills, using the instruments available in his studio. I also started sharpening my skills on his recording equipment. I now had access to top-line musical gear, and I dove into it like a fish to water, practicing all day and all night; bass, drums, piano, acoustic guitar. I started writing songs on a steady basis and some of them were getting pretty good. Rob turned me on to new writers and singers I'd never heard of, but whose music greatly inspired me. He would play me albums by Tim Buckley, Tim Hardin, Leonard Cohen, Joni Mitchell and Gordon Lightfoot. I couldn't get enough. Each album inspired me to grow rapidly as a writer and musician. It seemed that I practiced fifteen hours a day in that music room of Rob's.

Eventually, I was ready to take the next important step in my career: to get onstage and play at The Troubadour's now-famous Monday Hoot-Nights. I was ready, but still scared half-to-death. While I'd both composed and played in several bands, I'd never performed before a live crowd as a solo act, let alone one as serious and sophisticated as The Troubadour's. It was well known that all kinds of media people attended Hoot Night, all on the lookout for the next big talent. Hollywood producers, agents, and managers would all show up in the hope of discovering some new chart-topper. Many acts that played Hoot Nights wound up with recording deals and went on to big success. It was a very important stage to find yourself on and you had better be good, because the competition was frightening.

Rob dropped me off in the late afternoon. The line of singers, songwriters and musicians had already formed, most sitting on the sidewalk, playing guitars and trading riffs and tunings with each other, anything to pass away the long hours that remained until the ticket-booth opened. Only a certain number of acts were selected for that night's *Hoot*, so it was vital that you found a place in line early enough to get on stage. Once inside, you would pass through the Troubadour bar, where it wasn't uncommon to find familiar stars from television, film, and music all hanging out together, getting drunk and loud. On my first night there, I spotted a blind kid sitting cross-legged on the floor with his guide dog. He was playing a Spanish guitar and singing away, oblivious to the loud racket coming from the bar. And, he was incredible. Nobody seemed to be paying much attention to him, but I did. Through the Troubadour's gate, one year later the rest of the world would get to know and admire the great Jose Feliciano.

Inside the showroom, a dynamic emcee for the night's showcase was busy entertaining the crowd with homespun jokes and funny stories as he positioned the microphones for the next act. He was a very cool character and very popular with the crowd. His name was *Larry Murray,* and when he wasn't performing with his folk-rock group, *The Hearts and Flowers,* he ran the Hoots on Monday nights. Larry was from Waycross, Georgia with a smooth, southern style to his onstage personality. He was a sharp dresser, too: white sneakers, jeans with a sash around his waist, topped off by a colorful cowboy-style shirt. He was a favorite with the audience, and they laughed at everything he said. A competent Ringmaster, Larry kept the night moving happily while various acts were setting up. In the back of the club, by the balcony stairway, Larry would tell you when you were scheduled to hit the stage. You'd get 15 minutes, as well as an encore— if you got it. It seemed like everyone was walking around strapped to a Martin guitar, including me. I had Rob's small Martin D35 as I made my way up the stairway to the balcony to watch the other acts perform until it would be my turn. Some of them were Dylan clones and Donovan wannabe's, but every once in a while, an act would get up there, and simply *knock everyone out*. One in particular was a lean, handsome, clean-shaven kid with long hair and deep brown eyes. He sang the most beautiful songs, and played guitar with grace and style. He had a way of commanding the stage; you could hear a pin drop when he started singing. *"... Well I've been out walking ... I don't do too much talking these days."* His name was Jackson Browne, and the word backstage was that he was being courted by every major label in town. And, I could see why: the applause was thunderous, and he was quickly called back for the encore. Browne had made the top grade, and he was *in*.

Another great act was a young, cute, long brown-haired girl who played a small Martin, and *boy*, could this girl play—finger-picking like Chet Atkins in all sorts of weird open-tunings! And then came her mesmerizing voice. Her name was *Mary McCaslin*, and she stole my heart away, instantly. With her long brown hair and bangs and her ever pure, magical vocal style, Mary would take Beatle songs and weave them into the most beautiful folk arrangements imaginable. Again, the crowd ate it up and always called Mary back for an encore, then still not wanting to let her go.

As I hung over the balcony railing, I started to really worry, watching then-unknown's like Jackson Browne and Mary McCaslin *slay* the crowd below. I wasn't *anywhere* in their league, feeling as if I was headed out to the Guillotine as my turn neared. I noticed a back door at the bottom of the stairway and gave some serious thought to using it. But I knew I was never going to get anywhere if I didn't take the initial plunge into the deep water. If I bombed, it wouldn't be a total loss. Going to the Monday Night Hoot offered me a chance to see some really inspirational talent, and learn from them. It wasn't so much about getting a big audience response as it was a golden opportunity to learn my craft by studying those around me. So, as Larry Murray announced, *"Let's give a super-duper Troubadour welcome for singer songwriter, John Beland!"* I made my way up the two steps to the beautiful stage that I would eventually stand upon so many more times in the near future.

5 OFF THE STREETS AND INTO THE STUDIO

"So you want to be a rock and roll star?
Then, listen now to what I say:
Just get an electric guitar!
And take some time, and learn how to play!"

–The Byrds

I'd like to say that I dazzled them, that first performance at the Troubadour. But I didn't. I did get a good round of polite applause. Lord knows it could have been much worse. But, to my amazement, I discovered that once I reached the microphone I felt a sudden *calmness* and found it quite easy to speak onstage. It felt natural and fun, instead of the expected panic attack. Over the coming weeks I would fine-tune my act, trying out new things that I picked up from the other musicians who were now all around me.

Religiously, I was there every Monday. Over time, I started making friends with my fellow players and learning how to improve my skills by watching them. It was a close community of singers, and musicians, and writers I had fallen in with and I soaked up everything around me.

Back at Rob's, I kept rehearsing and writing until one day he told me he wanted to take me into a real studio and cut a two-song demo. He would pay for it, including three studio musicians to back me. I was in the clouds. Rob booked time at the *Hollywood Central Studios*, a little four-track studio on Cuenga Boulevard in the town's center. It was a small room, but it was a real studio, with baffles, microphones, headphones, a Hammond B-3 organ, and a finely-tuned and voiced baby grand piano. The musicians were setting up when Rob and I arrived. The drummer was an older black fellow, looking as if he had been in the business for years. I walked over to him and introduced myself. He smiled and gave me a warm handshake and told me his name was *Sharkey Hall*. In our conversation I learned he had recorded with Lou Rawls and Ray Charles to name a few. I was in awe listening to him go through his credits, and thrilled that this guy was playing on *my* first recording session.

We recorded two forgettable songs I'd written, but the

unforgettable part was playing on a real session in Hollywood with top studio musicians. I played harmonica, guitar, and B3 organ, and it was as natural as putting on my socks. I had pulled my weight with the session guys, and when it was over I felt I had grown several feet. *This* is what I had dreamed about back in Hometown, and now I was doing it—recording with pro's at *a real studio in Hollywood!* Suddenly, there was no more doubt about it: I knew at that moment *this* is what I would be doing for the rest of my life.

Continuing to use the Troubadour as my base, my appearances got better, and my playing improved dramatically. I became friends with emcee Larry Murray, who, for some reason, took a liking to me. He would always put me onstage at a good time when the audience was full, and important people were in the crowd. I idolized Larry; the great way he talked; his sense of humor, as well as the way he dressed. He became my role model and a mentor. Larry played in The Hearts & Flowers trio, a mixture of bluegrass and pop, featuring himself on guitar and lead vocals, *David Dawson* on auto-harp, and *Bernie Leadon* on banjo. Years down the road, Bernie would hit fame and fortune as a founding member of *The Eagles.* The Hearts & Flowers, a Capital Records act, were extremely popular at the Troubadour. Their show featured tight harmonies with fabulous songs, and a lot of comedy. Whenever they appeared at the Troubadour, all the mic stands were decked out in flowers. They were always exciting, and a lot of fun to see. There were other local favorites, as well like *The Dillard's,* a terrific bluegrass group, popular for their portrayal of *The Darling Family* on the *Andy Griffith Show.* When I saw the Dillard's for the first time, they had replaced their famous brother Doug with *Herb Pederson,* one of the greatest harmony singers I'd ever heard. Herb's influence and direction changed the Dillard's from just another bluegrass band to a ground-breaking, pioneer country-rock act. Their two albums, *Wheat Straw Suite* and *Copperfield's* influenced nearly everybody who played the Troubadour, with their fantastic musicianship, lots of humor, and their incredible, intricate harmonies. I never missed a performance when *Mitch, Dean, Herb,* and *Rodney,* the Dillard's, appeared at the Troub.

Another big favorite at the club was *The Nitty-Gritty Dirt Band,* a kind of cross between jug and rock bands. They all wore crazy clothes onstage; Mounties' uniforms, sailor outfits, and even outrageous cowboy get-up's. They were sensational, and a huge hit with the crowd.

They also attracted the most beautiful girls imaginable; the Troubadour was a haven for beautiful women, a feature never unnoticed by me. I had a real weakness for the long-haired, granny-glassed, hippie-folkie type in a peasant dress. And these astonishing beauties were all around at the Troub, especially when the Dirt Band played.

It was at one of the Dillard's Troubadour appearances that I met a pretty, long brown-haired, dark- eyed girl from nearby Beverly Hills. I thought she was really cute. Since she seemed to be alone, I walked up and introduced myself. Her name was Charlotte. She had just graduated from Beverly Hills High School, and had recently become a regular at The Troubadour. We talked for the whole night and I quickly fell head over heels for her. It seemed she felt the exact same way. Charlotte still lived with her parents in Beverly Hills, and drove a cool, pink Mustang. Soon we were cruising everywhere together all over Hollywood, most of the time on her dollar. She knew I was dead- broke, but never said a word about it. Charlotte taught me how to drive by letting me take the wheel and coaching me as I tried to get familiar with everything necessary to operate a car. But, that's not all Charlotte taught me. One night, after driving me back to Rob's following another Monday night Hoot, Charlotte ended up in my room, and then quickly in my bed. I had never gone all the way with a girl before, and this was obvious as I fumbled my way through it. But this seemed to make her happy. Then, in the same patient, loving way she taught me to drive, she taught me intimacy. I completely fell for her from that moment on.

She came to pick me up at Rob's for our weekly Monday Night trip to the Troubadour. But, before we left Rob's house, she hesitated, asking me if I knew he was *gay*. I hadn't picked up on it, being so uninformed on the subject, but Charlotte pointed out things that opened my eyes. I now understood why Rob's roommate, Bill, was always being so friendly to me when Rob was out of the house; why there were never any women at the house when Rob threw a party. What had I walked into? Not knowing what to do, I began to panic as Charlotte and I gathered what few belongings I owned and quickly left the home of Rob and his lover, for good. I felt like an idiot as Charlotte drove us back to Hollywood. As grateful as I was for Rob's help, I felt betrayed, wondering if there was an ulterior motive for his kindness and belief in me. As I look back now, I realize there probably wasn't. But, what did I know about any of that stuff? I had bounced back to square one, alone and broke, and, worst of all, homeless again. But for some reason and one I could not fathom, *Charlotte loved me.* She wasn't about to let me end up on the street this time. After the Troubadour closed that night, she found a little hotel on Sunset Strip, across the street from Hollywood High School, and got a room for us. She bought a bag of groceries so that I wouldn't starve while she was home with her parents. She happily assured me things would be better, and not to let this incident in any way dampen my hopes of a career. Something would happen that would turn things around. Charlotte *believed* in me. I hoped she was right, because I knew I couldn't last much longer in the shape I was in.

Charlotte and I in the Troubadour Bar 1967

I stayed in the hotel for the week. Charlotte would come to see me every morning, carrying in groceries and sundries, and then take my clothes home, laundering them when her parents weren't around. During those days, we would have lunch at hamburger stands along The Strip as she did all she could to build up my confidence and optimism, but there was little left. At night we would go back to the hotel and fall into bed together, and for those moments, my troubles would vanish completely. But, as she finally kissed me goodnight and departed for home, I was once again confronted by the realities: I had no plan, no contacts, and no friend in the world but Charlotte. I'd lay in my bed, racking my brain for a plan; my thoughts interrupted by police sirens screaming by or drunken brawls in the hotel courtyard. I had never been so alone or scared in my life as when I watched Charlotte smile, waving to me as she pulled away.

As Monday came around again, she suggested we go to the Troubadour and get our minds off our troubles. Half-heartedly, I agreed. When we arrived, a grinning Larry Murray said he had an opening in ten minutes if I wanted to get up and do a few songs. I didn't feel like singing at all but borrowed a guitar from one of the acts and hit the stage to play a few songs and joke a bit with a half-capacity audience. It felt so natural. The response was pretty good, considering the sparse crowd. *Not bad at all,* I thought. *Funny ... considering the mess I was in.* Following my 15 minutes onstage, I headed for the back stairway to the balcony section when someone called my name. I turned to a very pretty, blonde-haired woman. "Hi, John," she said, a warm smile on her face. "I'm Lois Dalton, and I really enjoyed your performance." I thanked her, but felt a bit embarrassed. Besides being very lovely, she looked important. *Did she really think I was good?* I wondered as Lois explained to me that she and her husband, Dan, had a production company, and asking if she could give me their card.

"Sure!" I answered professionally. "Now, that would be *great!*" She handed their card to me, telling me that if I needed any help or advice, to stop by their office in Hollywood at any time. I thanked her with a half-smile, tucking the card into my jeans.

"Give us a call, John. ... I hope to hear from you," she said, then walked away, disappearing through the front doors and into the warm, glittering night.

Charlotte took me back to the hotel, once again paying for the room, and everything else. I felt beaten to the ground. Unable to hold back any longer, I began crying. She held me in her arms trying to comfort me as I shook uncontrollably. Now I understood how my dad must have felt when I heard him crying to my mother only a month earlier, the way I now cried to Charlotte. He thought he was a failure and now, so did I. She held me closely as I fell apart, all the while stroking my hair as she tried to reassure me that everything would turn out alright. But I couldn't see how it would. I had hit the wall with absolutely nowhere to go and not a penny to my name. I was a man-child dependent upon the love of this beautiful woman-child, petrified at my prospects and the dark gray wall that was my immediate future.

"So ... what about that card the woman gave you at The Troubadour?" Charlotte asked. I dug into my pocket and pulled out the little green scrap that said *Dan Dalton Productions on Selma Avenue. 461-3531.* I showed Charlotte the address. She smiled confidently.

"I know where that is! I'll take you there tomorrow morning, John," she said with a sympathetic smile. "You know, it couldn't hurt to see what they want."

Knowing full well that the names in my hand were my final glimmer of hope, I agreed with her. "I'll come and get you in the morning," she said as she walked towards the door, again needing to return to her home. "... Maybe these people can help". I watched her get into her pink Mustang, smile and wave and then drive off. I looked down at the pastel card in my hand, folded and creased from hours in my pocket. "... You're my last shot, little fella," I said as I turned out the light.

Charlotte was on-time to pick me up in the morning. I was still an emotional mess as I sat down in her car. She thought it best to drop me off at Dan Dalton Productions while she stayed out of sight. I wanted her to stay with me, but she felt she would just be in the way. When we arrived at the address on the card, I got out of the car slowly. She wished me good luck and drove away. The office was a little place adjoining the Moonglow Recording Studios, where the Righteous Brothers had recorded. I walked up to the door and knocked, but nobody answered. I had arrived too early. Sitting down by the door, I waited. Was this just another false lead? Was I just wasting time fooling myself? In a few minutes, the Dalton's arrived in a light-tan Karmann Ghia. From the small car stepped Dan Dalton, a tall, red-headed guy looking more Irish than a keg of Guinness. Next to exit the car was a floppy-eared Cocker Spaniel named Murphy. Lois finally stepped out, immediately spotting me waiting at the door.

"Hi! ... John?" she asked, worriedly. "... Are you O. K.?"

"Well ... *No,*" I said, looking down at the ground, "not really." And with that, I began to shake and then cry as I tried to explain that I'd hit the wall, and didn't know what I was going to do. Dan came right over to me. "Come on in, John," he said in a reassuring voice, leading me into their tiny office with a single desk and a few chairs. I took a seat and began pouring my heart out to them.

"John," Lois said tenderly, "I told Dan all about you ... maybe we can help?"

Dan had a very charming Irish way about him. He was a dynamic personality and very animated as he spoke. I liked him and his wife instantly. Her genuine concern would calm me in a few minutes. They told me all about themselves. Both were former members of the popular folk-group, *The Back Porch Majority,* a sister group to the nationally-known ensemble *The Christy Minstrels.* Before that, Dan had been part of a folk trio with his brothers, called *The Dalton Boys.* He played the tenor banjo as well as a twelve-string acoustic guitar. Both had recently left the *Back Porch Majority* to start their own production and publishing company under their current name. It had been a risky venture, but Dan was an experienced producer who had already landed his acts recording contracts with several labels. And lately it was starting to look like they might be on the verge of major success with a band Dan was producing, called *The Peppermint Trolley Company,* a four- piece folk-rock group with great harmonies, led by two talented brothers, *Danny* and *Jimmy Faragher.* They had just finished recording a *Jessie Lee Kincaid* song, *Baby You Come Rollin Cross My Mind, a soft country folk song with sweet harmonies and reminiscent of the Byrds and the Lovin Spoonful.* The perfect summertime record for 1968's Summer of Love. Everyone easily agreed it was going to be a hit.

After playing them the demo session I did for Rob, Dan and Lois offered to take me in and work with me in the studio, as well as sign me up as a writer to their publishing company. I couldn't believe what I was hearing. That office was tiny, but there was enough room for a couple of large Guardian Angels. I felt relieved and thankful, still not quite believing what I was hearing. But it seemed the first order of the day would need to be a phone call to my worried parents. I dreaded it. Lois took on the task of phoning them and explaining the situation. They immediately hopped in the car and drove up to Hollywood. In the meantime, Dan asked if I was hungry, and I certainly was. He called in *Sid Kessler*, his jovial assistant. Dan asked Sid to take me to a nearby coffee shop for breakfast, while he and Lois met with my frantic parents. Off I went with Sid as mom and dad showed up and were greeted by Lois. She assured them that I was alright, and would be back shortly. In the meantime, Dan explained to my mom and dad that they saw something in me that interested them enough to want to take me under their wing, and possibly get me a record, as well as a publishing deal. My dad didn't have a clue as to what Dan was saying; all this entertainment talk was foreign to his ears. But Dan was very frank with my folks. "Look," he told them, "you can take John back to La Puente right now, but he'll only run back here the first chance he gets. ... Let Lois and I work with him. We'll find him a safe place to live, and we'll put him on a salary as one of our writers. We believe in John, and we did so right away. We genuinely want to help him."

My relieved folks looked long and hard at each other, agreeing this was, in fact, an opportunity for their eldest. My dad had missed his, he confided, but he wasn't about to let me miss mine. They seemed to trust Dan and Lois, giving them their complete approval as I walked in the room. Both my parents jumped up and hugged me tightly. My mom, in tears, told me that I looked terrible. *Terrible?* I thought. *Well, not for long! I had just landed on Cloud Nine!*

The first concern was where I would live. Dan and Lois had a close friend, *Attley Yeager*, a very popular and colorful rock-and-roll musician in the San Fernando Valley music scene. Both Attley and his wife were more than happy to let me stay with them until I made enough money to afford my own place. Attley was a complete character: skinny as a rail with a Black Jack mustache, long sideburns and always decked-out in the finest rock-and-roll threads. He gravely beat-nick voice sounded like *Wolfman Jack*, and his friends included some of the top rock musicians in southern California. There was always a parade of musicians marching through their house as I'd listen to their battle stories about this tour or that, all the while wishing I could be part of their circle. Charlotte was ecstatic when she heard the news about my working with the Daltons. Together, we started going to the studio with Dan while he produced an album on The Peppermint Trolley Company. The band recorded at an old radio studio on Western Avenue in Los Angeles called CP McGregor Studios, a big, old building with a huge main room. You couldn't help but notice the ancient sound effects equipment in the far-off corner, used for old radio programs. From the producer's booth, I watched Dan directing the four-piece band out on the floor, running through the song they were about to record over, and over again. I became fascinated by the way he took charge of the session, shuttling back and forth between the production booth and the main room. I admired the way he took command, extremely confident and completely knowing his craft. I stood behind Carl, the studio engineer, keeping my mouth shut as I watched and listened with all the intensity in me. I was learning to live that wonderful dream I'd had back in Hometown. Sometimes, during Dan's session, I had to pinch myself, making sure it was no longer a dream. Not only was I learning a great deal about the studio, I was also learning how to act like a professional. There would be no more behaving like a kid; all that would need to stop completely, and right now.

Dan and Lois taught me how to dress and how to conduct myself around other professionals. They took me to the top restaurants in town, teaching me how to act properly when at the table. Whenever I screwed up, Dan was on me like a drill sergeant, reminding me again and again not to blow the golden opportunity I was being given. When I succeeded at something, like writing a good song, Dan was a cheerleader to the max, pumping up my confidence, and making me feel that my talents were special. Whenever Dan burned me for something or another, Lois would take me off to the side and in a sweet way reassure me that he was only coming down on me because he believed so much in me as an artist. These loving people became my musical parents. A few, bright words from Lois always got me back on my feet again. I never wanted to let them down, and always remembered not to mess-up again.

Both knew I desperately needed a good guitar. Dan knew everybody in Hollywood from singers, to musicians, to label executives. He had heard through the grapevine that songwriter Jessie Lee Kincaid was selling his beautiful Guild F50 acoustic guitar. Dan was friends with Jessie, whose song *Baby You Come Rolling Cross My Mind* had recently become a big hit with the Peppermint Trolley Company. Excited, Dan and I drove out to Jessie's home up in Laurel Canyon. The guitar was as beautiful as anything I had ever seen. When I played it for the first time, it sounded like a *grand piano*, almost bringing tears to my eyes. Dan gave Jessie a check, and the guitar was mine—all the years of borrowing guitars were now over. I was the new owner of one of the best acoustic guitars in the world!

Charlotte and I continued to go to the Monday night hoots at the Troubadour, *this* time with *my own* exquisite guitar in-hand. From the moment I first held it, I never put it down. The result was that my playing improved dramatically. I started backing up different singer songwriters at the Troubadour, becoming more and more eager to get back up on that stage.

One Monday night, Larry Murray asked me if I would play guitar behind a friend who'd just hit town from Nashville. He had been staying with friends around town, trying to get his career jump-started. Larry went on to tell me that he wasn't very good on the guitar, and could really use someone to back him. Always jumping at a chance to get myself up on the stage, I answered before Larry could finish his request. "Sure thing, Larry!" Then up the back stairs we went, walking down the dark little hallway just behind the sound booth where two dressing rooms stood next to each other. The larger one was for the headliners who played during the week; the tiny one was for opening acts. Larry knocked on the door of the small room. When it opened, there stood this guy with long greasy hair combed back. He was thin, clean shaven, wearing a black T-shirt and faded, worn-out suede pants and worn-out boots. He held an old, beat-up Martin D28, with a lot signatures scratched nastily into the body.

"John," Larry smiled, "I'd like you meet my friend, *Kris Kristofferson.*

6 KRISTOFFERSON AND MORE

When I first encountered Kristofferson, I was struck by his humility as well as his insecurity for performing. At the Troubadour it was obvious he was quite uncomfortable about walking onstage to an audience of casual, long-haired hipsters used to seeing legendary acts appear right where he stood. Kris was fresh off the boat from Nashville, a town that represented the red neck conservative right-wing part of the political landscape. This crowd down below the stairs was the direct opposite. Anti-war protesters, hippies, radical left wingers all siting front row center for the next act up on Hoot Night. So, there was Kris with his beat up old Martin guitar, suede pants that looked as if they had seen better days with his hair all slicked back, red neck southern *good ol'* boy ready to enter the lion's den.

As I strapped on my new Guild F-50 to check our tuning, he was humbly apologetic about his playing and singing before he ever hit a note. "... These songs are pretty damned easy, man," he mumbled in a low, gravelly voice, and then turned slightly, standing upright, seeming proud "... I'll, a ... start off with this one."

He began to play me the songs we were to soon play together, trying to sing and voice his guitar as best he could. First came an easy-going, laid back tune he started off sloppily and stiff-handed on the guitar. But, when he began to sing, I was suddenly struck by how good this song really was.

"Busted flat in Baton Rouge.
Headed for the train. ...
Feeling nearly faded as my Jeans."

I followed him, highlighting on my Guild, thinking *"Jesus,* this guy is *good ...*

"Freedom's just another word for nothin' left to lose.
Nothing ain't worth nothing, but it's free."

These lyrics were so good, I couldn't help but smile as I played along. I had never heard this kind of a country song before.

"... Feeling good was good enough for me.
Good enough for me, and Bobby McGee ..."

"That's ... a great song, Kris," I said, a bit stunned as our final chord faded.

"What else do you want to do?"

One by one, we played them together up in that crappy dressing room: *For The Good Times* , *Sunday Morning Comin' Down*, *Help Me Make It Through The Night*, and a few more jaw-droppers. There, in that little dark room reserved for the unimportant opening acts, he proceeded to teach me the very songs that would eventually change the course of modern day country music, marking him as one of the most important songwriters since Bob Dylan. Nobody in the audience downstairs had ever heard of *Kris Kristofferson* or these wonderful songs before, but they were just about to. I wondered how they would react; if they'd be as knocked-out as I was.

We hit the stage following Larry Murray's intro, followed by a few mercy-claps from the crowd. I stayed close to Kris's right side, so I could watch his fingers in case he missed a chord. I also played counter-chords to his; that is, if he played in standard *E major* on his guitar, I would capo two frets up and play the same Sonics in a *D* position. That way, the two guitars would fill-out more, rather than the both of us playing the same thing. Kris liked it, seeming to relax a bit as he voiced those magic words over our now-lush and easy guitar work. His tempo was erratic, so I just followed his tapping foot. No problem. But the crowd wasn't very responsive and talked blithely away while we played. I guess Kris looked too much like *a redneck*, a big strike against him at the Troubadour. But *I* thought we sounded pretty damned good and loved playing his songs. The crowd seemed to be less than impressed, dismissing him as we finished *Me and Bobby McGee* with hardly any applause as we quietly left the stage. Kris was delighted with what we'd delivered, joking about how we *really knocked 'em out*. He sincerely thanked me for playing behind him. "I mean it, man," he said as he shook my hand. I told him that it was my pleasure, and if he needed me again I'd be more than happy to play guitar for him anytime, anywhere.

This was the first time Kristofferson had ever seriously stepped onstage in Hollywood. His rough image didn't fool me. He was a truly cool guy, as friendly as anyone I had ever met. I wondered if I would ever hear from him. Maybe the audience didn't *get it* but I certainly did. There was something about him that told me this wasn't the last time I'd be hearing from that Silver Tongue.

I continued to work for the Dalton's while starting to pick up outside work doing songwriter's demos for publishing companies. As a multi-instrumentalist, I would get paid to play everything on the track myself for a total of twenty-five dollars a song. It was a streamlined package. The publishers knew that they were saving big money using only me, instead of a full band. Many times the *complete* crew would be only myself, the writer, and the studio's engineer. I'd play guitar and then drums, finishing with bass and piano. Then the writer would either sing, or hire a studio singer. I would have done it for *free* just to get the studio experience. And, back in sixty-eight, twenty-five bucks was big money to a po' kid like me.

One day I got a call from David Nelson *(not the brother of Ricky, but that's another story),* the music director at *Four Star Music.* I had met David months ago at the Troubadour, and had already done a few demos for him. This time he had just signed a new writer named *Sonny Childe,* and wanted to book a four-song demo date at *Hollywood Central Studios* on Wilcox Avenue. But first he asked me to meet with Sonny at his house to go over the material and it meant a hundred dollars in my wallet! Sonny lived in a cool, Spanish-style bungalow in the Hollywood hills. The fellow who answered the door reminded me of someone I couldn't quite put my finger on.

"Hi, John?" he smiled. "I'm Sonny. Come on in!"
As I walked down the hallway, I noticed all these pictures of the late *Sam Cooke* hanging on the wall. *That's It,* I thought. *He looks just like Sam Cooke!* We sat down in the living room.

"Did you know Sam Cooke?" I asked as I opened my guitar case.

"I sure did," he answered suddenly looking sad. "... He was my uncle."

Well, if I hadn't guessed it by then, I surely would have once Sonny started singing—he sounded *exactly* like his uncle. It was eerie. He was a clone of the late pop legend. Sonny picked up his guitar and we went through the four songs: *That's What I've Got, Santa Never Came, I Can't Let You Go,* and *Take A Letter, Maria.* The first three songs on the list were quite good. However, the fourth was a killer. When Sonny sang it, I got goose bumps because it was an obvious smash-hit. The next day we put down the tracks and then Sonny laid down his vocals. *Take A Letter, Maria* was smoking! I played my Guild, doing a solid rhythm while I overdubbed another guitar for the Spanish-style answers. I also played Motown-style bass and straight drums. It sounded fabulous once Sonny laid down his vocal. Everyone was knocked out and I earned a crisp, new C-note for my efforts.

On tour a year later in the Midwest, I was sitting in an Illinois coffee shop near Hometown as I reminisced to my band mates. Over the radio came a familiar sound that I instantly remembered.

"*O.K., baby!*" The DJ laughed.

I'm not your baby, dumb-ass, I thought, snickering.

"And, that's *R.B Greeves'* number one this week on the WLS Silver Dollar Survey, *Take a Letter Maria!*"

I couldn't believe it! Sonny had changed his name and re-recorded the tune down in Muscle Shoals, Alabama with famed producer *Ahmet Ertegun* for *Atco/Atlantic.* It was *Number Two* on Billboard Magazine's Top 100 and had gone *solid gold!* The record would go on to sell two-million copies and the song itself would be covered by many other major artists in the years ahead. All of a sudden, my one once-fat hundred-dollar paycheck from Four Star seemed a good deal thinner! But such was the business of being a studio player. You were paid for hire and if the session turned out to become a hit for the artist there was no reward, but the union scale you were paid for the three-hour date. I really never cared about it. I was thrilled to be a part of the process. For me, that was worth a million bucks.

One night, Charlotte came over to my apartment to tell me about a new coffee house. It had just opened up on Sunset Boulevard directly underneath the *Guitar Center*, the brand new, giant music store that had just recently opened in Hollywood. *Artie Fatbuckle's Cellar* was a tiny room that featured acoustic acts, exclusively. Absolutely no electric instruments were permitted. This was a bit funny, considering it was situated in the basement of the biggest electric guitar shop on the west coast. We decided to check it out for ourselves. The Cellar was in a dirty alleyway right off Sunset Blvd. Accessible only from the rear of the Guitar Center, you had to walk around the back and down a few steps to find your way inside. The club was run by a guy named *Bill Malone* and his girlfriend, *Camille*. It was very small, with only a few tables and no stage for the performers, just *the floor*.

The tiny room looked like the set on a low-budget TV show. Still, at times you could go hear some great acoustic music at the Cellar, like Jackson Browne, Mary McCaslin, *Hamilton Camp,* and other top artists on the acoustic scene.

The night Charlotte and I first arrived at the Cellar, it was nearly empty except for Bill, Camille, and a duo playing that night called *Longbranch & Pennywhistle*. We decided to stick around and listen. Longbranch & Pennywhistle were two incredibly talented singer songwriters named *John David Souther,* from Texas, and wise cracking *Glen Frey* from Michigan. They played beautiful jumbo Gibson guitars, wrote their own songs, and sang as well as the Everly Brothers. I was floored—these guys were incredible, with their edgy country-rock style of music, combined with their soaring harmonies. Both of them skinny as rails with long hair, they wore faded jeans with patches sewn all over them. JD and Glen were cool, and I wanted to meet them. After their last set I walked over and introduced myself. We hit it off immediately, and when they invited me to play guitar with them, I gladly jumped at it. They had a new sound I hadn't heard before; kind of a mixture of The Byrds, The Everly's, and the Buffalo Springfield. They were too damn good to not make it. I just knew they were going to be big someday. Their fuse was lit.

As band mates for the next couple of weekends, Charlotte and I followed Glen and John along the southern California coastline, her pink Mustang hot on the tail of their beat-up 57 Ford. We played a number of mom-and-pop folk rooms, most of the time being paid with dinner and a place to sleep. But the music was fantastic, and I had a ball playing with them. We shared a common love for guitars, and their style of music was right up my alley as a player. I wasn't shocked when Glen started *The Eagles* a few years later. He was too good to *not* hit it big-time.

But that was a few years off. For now, it was old and new

Ford's, pickin' for lodging and a meal.

Playing with then struggling Longbranch & Pennywhistle.
Glen Frey and John David Souther

Backstage tuning up with Glenn Fey 1968

14 JB, Glen Frey & JD Souther

I couldn't wait to tell Dan Dalton about Glen and JD. Soon, I was jumping up and down in his office. But Dan was disinterested, and just stared at me.

"I don't like their attitudes," he told me. I couldn't believe my ears.

"You don't like their attitudes? Jesus, Dan, so ... you've *already heard* Longbranch & Pennywhistle?

"Alright. ...So, you don't have to sell their attitudes," I told him. " These guys are *fabulous!* They're going to be the next Everly Brothers!"
Dan wasn't fazed.
"That one kid, Glen, is a smart ass. I'm just not interested."
And that was that!

I didn't realize it at the time but Dan had already signed up a duo called Sampson & Hagar. Pete Sampson and Sammy Hagar were two great singers but their singles failed to score any serious airplay. After Sampson and Hagar split up a year later Pete soon disappeared from the business forever while Sammy went on to a great solo career and later an even more meteoric career as lead singer for the muliti-platinum band Van Halen. But that was years away.

One thing about Dan was that he would run the show *his way,* and Longbranch & Pennywhistle were a major conflict of egos. I had brought Dan an absolute smash act, only to see that he'd already rejected it, and had never been interested in my opinion. *It infuriated me;* that my creative ingenuity could be so easily dismissed, down through his trap-door, never to be discussed again. I knew that Glen and JD were going to become *huge,* and would have easily bet *my Guild* on it. But, I would stay faithful to Dan and Lois. We had a good relationship and had always been honest and fair with each other. Dan was the boss. He had always tried to help me, but I didn't always agree with him. Finally, the day came for me to sign with Dan's production and publishing company.

I was still under age, so my parents had to drive into the Los Angeles Federal Courthouse, where they would sign the deal on my behalf. I wondered what my dad's thoughts were, allowing me to sign a real Hollywood Management and Production contract in a Federal Court Office. He must have wondered about his own dreams of being a cartoonist; dreams that never materialized. He no doubt wondered if he was doing the right thing by signing the contracts before a judge. This must have been something he couldn't quite understand, but agreed to because he didn't want *my* dreams to end up like *his*. For my careful and conservative parents, putting their signatures on my contract and encumbering themselves for heaven only knew what, was an incredibly brave thing to do. Their love and their faith in me were never more apparent.

Very quickly we all went to work, and Dan set a date for my very first official solo effort. He had made a *single's deal* with *Ranwood Records*, a lucrative agreement that called for the release of two singles with an option for an album; in other words, if I scored a hit single, an album would quickly follow. Ranwood was a good start-up label, run by professionals. Owned by *Randy Wood*, founder of *Dot Records*, a dynamic guy who prided himself in his business daring, it was also well-managed by *Larry Welk*, son of the famous TV bandleader. Dan had found a great song written by none other than Larry Murray, from The Hearts & Flowers called *As If I Needed To Be Reminded*. It was a Johnny Cash-style song about a widower who, no matter how hard he tries, can't continue living without the woman he lost. It was a dark song, but we decided to record it. Another dark song had recently hit the top of the charts called *Ode To Billy Joe*. Dan planned to cash-in on the sudden popularity of country-styled tragic-pop songs like *Bobbi Gentry's* hit, and move in the same direction with *John Edward Beland*. Everybody felt I could sell the lyrics.

My session was held at CP McGregor's studio, where I'd watched the Peppermint Trolley Company complete their first album. I played acoustic guitar, along with session *musicians Larry Brown* on drums, *Steve LeFever* on bass, and *Bernie Leadon* on the very same Gibson five-string banjo he used on The Eagles' *Take It Easy*. For the violins Dan hired the renown arranger George Tipton, famous for his score on the Jose Feliciano hit "Light My Fire." I was in the clouds.

Working with Dan in the studio was both amazing and terrifying; a feeling that occurs only in the shadowed but highly-charged labyrinth of a multi-track recording studio. I was thrilled to be the center of it all, but nervous that I would blow it in front of these great musicians, and most of all, Dan himself. But, for some reason, whenever the red recording light came on, I always found myself calm and secure. I pinched myself at the microphone to be sure I wasn't back in Hometown, asleep and dreaming all this up. It hadn't been that long since we'd moved away and everything in my life became dismal.

Now, here I was center-stage in the heart of Hollywood with my brand-new image, making a real record. It also didn't hurt that Dan knew how to run a session like clockwork, which is precisely what a recording session is. It seemed to be instinctive with him. I just followed his lead and by the end of the day, we had a record. I'd made it through, yet again. It was mind-boggling.

Charlotte and I continued to be regulars at the Troubadour Hoot-nights. We'd sit in the corner with our friends and burgers and cokes, watching the parade of talent. One-night Larry brought on an interesting band called *Spectrum,* featuring *Karen,* a girl drummer who sang in a warm, smooth beautiful style. With their short hair and squeaky-clean, Ivy League appearance, the band looked a bit out of place. We all wondered to ourselves what they were doing at the Troubadour! They seemed better-geared to *Disneyland.* But when they started playing, there was no doubt as to their talent; the girl drummer was exceptional, and the band's harmonies were brilliant. Eventually, Spectrum would change their name the following year, and the world would come to know them as *The Carpenters,* Kevin and Karen.

One Monday night Larry told me to stick around and check out this new band featuring former members of The Byrd's. *The Byrds!* Being a rabid fan, I naturally couldn't wait to see this new group now calling themselves *The Flying Burrito Brothers. OK,* I thought, laughing, *what could be the hip, hidden significance of this wacky-cool name?* As they set up, I was surprised to see a steel guitar onstage, an instrument rarely seen at the Troubadour. Soon, all dressed up in rhinestone cowboy suits, the band walked confidently onto the stage and took to their instruments. It was a shocking sight because at the time, anything to do with country music represented the redneck element and the *country, Love it or leave it* crowd. So, here came these five, long-haired, rhinestone outfitted musicians dressed and tasseled like they were members of Buck Owens band. Instantly, I recognized *Chris Hillman* from the Byrd's, as well as drummer *Michael Clark.* The others I hadn't seen before. I was very excited about seeing the Flying Burrito Brothers, especially being such a fan of the Byrd's and their incredible harmonies back when they were led by Roger McGuinn. This was going to be absolutely great! But once they started playing, I quickly changed my opinion. *They were rough. Very rough!* Not only were they too loud and out of tune, the lead singer *Gram Parsons* seemed very high, and singing in a semi out-of-pitch, nasal voice. Even Chris Hillman's great harmony singing couldn't help. And it also didn't help that *Sneaky Pete Kleinow* was ear-piercingly loud as he played his steel guitar through a distortion box! I couldn't believe how removed from the sweet sound of the Byrd's these guys were! It all made me squint. I sat, disappointed as they played songs off their just-released debut album *Gilded Palace Of Sin* to a Luke-warm reception.

"... So, what do you think, John?" Larry asked me as the Flying Burrito Brothers blasted everyone's eardrums.

"I'm sorry, Larry," I answered hesitatingly, "but what a letdown! Just listen to them! I'd *never* join a band like this in a million years!"

But my jaded prophesy was as bad as the terrible noise they were making; it would only be twelve years before I would be called on to become their musical leader. Frustrated, almost angry, I decided to buy their album the next day. *Hell,* I thought, *nobody could actually be that bad! Surprisingly,* I *loved* most of it, and a few spins slowly began to respect these guys. *The Gilded Palace of Sin* was groundbreaking stuff, alright. The record was a delight; a hundred-percent better than the rag-tagged band I'd I witnessed the previous night; literally, *Night and Day.* I laughed as I found myself playing their album over and over again. Some of it was truly inspiring. There was something unique about this album; something different than anything I had ever heard before: *Country music with a Rock-and-Roll edge and attitude.* I became an instant fan of a new style of music going down, a style the locals starting coining, "Country Rock."

7 THOMAS WOLFE SAID IT ALL

One day from out of the blue I received a phone call from my old guitar buddy Carmen back in Hometown. He wanted to know what I had been up to in Hollywood and then said he had a gig for me.

"A gig"? I questioned.

"Yeah, JB, a very cool gig" he answered back with great enthusiasm.

It seemed that some of the guys from my old high school band had put together a new group called the Chicago Diplomats, and they needed another guitarist. Carmen suggested me and the guys agreed that it would be great to have me back. They were working steady in and around the south side of Chicago appearing at lounges and teen dances and playing a mixture of rhythm and blues and soul music, a very popular sound on the south side. Now I would have the opportunity to fulfill another dream of mine, a dream that was born the day we left Illinois for California and that dream was to return, to come home. As exciting as Hollywood had been there was still a void inside my soul, an emptiness of sorts and a longing to get back to my roots. My heart was filled with joy and anticipation as Carmen told me about the band and the many gigs they were doing.

Although Thomas Wolfe had warned "You can never go home again" something inside told me to take the offer and go back to Hometown and find out for myself if the dream of returning home was all I had imagined it to be. I knew I had to go but first had to tell Dan and Lois about my decision. I was nervous as hell and the last thing I wanted to do was to seem ungrateful for all they had done. I surely didn't want to burn a bridge but I had to confront them. Although sorry to see me go, they knew I had to find out where "home" really was for John Beland. I believe that in their hearts they knew I would be back but realized that in the end that decision was mine and mine alone to make. They wished me well, which made it all the more harder to leave.

With Charlotte, it was another matter. Although she supported me as always, I knew her heart was breaking as she pondered the thought of my not returning to California. Would this be the last time she would ever see me? Although we had never looked at ourselves as a steady couple, we never had to. It was clear to both of us that we cared for each other dearly. There was no need to hang a sign on it. The next week Charlotte drove me to the airport for what was to be my first airline flight ever. She walked me to the gate trying to hold back her emotions. When the time came to board I kissed her and told her that I would return, the same promise I made to my girlfriend back in Hometown the night before we moved to California. I boarded the plane for what would be the first of a million flights I would take in the years ahead. I was scared, not about the flight as much as the uncertainty of my decision to leave. Was I making a mistake?

Would things be the same as I remembered back in Hometown? As we took off I stared out the window gazing down on the lights of L.A feeling as if I was leaving my real home, once again feeling the same sense of loss, I felt when we moved away from Hometown. What lay ahead? Little did I know?

I arrived back in Chicago late on a winter's night in 1968. It was a thrill to see Chicago from the window of my plane. There below were the sparkling lights of the city twinkling like a big "welcome home". I was thrilled and full of curiosity of what the days ahead would hold. I felt a sense of home mixed with a sense of apprehension as the wheels hit the runway. Would I find things the same as when I left? I was met at the airport by the band's manager Terry Hoch, who was elated to see me.

"Hey JB" he said. "It's so great to have you back! All the guys are excited to see you again. It's going to be a ball to have you in the new group."

As we hopped in his car I said, "Hey Terry, would you mind if we drove through Hometown on our way to your house"?

"Sure thing, JB. It hasn't changed much since you left. We'll take a drive through it."

It was nearly midnight when we pulled into Hometown and headed down my old street. It was eerie looking out the window as a winter's frost cast a slight fog that hung over the snow filled little street I grew up on. There it stood, my old house, silent and still in the late hours, the only sounds being a faint bark from a dog or the clanging sound of the nearby railroad gates warning of an oncoming train. Where there once was activity and laughter and a sense of security now seemed dead and frozen in the winter's harsh cold. Only the echoes of family and friends remained, imaginary images of my younger self running in the yard throwing snowballs with my brother Bob and hearing the faint voice of my mother calling us in for supper. Images, echoes.

"Let's go, Terry" I said in a quiet voice, as not to break the haunting silence that surrounded us. And as we pulled away my heart felt a heavy weight in the realization that time waits for no one.

I found out that instead of being asked to stay at any of the band member's homes I was informed by Terry that I'd be staying with him in his basement on an army cot. "Strange" I thought. Why wouldn't my old bandmates offer me a room at their homes? I thought they would have opened their doors wide open for me! But that didn't happen for some weird reason.

I didn't make a big deal about it. However, a flag went up in my mind, a small one but a flag just the same.

Despite my living conditions it was great to see my old band members again. They had found an electric guitar for me to use, as the only guitar I owned was back in California with Charlotte, and that was an acoustic guitar. The band sounded tight. Carmen and I handled the guitar section while Johnny Livigni handled drums and lead vocals, Tony Sicilliano was on the bass and his cousin Larry Klimas played the sax. In the years to come all three would eventually move to Hollywood. Johnny would change his name to John Valenti and have a number of major dance hits in the late 70's. Tony would become a much in demand bass player working with Mac Davis and Rick Nelson and Larry would go on to become one of the top sax players in the business, playing for Neil Diamond, The Manhattan Transfer and many others. But that was a long way up the road. For now, we were just another south side band working the same circuit as a hundred other groups in the surrounding area.

One of the more important gigs we did was to back up Chicago radio legend Dick Biondi on a live show he had put together for high school dances and lounges. He called it "Dick Biondi's History of Rock and Roll." Dick would give the audience a brief history of various rock and roll pioneers and for everyone he mentioned we would perform one of the acts big hits. Working with Dick was a thrill. I literally grew up listening to him on WLS Radio, the hottest station in the Mid-West. He had the voice and the personality to win any crowd over. In Chicago he was king of the airways and everywhere we performed with him kids from far and wide flocked to see him. He was a wiry little guy. Thin as a rail with a head of curly black hair and Buddy Holly style glasses. I was amazed at his easy-going demeanor off stage. He was a genuinely "nice guy" with absolutely no ego. But on the mic he commanded the room with that golden recognizable voice. Kids worshiped him. Years later Dick would be inducted into the Rock and Roll Hall Of Fame, and rightfully so. Today, well into his 80's, Dick is still on the air in Chicago, playing oldies, as popular and loved as ever.

But after the fun gigs we did I had to return to Terry's basement, alone and wondering where any of this was leading to. While the other band members were at home, comfortable in their warm beds and eating home cooked meals and surrounded by family, I was in a cold basement, living on cheap burgers and without any kind of social life at all. Furthermore, it felt surreal to be staying in Terry's basement, so close to the house I had grown up in back in Hometown, only a mile or two away. I felt like an outsider, not an old friend from a few years ago. As the weeks went by I grew despondent and longed to be back in Hollywood with Charlotte, Dan and Lois, back at the Troubadour, back to the environment I had struggled so hard to be a part of only to leave it for this, an army cot and a false sense of friendship.

One night on June 6, 1968 I was upstairs watching Terry's family television. Nobody was home, so I sat back and watched the California election primaries live on TV. Robert Kennedy had won, and it looked as if he was sure to be the next Democratic presidential nominee. "Now it's on to Chicago" he announced to an adoring crowd of supporters all packed into the banquet room of the Ambassador Hotel in Los Angeles. Suddenly the celebration turned to panic as the reporter announced that Kennedy had been shot while exiting the podium. I was frozen to the screen thinking "Oh no, not again!" I truly felt that he would be alright and that there was no way this would be a repeat of 1963. But then the announcement came. "Robert F Kennedy was dead."

I felt detached from the world as I watched the horror unfold on TV. It was strange to not have friends and family around me at this terrible moment. I ached for Charlotte's comforting embrace, but I was alone, watching the country's bright future disappear in a second. It was then and there that I realized I had to return to my beloved California, back to Charlotte, The Daltons, the Troubadour, the studio, the life I missed so much. My place wasn't here in a basement just down the road from where I grew up. My parents, my siblings, my relatives had moved on. Hometown was now just a ghost from the past. My place was back in Hollywood and I decided to do something about it. I called Charlotte and told her I was coming "home." I had enough money from the band gigs to buy a one way red-eye flight to LA and I would be leaving that very night. Charlotte was elated and told me she would inform Dan and Lois and that she would be there to pick me up at the airport. I went downstairs to the basement of Terry's and wrote a short note:

"Guys, This isn't working for me. Going back to California. Good luck with the band.
JB"

I left the note on my pillow on the cot, called a cab and caught the next flight out to Los Angeles. This time I didn't stop in Hometown on the way out. I had seen enough to know that all I had foolishly longed for was forever imbedded in the past. Now I was more intent on heading towards my future. California was calling me home and I headed back as fast as I could.

John Beland

8 HOME IS WHERE YOU FIND IT

Back in Los Angeles dear Charlotte was waiting for me at the gate just as she promised. She had always been there for me and this time was no exception. With a larger than life smile on her face she ran to embrace me as I stepped off the plane. Once in her arms I felt the weight of the world lift from my shoulders. The very next day I met with Dan and Lois. Immediately I noticed some changes … all great. While I was gone Dan's main act, *The Peppermint Trolley Company* had scored a top 10 single and there was great excitement in the office. Speaking of "office" Dan and Lois had now moved headquarters to Sunset Blvd just above the lush surroundings of the popular Mouling Chinese Restaurant, a popular industry watering hole frequented by an array of celebrities, producers, agents all wheeling and dealing at lunchtime in the beautiful outdoor gardens just below Dan's window. The Daltons were now finally enjoying the fruits of their labors thanks to the success of the Peppermint Trolley Company's new hit record "Baby You Come Rolling Cross My Mind." Dan knew how to make records and he scored big on this one. The single now gave Dan status with the major labels and money to operate on a higher level than before I had left for Chicago.

When I walked into the reception area of the Dalton's new office, Lois greeted me with open arms and a warm familiar smile. She filled me in on everything that had happened while I was away and painted a very positive picture for days ahead. She led me into Dan's new office, a big Spanish style room with a baby grand piano in the corner and a big oak desk filled with papers, tapes and demo records.

"Hey John" Dan shouted out as he jumped up from his chair. "Welcome back. We've really missed you!"

It felt like a million bucks being back with the Daltons. They were now flooded with projects and the energy in the office was electric.

Now that I had made it clear I was staying in Hollywood for good, Dan signed me to an exclusive recording, publishing deal. Being underage my parents once again had to drive into the Superior Court in Los Angeles to sign the contracts on my behalf. I was walking on a

74

cloud as we celebrated at a local Hollywood Bistro. Mom and dad were thrilled and concerned during the entire day. All of this was so foreign to them, but they put their trust in the Daltons and left me in their capable hands. To this day I still wonder what went through their minds as they signed those contracts.

Once I signed with Dan and Lois the doors started opening. First off, my old friend from the Monday night Troubadour Hoots, Larry Murray was now a staff writer on the new CBS TV Show the Glen Campbell Goodtime Hour. Campbell, a former A-Team studio guitarist had recently scored big time with his number one hit single "Gentle on My Mind" written by John Hartford. CBS quickly signed Glen as a summer replacement for the Smothers Brothers Show which led to his own prime time slot for the network. Larry had called Dan Dalton

Glen Campbell Goodtime Hour

to see if I would be interested in working on the show as a singer to entertain the audience waiting in line to get in for the tapings. I would have to sing country oriented songs and answer questions from the audience about Glen and the show. The gig paid $250.00 a week. I jumped at it and soon I was walking into CBS Studios, acoustic guitar in hand ready to start working on my first paid gig in Hollywood.

Since I was working on the show I was allowed access backstage at CBS where I became good friends with the great banjo playing songwriter John Hartford who was a regular on the show. John took a liking to me and we started picking together every week before the audience showed up. Playing with John opened my eyes and ears to bluegrass music. We would take Beatles songs and do them bluegrass style and it sounded fantastic. What fun we had during those weeks I worked at the show. I also got to meet some of the biggest stars in the entertainment industry as well. In fact, I used to get to work early so I could catch who was Glen's guest star for the week. From Johnny Mathis to John Wayne I got to meet them all backstage.

Backstage with John Hartford 1968

Two guests in particular will forever stay in my memory. I was backstage one day when I noticed two familiar faces walking my way. I couldn't tell who they were until they finally came into view and then I nearly jumped out of my jeans. There before me headed my way came none other than my boyhood hero, Roy Rogers and Dale Evans dressed in their sparkling Nudie's western cloths with dual six guns strapped around their wastes. Like every other kid my age, I grew up with Roy and Dale and idolized the two of them. Well, I ran and grabbed the house photographer, Jasper Daley, and told him to follow me.

Then, with a deep breath, I walked up to Roy and said with a shaky voice: "Mr. Rogers, my name is John Beland and I work here at the show. I'm your biggest fan. Could I get my picture taken with you, sir?" Roy smiled and threw his arm around a grinning me as Jasper snapped away. I kept thinking "How many times had Roy been asked the same request by millions of fans?" But he gladly obliged and was everything I would have expected from my boyhood hero. What a huge thrill. If only the folks back in Hometown could see me now!

One of the most embarrassing things that happened to me on the show was the day the announcer, Roger Caroll, came up to me and said, "John, I have to talk to you about something." I wondered what the hell I did wrong.

"Listen John, if you're going to work on the Glen Campbell Goodtime Hour it might be a good thing to get to know just exactly Glen's history before you answer questions from the audience."

Seems I had been making up answers about Glen when answering questions from the audience. For example, I would tell the folks that Glen was born and raised in Texas, when in fact he was born and raised in Delight, Arkansas! I was busted and promised Mr. Caroll that I would get my facts straight before next week's taping! I also became friends with comedian Pat Paulsen, one of the funniest people I had ever met. What a great guy who made everybody backstage laugh their ass off! The guests that year included Linda Ronstadt, Ann Murray, Jerry Reed, John Wayne, Dione Warwick, the Monkees, without Mike Nesmith, Tom Jones and Neil Diamond to name a few.

I loved working at the Campbell Show and looked forward to every Sunday afternoon taping. I learned so much from hanging with Glen's band, Bob Felts, Norm Cash, Billy Graham and John Hartford and studying Glen himself, a master guitarist and amazing singer. What an education it was for an 18-year-old kid from Hometown.

With the money I earned from the Campbell Show I got a studio apartment just below the Hollywood Hills on a little cobblestone street called Vista Del Mar. It was above an old house next to a little church. Only two rooms, a tiny bath and a main room with a kitchenette but it was all mine, for $65.00 a month. I was on my way! I was starting to become a good songwriter by this time, influenced by the enormous talent I would see at the Troubadour as well as some of the big-name writers that would pass in and out of Dan's office pitching him material, writers like Paul Williams and Jimmy Webb.

John Beland

My first apartment on Vista Del Mar in Hollywood

One-day Dan called me into the office all excited.

"John, I have some great news for you."

I was all ears.

"Two weeks ago, I met Gordon Mills, who produces Tom Jones and Englebert Humperdink. I met him at Sy Devours Clothes Store while he was trying on a suit. I happened to have a demo of your song "Nashville Lady" in the car and ran out and grabbed it in time to give it Gordon. Well, Gordon's office called today and Englebert Humperdink recorded it on his new album! *"The Eagle Shit!"*

That was Dan's favorite expression whenever he landed a money-making project.

At that time Humperdink was selling a lot of records and to get a cut on one of his albums meant thousands of dollars for the writer and the publisher. I jumped for joy! My first cut as a writer, and a huge one at that! I was able to get a $1,500.00 advance which Dan and Lois paid me a weekly draw from. With that Charlotte and I went shopping! I bought a new wardrobe of high dollar leather boots, western shirts and pants. Things were turning out incredible.

Meanwhile, Dan started to record me as a solo act. I had come up with a new arrangement for the Peppermint Trolley Company's hit from a year earlier, *"Baby You Come Rolling Cross My Mind"* which knocked Dan out. I had added new chords and slowed it down to a neat ballad and the song took on a whole new original feel. It sounded like a hit. Dan called a session and we cut it with a full string section and background vocalists. It sounded like a smash. Armed with a potential hit in his hands, Dan landed me another singles deal with Ranwood Records. Ranwood was getting hot with a massive pop hit by the duo Zager and Evans called *"In the Year 2525."* It claimed the number one spot in the country for six weeks. So I now had a publishing deal, a major cut as a songwriter and money in the bank. Not bad. Not bad at all.

9 MEANWHILE, BACK AT THE TROUB

While my version of *"Baby You Come Rollin Cross My Mind"* was getting ready for release, Charlotte and I continued hanging out at the Troubadour where I would continue to play on the Monday night Hoots. We witnessed an amazing parade of talent on those open mic nights, some acts would go on to fame and fortune while a majority would blaze across the Hollywood sky for only a moment before burning out and vanishing.

Steve Martin was a regular Monday night feature, throwing the whole place into hysterics with his offbeat original brand of humor. One night the winners of the popular game TV game show THE DATING GAME, were due to visit the Troubadour as part of their prize. Steve told the audience that when the winning couple came through the door to start laughing and applauding him like crazy regardless of what he said onstage. When the couple came in, dressed as if they were going to the prom, they found their seat and watched Steve do his act. Steve said something like "I went to the store and bought myself twelve bananas!" The place went crazy with laughter and wild applause. But sitting in the VIP section, the Dating Game couple only looked confused and baffled. "Then I went to the kitchen and poured myself some java" Steve would say. Again, the crowd roared with delight and pounded their approval on the tables. The Dating Game couple looked like deer in the headlights, totally clueless to the inside joke but halfheartedly clapping as not to look cool like everyone else. This went on for about five minutes until the couple, with their chaperone, eventually got up and left. Steve was brilliant, and everyone loved him.

One act that made its debut on a Monday night was a band consisting of past members from the legendary Buffalo Springfield. They wore very cool western shirts and jeans and full of energy with a powerhouse of talent. Like the Flying Burrito Brothers they also featured a brilliant steel guitarist, Rusty Young. And when they sang they sounded like choir boys, beautiful harmonies and incredible instrumental work. They called themselves Poco, and would become one of new breed of country rock architects gracing the stage of the Troubadour in the late 60's.

Other acts that made their debut on Monday night were The Five Man Electric Band, Sunshine Company, folk duo Hedge &

Donna, The Nitty Gritty Dirt Band, Jennifer Warren, The Merry Go Round, The Hearts & Flowers, The Dillards and many more.

One-day Dan called me to his office to tell me of a recording project he had for me and Lois. ABC had a new sitcom coming out and they had signed Dan's group the Peppermint Trolley Company to sing the show's title theme song. Unfortunately, the band broke up. Not wanting to work with Dalton any longer Dan, who owned the name, had to quickly put together another *"Peppermint Trolley Company"* to sing the theme song. He chose myself, Lois, and one of his latest finds, songwriter arranger Paul Parrish. The three of us worked up the silly title song and went down to Paramount Pictures to record it. I found it ironic that just a couple years earlier I was sneaking into this movie studio to watch them make films. Now, my name was actually at the gate and the security guard happily waved me through. We took our positions around one microphone in the dark, almost ancient sound stage and did a run through. I noticed that behind us they ran the visuals to the opening credits as we sang. I recognized one of the stars from the old Bob Cummings Show "Love That Bob" but didn't recognize anyone else. A loud school bell rang as we prepared to do a take. 3, 2, 1…..

"Here's the story 'bout a lovely lady
Who was raising three very lovely girls?
All of them had hair of gold like their mother.
The youngest was in curls.
Here's the story about a man named Brady
Who was busy with three boys of his own.
They were four men living all together
Yet they were all alone.
Till the one day when the lady met this fellow
And they knew that it was much more than a hunch
That the two would someday for a family.
That's the way the all became the Brady Bunch."

Well, it wasn't "Blowing In The Wind" but it paid a whopping $250.00 and that's all I thought about. The rest, as they say, *is TV sitcom history.* But at the time I wasn't interested in the show one bit except for wanting to cash the check as fast as I could. To this day I have never seen a complete episode of the Brady Bunch. But it seems like every other human being on the planet sure has!

Knowing I was a lifelong Ricky Nelson fan, Charlotte called me one day all excited.

"John, guess who's playing this week at the Troubadour?"

"Beats me" I answered. "The Beatles?"

"Very funny, but maybe just as interesting to you. Rick Nelson and his new band."

I was stunned! "Are you kidding me?" I answered back.

"Of course not!" Charlotte snapped back. "He's debuting his new band called the Stone Canyon Band. They're doing a sound check this afternoon. Why don't we go down there?"

There was a recording sound truck parked in front of the Troubadour when Charlotte and I arrived in the early afternoon. Cables were everywhere, and the sound crew was busy carting in speakers and mic stands, getting ready to record Rick and the band's debut later that evening.

We both strolled inside and made our way to the top balcony. The Troubadour staff was busy setting tables and cleaning floors, so nobody questioned our being there. From the top of the stairs we had a perfect view of Rick and the band tuning up and preparing to run through a few numbers for a sound check. There he was, the guy I idolized back in Hometown whose records had such a profound impact on me. He looked the same as he did in films as well as on the old TV show "*The Adventures of Ozzie & Harriet*," with the exception... a longer hairstyle, faded jeans and T-shirt. I noticed that the band featured yet another steel guitar player and I wondered what kind of music Rick was going to play that night. Rock, country, folk? It was a real mystery to me as I watched the band get ready to launch into one of their songs. When they kicked off the first number it was evident that this was no "oldies but goodies" concert. The band was sensational, a mixture of Poco and Dylan and when Rick walked up to the mic and sang, there was that undeniable voice that sold millions of records. Furthermore, the band members sang beautiful harmonies, especially Rick's bass player Randy Meisner. In the years to come, Randy would wind up as a founding member of the Eagles, writing and singing one of their biggest hits "Take It to the Limit."

Another surprise was Rick's brilliant steel guitarist, Tom Brumley. For years Tom had played with none other than country legend Buck Owens. Now he was part of Rick's new band and the blend of his steel with the rock edge of the rest of the band was incredible. As we watched the rehearsal I secretly envied his guitarist, Alan Kemp. I wanted his job. How cool would it be if I actually was the lead guitarist for Rick Nelson? I certainly imagined it as Rick and his Stone Canyon Band ran through their set list. It was funny. Back in the early 60's Rick's rock and roll records really connected with me and now even his new direction seemed to have the same effect. Little did I know that a decade later I would be standing in Alan Kemp's place, playing behind my idol and once again living out another dream. But that was 10 years off. For now, Charlotte and I watched the rehearsal, thrilled to hear Rick and the band pioneering a yet another new style of pop music.

10 WELCOME TO THE ROAD

At the start of 1969 Dan called me into his office to tell me about a project. He and Lois had seen an ad in the Hollywood Reporter about the former hit group Spanky and Our Gang looking for a new guitarist. The ad called for a young, good looking, skilled guitarist who could handle harmony vocals. Spanky and Our Gang was known for their exceptional, complex harmonies on such stand out hits as *"Sunday Will Never Be the Same" "Sunday Morning" "I'd Like To Get To Know You" "Give a Damn"* and many more. Both Dan and Lois felt that it was a great opportunity for me. They also felt that it was time for me to finally leave the nest. Thanks to the guidance of the Dalton's I now had the experience and the training to handle being in a major group and now it was time to test it all out.

The audition was held at an office on Sunset Blvd and I went there armed with my Guild guitar. I was one of a half dozen musicians sitting around waiting for their turn. None of them spoke a word to me. Finally, after a half hour wait I was called into the office where I was greeted by the band's manager, a very warm and friendly man named Curly Tate.

"Hi John, I'm Curly the manager and this is Nigel Pickering and Kenny Hodges."

I shook hands with Nigel and Kenny, recognizing them from their many TV appearances. Nigel was a tall, thin, neatly groomed David Niven looking sort of fellow, skinny mustache and all. He was much older than I expected, probably 20 years older than myself. Kenny was a jovial kind of guy with a big warm smile and a slight stutter. All three were exceptionally friendly and I instantly felt quite calm and relaxed with them.

"Hey John" Nigel said "How are you with harmonies?"

"Well, I'm good at it. I love the Beach Boys, Byrds and of course the Beatles."

"That's great. Let's try singing something."

With that Nigel pulled out his big old beautiful blonde Gibson jazz guitar from its case. "I call her "Mama" Nigel said with a smile as he strummed a few chords. Kenny suggested we play a Beatles song since I was a devout fan. "How about "I've Just Seen A Face?" Nigel strummed away on "Mama" while I trailed behind on my trusty Guild F50. They both sounded great when they sang but when I added a third part harmony to the chorus, we all sounded fantastic! When we finished Nigel and Kenny looked over at Curly, who was nodding his head in agreement.

"That's great John. Play a little guitar behind this next song" said Kenny.

They launched into a rocking original song of theirs called "Freeborn Man" and I filled in all the lead parts as well as impressive solo. When it was over all three asked me if I'd be interested in joining the band.

"You bet" I said with a huge smile!

The three of us sat down to talk about the project.

"John, here's what the project is all about" started Curly. "As you know, Spanky has been the Gang's lead singer since the beginning. She's sung on all the records and tours and she's irreplaceable. Well, last month she informed us that she was quitting the band for personal reasons. Rather than replace her with another sound alike singer, the guys and myself have agreed to start an entirely new group called "One Man's Family."

I was surprised to hear that Spanky and Our Gang was no more. But Curly went on.

"We still want to feature the harmony vocals that made the Gang so popular, but now we want to stretch out even more with a harder edge and slight change of direction more towards a country rock feel." Now I was getting very interested. Curly continued. "There's already a lot of interest in the new band from promoters and labels and all we have to do is deliver the goods. A tour is all set to begin in Vail, Colorado and it will take us all the way to Chicago where we'll open for the Byrds. There will be record people at that gig and I'm confident that if the band goes over well we'll land a major deal shortly afterwards."

"What do ya say, kid?" asked Nigel "The road awaits!"

Kenny chimed in "We love your playing and singing John. You're perfect for us. Hope you'll come aboard!"

I didn't have to give it a few days to think about it. I could see the opportunities and I admired Nigel and Kenny, two seasoned vets of countless TV and recording work. I'd be a fool not to jump at it.

"Count me in, fellows!" I announced, shaking their hands. I couldn't wait to start work with these guys.

Onstage at 2nd City, Chicago with Nigel Pickering & One Man's Family 1969

Rehearsals took place in a funky old house in Topanga Canyon, not far from the Pacific Ocean. Topanga was laid back community of actors, artists and musicians, some very well-known musicians, too. Nigel had been dating a beautiful long-haired blonde named Brook, who lived close by where we rehearsed. I noticed that Brook usually brought her roommate along, who always stood in the background watching and listening. I wondered who she was but never found the nerve to inquire although she looked mighty familiar. One Man's Family consisted of myself on guitar and vocals, Nigel on guitar and vocals, Kenny on bass and vocals, Thad Maxwell on drums and a cute little redhead singer named Sue Richards. Sue was a great singer who had even sung with George Harrison in the Concert for Bangladesh. She was painfully shy but certainly could belt out a song as good as anyone in town. Together we sounded terrific. Our repertoire consisted of a few Spanky and Our Gang favorites as well as some rocking versions of classic old country tunes such as the Osborne Brothers *"Once More"* and the Everly Brothers *"When Will I Be Loved?"* We also worked up some short comedy bits to fill in between songs. Nigel and Kenny's timing was spot on. They were hilarious. It was a real rush to be amongst such talent. I watched, listened and learned everything from harmony to timing. These guys were pro's and I felt damn lucky to be working with them.

I had to tell Charlotte about our upcoming tour, and that was difficult. Once again I was leaving and had no idea when I would return to L.A. We both knew that it was inevitable that I would go off on my own and continue to follow my career. There was no room in my life for a steady relationship no matter how deeply I felt for her. We would remain friends, but just like with the Daltons, it was time for me to move on. I knew it hurt her and I felt terrible about it. She meant the world to me and had it not been for her I would have been swallowed up on the streets of Hollywood long before I ever stepped into a recording studio. I owed her everything. But Charlotte never complained or caused any scene. That was typical of her. She still supported me and wished the best for me. Dearest Charlotte, you were a guarding Angel when I was down to my lowest point. In my heart I wished her happiness and love. I never saw or heard from her again except for one day in 1980. My mother had died and we had just buried her high on a hill next to dad in Napa, California. When I came back to mom's house following the services I was told by the lady taking care of mom's place that a call had come in for me. The person on the other end wouldn't leave a message, only her first name. Charlotte.

Dear Charlotte and I in Bel-Air 1968

"Hey kid" Nigel said to me one day at rehearsal. "There's a party going on tomorrow tonight at photographer Henry Diltz's house up in the hills. He invited all of us and I've got you fixed up with a date." "A date? Are you kidding me?" I blurted out! "Yeah, yeah a date, as in female companionship" he said cynically. "She's Brook's roommate and you're going to thank me later. We'll pick them up tomorrow night so don't make any other plans." I was all nerves and begged Nigel to get me off the hook. "Nigel, I don't want to be fixed up on any blind date. Call it off!" "Too late kid" he said. "It's all set, so relax. It's going to be a great night!"

The very next night Nigel and I drove up to Topanga Canyon where Brook and her roommate lived. Their rustic old house was high on a steep hill. As we climbed up the steps I started getting nervous and sweaty and once again begged Nigel to take me home.

"Will you relax, kid?" he scolded. "Just follow my lead and you'll be fine." That was Nigel. Ever the suave lady killing man-about-town.

We got to the door and Nigel whispered "Ok, kid. Be cool and don't blow this."

"Easy for you to say" I whispered back. You know who your date is. I haven't a clue who the heck is mine!"

"Oh yea, that's right" he whispered again. It's Linda Ronstadt."

"What? I shouted out! Are you kidding me, Nigel?"

"Hey, be quiet, kid" he scolded in a whisper. "Just roll with the flow."

I was petrified as Nigel knocked on the big oak door, which was soon answered by Nigel's beautiful girlfriend, Brook.

"Hi guys" she said with a smile "Come on in and have a seat. Linda's still getting ready so we'll be a few minutes." With that she left us alone in the living room while she and Linda got ready. The girl's house was an earthy old place with lots of tapestries and antiques everywhere. Nigel sat on a big overstuffed chair with his leg slung across the arm rest, smoking a cigarette and looking like a combination of Errol Flynn and the Cheshire Cat from Alice In Wonderland. As for me, I was sinking deep into the sofa where I had landed. Looking like some helpless passenger from the Titanic.

"Hey kid" Nigel whispered. "Come here. And he motioned for me to lean forward.
I moved in a little. "What do you want, Nigel?" I whispered back. "Take a peek down the hall. There's Linda." I turned my head and glanced down the hall and froze like a deer in the headlights. There through the open door in one of the bedrooms was Linda Ronstadt, completely nude, back towards me bending over putting on her shoes! I nearly fell off the sofa in shock as Nigel chuckled away.

"God dammit, Nigel" I whispered in a fit of rage as he sat smiling in his easy chair puffing away on his cigarette.

The girls soon came out into the living room and I was finally introduced to Linda Marie Ronstadt. Linda looked terrific in a pair of shorts and a tiny t-shirt with a long flowing hair and big brown eyes.

"Hi Beland" she said in a bouncy cheerful voice. "I've been watching you at your rehearsals. I love your guitar playing!"

Now it made sense! She was the attractive brown eyed girl standing in the back of the rehearsal room with Brook so many times. Little did I know? From our first "hello" I felt like I had known Linda forever. She was fun and outgoing, sure of herself and of course, cute as a button. We arrived at the home of Henry Diltz, one of the premier rock photographers in the business. Henry had taken the iconic debut album cover of Crosby, Stills and Nash, and he had also taken my first publicity photos for Ranwood Records. Henry knew everyone, and everyone knew him. At the house we all made our way to the dimly lit living room where we formed a circle and played music all evening. It was a mellow laid-back scene as one by one each guest did a song. I played along with everyone, throwing in a few fancy guitar riffs hoping it would impress Linda, who sat by my feet as I played. I guess I succeeded because suddenly, in the middle of one song, I felt her foot going up the inside of my pants leg. I kept playing and doing my best to keep cool, but it was a losing battle. I kept remembering what Nigel had warned me when the girls weren't listening: "Kid, Linda wants you play guitar for her, so you've got it made tonight. But don't give in no matter what! We leave for Colorado in two days, so don't fall in love for Christ's sake!" Those words of his kept running through my mind as Linda's foot kept running further up the leg of my jeans!

On the way back to her place she leaned over and in a soft voice as not to let Nigel hear, she said

"Beland, why don't you play guitar for me? I'm putting a new solo band together and you would be great in it." I felt like Christ in the desert being tempted by the devil.

"Gee, Linda. I just can't leave the band hanging like that. We leave in two days. I just couldn't do that to them." Later that night she told me "That's OK, Beland. But listen, if the band should break up be sure to call me. You'll have a gig with me right away." I was relieved to say the least but a part of me regretted passing up the chance to join up with her. Linda was a terrific person, full of life and so much fun to be with. She was totally void of ego and made you feel as if you knew her all your life. I knew we'd cross paths again.

Linda Ronstadt

One Man's Family did a couple gigs around Hollywood to get us ready for the cross-country tour. One gig was at the Troubadour where the reaction was fantastic and very promising. The other show was in Glendale at the famous folk club called the Ice House. Same reaction. We knew we had a hit band. All of us could feel it. Now to take it across the country to see how the rest of America would react. We hit the road bound for Vail Colorado in the winter of 1969. The first "official" gig was booked at a local ski lodge and the place was packed with drunken ski bums and snobby rich women. Just before show time Nigel had some advice for me. "Listen, kid. The air is pretty thin up here so don't sing too loud in the beginning or you'll black out." I shrugged it off. I didn't need any advice. I certainly knew how to sing on stage without any last-minute pointers, or so I thought! Our opening song was a version of the Hollies classic "*Look Through Any Window.*" It was a full-on, four-part harmony number and a great opener. However, when I walked up to the mic and belted out the first sentence, the lights went out and I woke up on a sofa backstage. There looking down at me with a look of "I told you so" stood Nigel. "Nice way to start the tour, kid. Too bad you missed a great show."

We trekked across the country playing scores of colleges and a few concerts, sharing the bill with acts like Steppenwolf and the Hollies. It was a great experience and with every show I could feel us getting tighter and tighter. Not all the gigs went smoothly, however. At one college concert somewhere in the mid-west, and right in the middle of our set, some guy kept interrupting Nigel shouting out "Play some soul music!" Nigel ignored him and went on with the intro to our next song. Once again he was interrupted by the same guy "Hey, play some soul music!" The crowd started booing the jerk who was doing the heckling, but he wouldn't stop. Nigel had enough and said over the mic "Listen, my dear friend. We don't play soul music so why don't you leave and let the rest of the audience enjoy the show?" A roar of approval came from the crowd. Suddenly, the guy stands up, points a real gun at us and yells "I said play some fucking soul music!" The room fell silent as a church as I snuck off stage to get security while Nigel looked at the rest of the band and simply started singing a verse of James Brown's hit "I Feel Good." Eventually security yanked the guy out of the building. I thanked one of the security guards for coming to our rescue. "Ah, no problem. Besides, nothing would have happened anyway. That guy was old Bill. He does that all the time at our concerts!"

We arrived in the Windy City on a cold snowy night and immediately headed to N. Wells Street, better known as "Old Town" to Chicagoans. Situated not far from Lake Michigan, Old Town was an exclusive haven for actors, poets, folk and blues artists. The famed comedy improvisational group Second City was based in the heart of Old Town. It was there that such iconic names in comedy got their start, artists such as John Belushi, Jim Belushi, screenwriter Harold Ramis (National Lampoon, Ghost Busters) Brian Doyle Murray and SCTV's Joe Flaherty, to name a few. In the center of all this collection of talented people was a lady named Loraine Blue, nicknamed Mother Blue by those who knew her well. Blue was a big jovial woman who owned an apartment in an old brownstone building just over the famed Piper's Alley, one of Old Town's more popular tourist attractions. In the 60's Blue owned one of the most famous clubs in Chicago simply called "Mother Blues." It was the launching pad for such legendary artists like the Blues Project, Siegel – Schwall Band and Spanky and Our Gang. By the time we arrived Blue had long since retired from running a club and now lived in a rustic old apartment surrounded by young kids and musicians. I guess you could say it was kind of a commune.

When we showed up at her door Loraine was ecstatic. She had known Kenny and Nigel for years, going back to the very beginnings of Spanky and Our Gang. When she set eyes on her two dear friends from years ago she out a loud scream and proceeded to give us all giant hugs and well wishes. She led us inside her apartment which was buzzing with all sorts of people. Guitars were playing in the living room, food was cooking in the kitchen and everywhere you looked there was activity going on.

"Now come on in, make yourself at home and we'll fix you up with some food and drink and get you all settled in" she announced. I cautiously looked around, not knowing a single soul while Blue, Nigel and Kenny proceeded to pull up chairs and crack open a bottle of wine.

"Oh, my lord" she said with a huge smile "This is just like old times!"

While Kenny and Nigel were getting reacquainted with Blue and sharing one old war story after the next, I made my way to the kitchen where I spotted a very pretty girl, slim and tall with long brown hair flowing down her back. She had a warm friendly smile and big brown eyes and was busy cooking up dinner for everyone.

"Hi" she turned around and said. "I'm Suzy. Are you in the band?"

"Uh, yeah I am" I sheepishly said. "I play guitar and sing. Something smells good. What are you cooking?"

"Oh, just beef stew. Good for a cold night like this. Are you hungry?"

As a matter of fact, I was starved. We had been driving all night without stopping for dinner.

"Sure" I said, "if it's not too much trouble."

She threw me another warm smile and a very friendly look and for the next couple of hours chatted the night away over a bowl of beef stew and a couple glasses of wine. "My room is just down the hall" she said after we had eaten and downed a few wines. "Come on, I'll show you."

With that she took my hand and led me to her room. It was dimly lit with beads hanging from the doorway and black light illuminating posters on the wall. Her bed was a mattress all covered with furs and animal hides. Incense was burning on the table next to her bed and the whole room felt like something out of Alice in Wonderland.

"Do you like the Beatles?" she asked.

"Who doesn't?" I replied.

"I have a bootleg record of their new album that's coming out next month" she said. "Want to hear it?"

"Sure" I answered, still looking around her wild bedroom in wonder.

We laid down on her bed as the Beatles started playing "Back in the USSR." It didn't take long before she moved closer and closer with each new Beatle's track. By the last track, ironically titled "Goodnight" we were under her blankets, rolling and tumbling around until day break. Welcome to Chicago!

A few days later, One Man's Family began rehearsals next door to Blue's at the Second City Theater. There we became friends with the Second City Players comedy troupe consisting of Joe Flaherty, Jim Fisher, Brian Murray, Judy Morgan, Robbie McGuire and Harold Ramis. I used to get to rehearsals a bit early so I could catch the comedy troupe doing improvisation bits and working out new skits. They were brilliant, and I learned a thing or two about timing and comedy just by watching them rehearse. We stayed at Mother Blue's for a week up to our most important gig of the tour, the legendary Aragon Ballroom. We would share the bill with blues artist Al Kooper, the Second City Players and finally the one and only Byrds. Our manager Curly made sure that the show would be reviewed in all the top music trades hoping that a positive one would secure us a record deal with one of the major labels. It was all on the line.

One night after rehearsal, our drummer Thad Maxwell and I decided to brave the blizzard outside and grab a couple beers at the pub across the street from Blue's, the famous Earl of Old Town.

As famous as it was it was nothing more than a corner bar with one solitary microphone and stool tucked away in the corner. The Earl was practically empty when we arrived except for a lone singer playing to a room full of empty chairs. He was an awkward looking fellow with a Woody Guthrie kind of way about him. He wasn't the greatest singer in the world either. Thad and I whispered a few jokes between us as the guy continued to sing away to an empty bar. On our way out the bar we asked the bartender who they guy singing was.

"Oh, you mean John?" he said proudly. "That's John Prine. He's a mailman who comes in here and sings occasionally. Good songs!" I looked at Thad and we both raised our eyebrows and as we headed for the door I still recall the poor guy singing some song called "Sam Stone." One line in particular stood out as Thad and I headed out the into the snowy Chicago night;

"There's a hole in daddy's arm where all the money goes.
And Jesus Christ died for nothing, I suppose."

"Not a bad song" I said to Thad. "That guy's pretty good."

With that we left the Earl and headed back to Blue's. Little did we know that we had just listened to a guy who would eventually become one of the greatest singer / songwriters of our generation in the coming years. That's one we let slip right by us.

While at Blue's I continued to hang out with the lovely Suzy. We spent a lot of time talking music and rolling around in her hippie style bedroom, pure 60's. She was sweet and fun with a great personality. One could really get stuck on a girl like that. However, we had career business to concentrate on, namely the big concert at the Aragon coming up.

The Aragon Ballroom was packed to the rafters the night of our show. This was a very old and famous ballroom that dated back to the days of when my parents were teenagers. In fact, they probably jitterbugged at this very place to the famous big bands that appeared here through the 30's and 40's. Both Thad and I were diehard Byrds fans and couldn't wait to see their show, especially from backstage. But the most important musician we wanted to see firsthand was the Byrd's legendary lead guitarist, and master of the Fender Telecaster, Clarence White.

We had heard all about Clarence back in L.A where he was the "buzz" going around Hollywood whenever the subject of hot guitarists came up. Clarence first started as a bluegrass guitarist performing with his two brothers and father at festivals and small clubs in and around southern California. In fact, they even appeared as Andy Griffith's backing band in a few episodes of the Andy Griffith Show. When he got older and switched to a Fender Telecaster, he started playing on tons of recording sessions. His unique style was a combination of electric bluegrass combined with a steel guitar effect that he got from a specially created device installed on his guitar called a "B-Bender." It was a metal arm that was hooked to the back of his Telecaster that moved every time he pulled down on his strap. This would raise the pitch of his b string a whole step, similar to what a pedal steel guitar does. Thad and I couldn't wait to see Clarence and his B-Bender in person, so we found a place just above the stage in order to get a bird's eye view of his playing (no pun intended). And what a view we had! When the Byrds hit the stage the crowd went crazy, despite the fact that the only original member left was Roger McGuinn. I recall being disappointed in how they sounded. They were loud and more like a jam band than the sweet harmonic group that changed the folk-rock world with their classic version of Bob Dylan's "*Mr. Tambourine Man.*" The new Byrds harmonies were ragged with no blend and their volume was so loud that Roger's voice, once so smooth and sweet, was now raspy and gravely sounding. However, Clarence White was brilliant. To witness his playing was nothing short of an epiphany. It changed my whole view of playing and I couldn't wait to start learning to play like him. He played notes that seemed inconceivable to anyone who played a guitar. The Byrds may have sucked, as far as I was concerned, but the night belonged to Clarence White. The greatest electric guitarist I had ever seen or heard.

11 LINDA MARIE RONSTADT

"I've done everything I know
To try and make you mine.
And I think I'm going to love you
For a long long time"

One Man's family nailed it at the Aragon. The crowd loved us and we all headed back to Blue's, higher than a kite over our flawless performance with the Byrds. We celebrated at Blue's apartment that evening confident that we were on our way to a record deal. I did notice that Nigel was unusually quiet during the festivities, but I chalked that up to being tired from all the excitement. The next day when I woke up I saw Kenny sitting at the kitchen table staring into a black cup of coffee with a dead serious look on his face.

"Hey, Kenny" I said as I slapped him on the back. "Great show last night wasn't it? Man, I can't wait to read the reviews and......"

"I have some bad news. Sit down" he said in a dark tone. "Nigel quit."

"Very funny" I answered. "That's just what we need isn't it? I mean...."

"John, I'm not kidding. It's all over. Nigel's fallen in love with a local girl and has decided to leave the band. It's all over. With him gone we have no connection with Spanky & Our Gang. I'm tired of all this crap. I'm heading back home to LA."

I stood there frozen.

"Kenny" I said in a shaky voice "is this the truth? It's all over? How can that be, especially after the best concert we ever gave?"

We were in shock. How could he just quit when we were so close to a major record deal? It spelled the end of *One Man's Family*. The next day I was on the phone with *Linda Ronstadt*.

"Hi, Linda!" I spoke in my best upbeat tone, coming right to the point; the way she liked it. "I'm in Chicago—is that gig still open for me?" She laughed when I told her about Nigel and simply replied, "C'mon back, Beland. The gig is yours!"

A few days later Kenny, Thad and I rented a car and drove all the way back to Los Angeles, sadly leaving One Man's Family in ashes. I never did say goodbye to Suzy. I had much more on my mind than any romantic thoughts. On the trip home, a funny thing happened: I had a copy of the latest issue of Billboard Magazine, the bible for the music industry, and inside was a review of our final show with the Byrds. It read "*Also on the bill was One Man's Family, consisting of founding Spanky and Our Gang members. The band wowed the crowd with its impressive harmonies and solid country rock arrangements. Looks like these guys are going to be around for a long time.*"

"Yeah," I thought, laughing out loud.

When we hit L.A. I immediately called Linda who told me to meet her backstage at ABC Television Studios where she was taping a guest appearance on the Everly Brothers weekly variety show. Kenny, Thad and I said goodbye to each other and parted our separate ways. I felt bad about parting with Thad. We had become solid friends while working together. I hated to see that end. Meanwhile, Jerry decided to hang with me and go in 50/50 together on a house in the Hollywood Hills. And that's just what we did. We found a terrific old house in the hills up on Whitley Avenue just above Hollywood Blvd.

Immediately, I met Linda on the set of the Everly's Show at ABC. It was exciting to see Don and Phil up close. They were my idols and a huge influence on my career. They looked fantastic with their sharp western shirts and matching jumbo Gibson guitars. I watched Linda rehearse with them. Talk about three of the greatest vocalists in rock music on the same stage together! Linda then ran through a rehearsal of her new hit single "Long Long Time" a beautiful ballad she had recorded in Nashville. When Linda sang "Long Long Time" you couldn't help but get goose bumps all over. It was an emotionally powerful song with an amazing, almost orgasmic, vocal finale. And it was now a major hit all over the country. "Beland!" Linda ran and gave me a big hug and asked me what had happened in Chicago. I gave her the whole story and she couldn't believe Nigel would screw up things with the band because of a woman. But the band's loss was Linda's gain, according to her.

The next day Linda picked me up at the house and we headed over to a rehearsal hall to meet up with the other three musicians she had hired to be her band. On the way over she said "Now Beland, these guys are a bit weird but they're good players. They live up in Palmdale, of all places"!   Palmdale being a desert town a few hours away from Hollywood.

"The drummer used to be a fry cook and the bass player is the brother of Clarence White."

"Clarence White?" I asked "The guy in the Byrd's?"

"Yeah" she answered. "And the neat thing is that the rhythm guitarist is a monster fiddle player too. He's from Louisiana and he's a Cajun.

His name's Gib Guilbeau and he's a great singer, fiddle player and songwriter. He and Clarence White used to play in a band together called Nashville West. You're going to like him Beland"

I met the new band members at the rehearsal hall Linda shared with Avant guard rock genius Frank Zappa and his group the Mothers of Invention. All three of the new guys in her group were terrific with a wonderful sense of humor. And brother, could they play country rock! Gib Guilbeau was already known around Hollywood for writing songs for the Byrds and other artists. He was also one of the hottest fiddle players in town, playing his trademark grinding Cajun fiddle and backing it up with an incredible voice. His brother-in-law Stan Pratt played drums with a rock-solid driving beat while Eric White laid down a simple but solid bass guitar. Once I was thrown in the mix it was obvious we had something unique, especially Gib and I. It was a "gumbo" of sorts made up of my twanging Telecaster and high Everly/ Beach Boys harmony and Gib's Louisiana rockin' country fiddle. None of us, including Linda, had ever heard anything like it and for some strange reason it actually worked for her. Soon her country stage songs like *"Silver Threads and Golden Needles" "Break My Mind"* and

"Only Mama to Walk the Line" kicked serious ass. It was sensational and soon we were ready to unleash it on the public starting with the first gig, the Fillmore West opening for none other than the Byrds. It was time to buckle up our seat belts, because the days and the miles ahead of us were going to be fast and furious. Linda's star was on the rise. The word was out, and you could feel the momentum building with each passing week. No more tiny little coffee houses or non-paying Monday Hoots at the Troubadour. From here on out it would be planes, boats, trains, hotels, festivals, television and recording. Instead of a few drunks at the bar we would now be touring America playing for millions of diehard rock fans and sharing the stage with some of the most iconic bands of the day. This was the big-time and life for me would never be the same again.

It's hard to accurately describe what it was like to play the famed Fillmore West. It had been ground zero for the "Summer of Love" bands like the Jefferson Airplane and the Grateful Dead but the Fillmore also showcased an amazing lineup of rare blues and soul artists who up until that time had very seldom performed before a young white rock & roll audience. Many legendary blues artists like BB King, Freddy King, Rufus Thomas and Johnny Otis all appeared on the Fillmore stage. The crowd was mostly made of stoned-out hippie kids all grooving like a wave to the incredible music. At the front of the stage danced the groupies, all painted up with the most outlandish clothes and hairstyles imaginable. With their arms held up high they would sway to the music, eyeing band members and flashing their wears throughout the show. Combined with a trippy acid inspired light show it was quite a sight to see, especially for guys like us whose California backgrounds were relatively straight for the crazy San Francisco scene.

Backstage we hung out with the Byrds whose lineup was now Roger McGuinn, guitar legend Clarence White, bassist Skip Batten and drummer Gene Parsons. Since Gib and Clarence were such great friends, having played together in a country band prior to his joining the Byrds, I asked that he introduce me to Clarence White. I was a huge fan of Clarence's playing and couldn't wait to finally meet him. We walked over to the Byrds dressing room and in the corner a poker-faced Clarence White was sitting there alone playing his trademark Fender Telecaster with the strange device called the B-Bender, an attachment that allowed the player to automatically bend the b-string up a full step simply by pulling down on the guitar strap. This allowed the player to make the guitar sound like a steel guitar, and Clarence was the only guitarist that had one on his Telecaster. What he played on that guitar was pure magic.

Gib introduced me to Clarence who, behind the straight frowning poker face, was a real sweetheart of a guy. He shook my hand and acted as if he had known me for years. I told him what an influence he had been on my own playing and he smiled, all the while running his fingers all over his guitar neck. We became good friends that night and in the years that followed he would help me out by recommending me for sessions or subbing for sessions he couldn't make. He was truly one of the greatest musicians in the business, considered today to be the greatest Fender telecaster player of all time, almost a half-decade after his premature death by a drunken driver in 1973.

In all honesty, the Byrds were crap as far as I was concerned and a tremendous let down for a die-hard fan like myself. Noted for their sweet soft harmonies and Roger's jangling 12 string guitar so evident on their iconic hits like *"Tambourine Man"* and *"Turn Turn Turn"*, they now were a loud jamming band whose vocals were loose and buried in the tremendous volume they played at. Even Roger's beautiful lead voice was now raspy and barely able to keep up with the volume. It was a let-down. As for us, we scored big and the crowd loved Linda, who belted out some of the best singing ever heard on a rock and roll stage. Dressed only in a short skirt with no shoes, banging her tambourine, the hippie Fillmore crowd couldn't get enough. And when Gib pulled out his Cajun fiddle they simply went crazy. Strobe lights flashing, smoke blowing across the stage, the rumble and roar of the Fillmore crowd. Let me tell you dear reader, Linda's show was a slam dunk and it isn't simply boasting to say that NOBODY could follow us onstage.

After the show we were invited to a private party out in Marin County. Gib, Stan, Eric and I thought it would be a typical gathering of musicians, passing the guitar and smoking a few joints. However, when we arrived at the door we were in for a shock. The guy who answered the door was this tall skinny long haired bearded wacked out hippie who was stark naked.

"Hey brother's, can I help you?" he slowly muttered while looking us up and down as if we were Martians.

I spoke up "Uh, yeah. We're Linda Ronstadt's band and were

invited to the party."

Suddenly our door man burst with excitement and led us into the house. "Man, it's so cool you guys could make it. Follow me. Hey everybody, Ronstadt's band is here!"

Suddenly we were in the middle of a house full of totally naked people, all stoned floating from room to room to the loud acid rock music that was blasting from the stereo. The lights were low and incense filled the air. Beautiful, totally nude women surrounded us and before I knew it, just like the famous Blue Angel's synchronized flight team, a few of us broke ranks and headed off to various rooms for a night of San Francisco fun. I don't know about Gib, Eric and Stan but I was hijacked by two slim, trim beauties who proceeded to toss me on a water bed and give me a crash course in sex education. The next morning, we managed to crawl across the floor and find our clothes and call a taxi to take us back to our hotel. We each looked like the entire Fillmore West audience had run over us. Peace, flowers and free love. Welcome to San Francisco 1970.

It was then on to Hawaii and the 1970 Capital Records Convention, where Linda would share the bill with the amazing singer / songwriter from Atlanta Georgia, Joe South, singer Glen Campbell, Rat-pack singer Al Martino, the Al DeLory Orchestra and Apple Records new hit British band, Badfinger. It was to be a star-studded event and we were to treated first class all the way. However, there was a speed bump ahead just before we stepped on our flight to Hawaii.

As we were headed for our gate we were stopped by a number of guys in suits and sunglasses who asked us if we were the Linda Ronstadt show.

"I'm Linda Ronstadt" Linda said in a matter of fact tone. "What's going on?"

One of the suits said, "Miss Ronstadt we need you and your band to accompany us"

"Who the fuck are you guys?" she sarcastically blared out.

"We are from the Sherriff's office and FBI and we have it that you and your band are trying to board this plane with stolen airline tickets."

"What the…?" came all of our replies.

We were led away back out of the airport and taken in a van to the San Mateo jail for questioning. All the way there we tried to guess what the hell was happening. Linda's new boyfriend and producer John Boylan was now part of our entourage and became the spokesman for all of us. Immediately he called Linda's manager in LA, the notorious Herb Cohen. Herb informed us to stay cool and he would be jump on it immediately. Meanwhile, the cops took us to the men's part of the jail while Linda was taken the women's detention. Needless to say, we were all scared shitless being long haired rock and rollers, especially me with the longest hair and striped pants to boot! The cops never quite made it clear why we were being arrested, so we were getting close to panic.

Suddenly this middle age short stocky trustee comes up to us loaded with candy bars and all smiles. "Hi guys. My name is Bob and I'm a trustee here. Don't worry about a thing I'll take good care of you. I'm a fan of Linda's. You're in good hands." With that he led us to another room far away from the general jail population, and that was a huge relief! "There ya go, guys" Bob said as he passed out candy bars to us. "You'll be fine in here. Nobody will mess with you. I'll check in on you to see if there's anything you need. I'll check on Linda too."

We sat alone in this small meeting room for what seemed like an eternity, until suddenly the door opened and the cops came in as well as our guarding Angel, Bob.

"You're free to go. Everything seems to have been cleared up. Follow us and we'll drive you back to the airport" said one of the cops. "Hey guys, nice to have met you all" chimed Bob. "Maybe I'll come see you play when I get out of this place."

We told Bob that if he ever got out and came down to L.A. and heard we were playing at the Troubadour to let us know and he would be our guest. "You serious?" He said. "You bet, Bob. The night will be on us" we told him.

About six months later we were playing at the Troubadour. The place was packed as always and we were getting ready to launch into Linda's hit single "Long, Long, Time" when from out in the audience someone shouted "Hey guys. Hey Linda. It's me Bob from the jail!" We couldn't believe it! We all had a great laugh and picked up

Bob's ticket and dinner at the end of the night. And after Linda shared the story with the audience good old Bob was the real star of the night! I still I remember him walking off into the night, drunk, arm and arm with a tall blonde Troubadour waitress. I'm sure Bob felt that he was compensated good for his kindness and protection back at the San Mateo jail. Somebody must have taken responsibility for our arrest blunder because when we arrived at our gate for our flight to Hawaii we were informed that we had all been "upgraded" to first class. "First class!" I said to Gib. "We should get arrested more often!"

It was on to Hawaii where we played the 1970 Capitol Records Convention at the famed Ilikai Hotel in Honolulu. All the top brass from every division of Capitol Records would be in attendance for the big show in the Grand Ballroom. It was some event and I couldn't believe I was actually performing at it. Heck, it hadn't been that long since I first landed on the streets of Hollywood and sleeping behind the trash dumpster in the parking lot of Capitol Records as a young runaway. Now, there I was getting ready to hit the stage with Capitol's hottest new female singer. Life and luck can certainly turn on a dime.

We toured the country with Linda that year playing every kind of venue from small clubs and colleges to major rock clubs and festivals. We covered just about every major city and small town in America, all of us traveling in rental cars, crammed together with our gear and luggage, including Linda. Every gig was exciting, and the crowds went crazy for Linda wherever we played. With her mini skirt and bare feet, banging her tambourine on her ass to our driving Cajun rock music we killed every crowd we played for. It was some sense of power knowing how good we sounded each night we hit the stage. From LA's Troubadour, Philadelphia's Main Point, New York's Bitter End, Chicago's Quiet Knight to Boston's Paul's Mall we introduced a style of music seldom heard at that time. It was country with a driving rock edge fronted by this amazing sexy, gifted singer. I was in awe watching Linda sing, flawless and passionate making it look so effortless. She simply was the best female vocalist in rock & roll and we knew it.

Linda, Gib, and I onstage 1970

As good as we sounded on stage we knew we had a problem in Eric White's bass playing. Eric had come from an impressive bluegrass background playing upright bass with his famous brother Clarence and his brother Roland on mandolin. But Linda's songs were more complex than Eric could grasp and night after night he would hit bad note after bad note. simply lost. We finally decided to replace him. I wanted my best friend and band mate from One Man's Family Thad Maxwell to take over the bass position. The problem was that Thad was a drummer, but he also excelled on guitar. "How hard could it be to play bass?" I thought. So, I painted a picture to Linda of this great bass playing friend of mine who was one of the best I had ever heard. I pumped it up so much to Linda that she simply said "Well Beland, go hire him."

Back then Linda never wanted anyone to think she wasn't on top of everything relating to musicians. So, it seemed that I could bullshit her into hiring Thad simply by telling her that Thad Maxwell sounded just as good as Joe Osborne, famed LA studio bass player that everyone in town respected. Linda really never heard Joe Osborne play but she didn't want it to seem she was ignorant, so she went along with what I painted out and simply told me to hire Thad. Immediately I called Thad who was playing drums for a Tom Jones impersonator at a sleazy Italian lounge in Glendale called The Copa.

"Hey Thad, John here. What are you doing?"
Thad said, "Playing for this guy at the Copa Lounge, what's up?"

"Do you know how to play bass?" I shot back
"Well, yeah I guess so. Why?" he answered
"Because I got you the bass gig with Linda. I told her you played as good as Joe Osborne" I said with a laugh.
"What?" came his reply "Hell, I don't even own a fucking bass guitar!"
"Well, round one up fast. Rehearsals are starting soon". And then I hung up.

To Thad's credit he rounded up a beautiful old Fender Precision Bass, rehearsed on it and came into rehearsal fully prepared and won over everyone, including Linda. Now we would finally be a real tight band that nobody could touch. As for Eric, he was happy, and relieved, to remain on board as our roadie, and he was damned good at it.

After Hawaii it was back to Los Angeles where we were booked for a week's run at the good old Troubadour. And to make it even more special our opening act would be none other than my buddy from a few years ago, Kris Kristofferson. Since our first appearances together on the Monday night "Hoots" when he was relatively unknown to the LA crowd, Kris's career had started to blossom, and he had now become the latest "buzz" around town. Still not a household name he was attracting the attention of the media and people, important people, were starting to take notice of this new rough and tumble Nashville songwriter. Kris had also started to make a splash as an actor and had just starred in his first film Cisco Pike. The word on the street was out, and for me I was thrilled to be sharing the bill with him.

Since Linda was the headliner Kris opened our show, backed up by two of his old friends from Nashville, Dennis Lindy on acoustic 12 string guitar (who would go on to write "Burning Love" for Elvis) and on bass guitar singer – songwriter Billy Swan (who would score his own self-penned massive hit "I Can Help") a few years later. That was it as far as Kris's backing musicians went. Feeling that Kris could use a bit more sparkle in his back up musicians I volunteered to play electric guitar for him, since we were on the same bill together anyway. I was already getting paid by Linda so I asked Kris if I could join Billy and Dennis onstage at no charge. Kris was glad to have me and so that week I backed up both Linda and Kristofferson on what would become a ground-breaking gig for Kris.

Kris's performances were still a bit rough and his stage banter was terrible. He was very microphone shy and often stumbled painfully between songs and occasionally apologized for his flawed singing. I'm sure that he was very intimidated being on the same bill with one of the greatest rock country voices of the time. Another thing was that Kris just couldn't say "no" to old friends and down on their luck musicians. One case in point. Dewy Martin was the former drummer of the legendary band The Buffalo Springfield. Although not a commercial success, the Buffalo Springfield were a highly revered and influential band in rock circles with such a stellar line up as Neil Young, Steve Stills, Ritchie Furry and Jim Messina. However, the band broke up after a couple of critically acclaimed but low selling albums and the various members all went on to bigger success with other bands. Still's went on to Crosby, Stills and Nash while Messina teamed up with Kenny Loggins as Loggins & Messina. Ritchie Furry went on to form the pioneering country rock band Poco and Neil Young went on to a very successful solo career.

Dewy Martin went on to nothing. His career was over and by now he was just another drunk at the Troubadour bar, loud and obnoxious butting his way onstage with other bands while bragging to the world that he was once the drummer for the Buffalo Springfield. It was embarrassing but not surprising at the Troubadour, a place where stars were made and where stars' careers ended.

This one particular night during Linda and Kris's Troubadour run Dewey managed to barnacle himself to Kris and his drunken entourage and corner the singer/songwriter into agreeing to let him sit in during Kris's set. Since our drummer Stan's drums were already set up behind Kris onstage, Dewy could just hop on the seat and play. Kris tried to tell Dewey that he didn't need drums because his music was more acoustic and light country. But Dewy was loud and adamant.

"Fuck, man" Dewey would blare out in the dressing room "I played with the Buffalo Springfield and your stuff is a goddamn walk in the park."

Kris almost pleaded with Dewy, who was now leaning all over him almost shouting in Kris's ear. "Listen Dewy, drums just don't work for my stuff. I can't hear with all that going on behind me."

Again, Dewy ranted on "Fuck man, it'll sound great, man! I'll keep it quiet enough for you. It'll be cool, man. You'll see."

Kris finally and reluctantly gave in. So as Billy, Dennis and I set up on stage for Kris's show, we noticed this guy behind us rearranging Stan Pratt's drums. We looked at each other as if to say, "What the hell is this"? The place was sold out. Kris was introduced and walked up to the microphone to a well-received response from the crowd. He was still dressed in a t-shirt, leather pants, beat up boots and playing that same old Martin D28 guitar with autographs engraved all over the body.

We opened up with one of Kris's great story songs called "The Law is for Protection of the People", a light easy country groove feel. Suddenly, from out behind us came the loudest drum fills I had ever heard. Ear shattering. Mind you, the Troubadour stage wasn't very big to begin with, so a full drum set took up most of the stage and sat right behind whoever was singing at stage center, and this time it was Kris!

Bam! Bang! Crash" came the drums, sweeping over our little acoustic trio like Sherman's march to the sea. Kris tried to tell Dewey to turn it down but Dewey was too obscured behind Kris to see any signals. The audience started to talk amongst themselves like a lynch mob scene from "The Oxbow Incident." We made it through the song and during the faint applause Kris whispered to Dewey to keep things down. "Gotcha" came Dewey's oblivious, drunken reply.

The next song was Kris's classic "Sunday Morning Comin Down "which was a soft tender ballad. As soon as we started "Bang Boom, Crash" roared the drums. It was horrendous. Now people from the audience were yelling at Dewey saying, "Get off the drummer off the stage" and "the drums are too loud" or "The drummer sucks!" Dewey became belligerent and actually started yelling responses back to the crowd which just fueled the moment

"Hey man, fuck you!" roared Dewey's response to the crowd while rising from his drum seat. "I played with the Buffalo Springfield assholes so shut the fuck up!"

The crowd shouted back bigger and louder! "Boo, get off" "You suck" "Shoot the drummer" …. It was a madhouse. Kris started playing another one of his classic songs but the drums remained loud and horrible. Finally, Kris stopped and asked Dewey to leave. The crowd roared with approval and Dewey stumbled off the stage knocking the drums over as he left and then stopping to give the crowd the finger! Eventually the Troubadour settled down and we managed to salvage what was left of Kris's show. Dewy disappeared into obscurity never to really be heard of again.

However, there were high points to Kris's appearance that week. One-night Kris came to me before show time and told me that a guest of his would be sitting in during the show. I sort of panicked, remembering the Dewy Martin fiasco. But Kris assured me that I would enjoy this guest.

"Who is it, Kris? Anyone I know?" I asked.

Kris smiled and simply said "You'll know him" and that was it. I didn't ask any more questions and simply turned my attention to his show. In the middle of Kris's performance he said to the crowd "I have a good friend of mine from Nashville who's gonna come up and do a song. Let's have a round of applause for JOHNNY CASH!"

The roar from the crowd was deafening and for a brief moment it didn't sink in until he hopped on stage. There he was, Mt Rushmore. Billy and Dennis were friends of Cash's so they weren't moved one way or another, but John Beland was. I almost froze to death as he strapped on a guitar and shouted "Folsom!" We launched into the iconic song and Cash belted it out with that signature vocal sound. The place was going absolutely crazy!

"I hear the train a comin. It's a comin round the bend" He sang to an orgasmic Troubadour crowd. It was as if we were flying into the eye of a hurricane. John was bigger than life and full of unbridled energy and self-confidence. I mean, this was Johnny fucking Cash! My knees were shaking but I held on, mimicking the "dump da da dump" Telecaster I had remembered from his records. Suddenly it was time for my solo. I was flushed with fear and excitement as John made a swift and sudden turn from the microphone right and walked up to me with his nose touching mine and said in the deep Cash voice "Pick it, Luther!" The "Luther" he was referring to was the late Luther Perkins, his original guitar player who invented that style and who had sadly

died in a fire 2 years before.

My excited eye's opened wider than silver dollars as I launched into the trademark guitar solo, and I played it note for note over the deafening screams and clapping from the Troubadour audience. John smiled as he turned back to the microphone. I wanted to faint. As quickly as it came, it was over. John left the stage to thunderous applause while I wanted to smoke a cigarette, even though I didn't smoke. It was a night I will never forget.

On the last night of the week's run we had just finished the show and the crowd was headed out the doors and the houselights were on. The crews were tearing down the gear and lights and I was collecting my guitar and heading for the back stairway that led to the dressing rooms. Suddenly I spotted this amazingly beautiful knock-out blonde headed my way, and she WAS headed my way. Before I knew it, she had her arms around me and gave me such a deep French kiss that I should have been awarded the Legion of Honor!

"You were terrific tonight. God, it was incredible" she spoke out in a loud voice. Then she turned and was gone. Behind me I heard the familiar voice of Mr. Kristofferson, the Silver Tongue devil himself, laughing at what he had observed from the top of the stairs.

"Well Hoss, you're a fucking star now" he laughed.

"What do you mean" I asked.

"Well, it isn't every day that a guitar-slinging kid gets kissed by Faye Dunaway."

"THAT was Faye Dunaway?" I yelled out. "Relax, man" she's long gone by now. And she was.

"Hey, I want to give you something" Kris said as he searched the pockets of his worn-out suede pants.

He handed me $35.00 and said "Here man, I wish I could pay you more for all the guitar playing you did. "Hey Kris, keep the money, man. I was glad to do it. I had a ball and besides, Linda's already paying me so don't worry about it." But Kris was adamant about it, and as he put the money in my hands he said "No man, take it. Maybe someday when I'm a big fucking superstar I can pay you a lot more." That was Kris. A heart of gold and as loyal and humble as anyone I had ever known.

As I put the wrinkled notes in my pocket that night, I smiled and wondered if lightening should strike his career, whether Kris would really keep his promise. And Damned if he didn't!

Before Linda would arrive at rehearsals the four of us, Gib, Thad, Stan and myself, would jam a bit just to loosen up before she arrived. But it became crystal clear that the first time we played together we had a sound, a unique sound of our own. It was a mixture of Credence Clearwater, Poco, the Byrds all wrapped into one. Furthermore, Thad, Gib and I had a fabulous vocal blend that sounded like the Beach Boys meets Buffalo Springfield. It was a great sound and totally our own. No other self-contained band in town featured a fiddle in front of a driving rock beat along with sweet three-part harmony. We knew we had something so we decided to start our own band and we named it Swampwater.

Linda's manager Herb Cohen was also Gib's publisher and he had secured a solo deal for Gib on the Nashville based label Starday-King Records. But now he was so excited about Swampwater that he talked Herb into changing his solo deal to a band deal for all of us.

Both Gib and I contributed original songs and along with Thad we worked up some really great vocal arrangements. It was country, rock and Cajun influenced and it was fabulous! The label flew us to Albuquerque, New Mexico, between our touring with Linda, to record our first album at producer John Wagner's 4 track studio. We clicked with him immediately. John allowed us the freedom to follow our creative instincts without dictating what we should or shouldn't play. His ideas were always constructive and his good nature made the entire recording project a world of fun. This was a hit group if I ever heard one. Forget One Man's Family. We were our own band without any ties to any former group. Our sound was our own and like nobody else. All of us were thrilled at what we heard on the playbacks and in LA, so was Herb Cohen.

Swampwater's first album 1970

Now that we were a band with our own album set for release, Linda featured us in her show, which was a great shot for us. With Thad rounding out the band we were smoking onstage. Even though we were only 4 pieces, with Linda at the microphone there was no way anyone could follow us. Linda's powerful vocals and sexy image coupled with Gib's grinding Cajun fiddle and mine, Stan and Thad's driving country rockin' it was a home run every time we hit the stage. What a feeling it was to share the stage with all these fantastic musicians. No matter who we shared the stage with, Van Morrison, Johnny Winter, Poco or the Byrds, we held our own and never failed to knock out a crowd. We were the 27 Yankees of country rock!

Crossing the country in 1970 with Linda & Swampwater

12 THE CASH SHOW-WELCOME TO MUSIC CITY

In the winter on 1970 Linda was booked to appear on the Johnny Cash Show in Nashville, Tennessee. The Cash show was hot that year, a real ground-breaking program that featured a wide range of musical guests and not necessarily country stars either. John's past guests had included Deric & the Dominoes, Neil Diamond, The Monkees as well as a rare appearance by Bob Dylan. For the special two parts show we were to do, John's guests would be Neil Young, James Taylor, Earl Scruggs, Tony Joe White and Linda. It looked to be a great show and all of us were excited to be part of it.

I had never been to Nashville, Tennessee but had heard so much about it being not only the "Mother Home" of country music, but also home to a lot of early rock and roll hits as well. Elvis, The Everly Brothers, Roy Orbison, Jerry Lee Lewis cut many of their biggest hits right there on a 3-block residential neighborhood called Music Row.

It was very late in the evening when we arrived in Nashville. We rented a couple of station wagons at the airport and drove through the downtown area of the city, past the legendary Tootsie's Orchid Lounge, Earnest Tubbs record Store and of course the Ryman Auditorium, the "original" Grand Ol' Opry. Our faces were pressed against the windows of our car like schoolkids passing by Disneyland. Suddenly, we came to a dead stop.

"Shit!" someone in the car yelled out. "Take a look at that!" We all turned our heads to the left to see a line of elephants being led down the middle of Broadway. It was the Barnum & Baily Circus leading long procession of animals down the main drag of town headed towards the auditorium where they would open the next evening. "Holy crap" I said. "Are we in Nashville, or what?"

A winter storm had dumped a ton of snow shortly after we arrived and since the city had little or no snow removal system we were pretty much confined to either the Ramada Inn, the taping going on at the Opry or Vanderbilt University where a concert portion of the show was to be shot. Besides, there wasn't much to really see on the "famed" Music Row anyhow. In fact, it was a bit of a letdown because most of the music-related businesses such as publishing companies, recording studios and record labels were located in houses all within a 3 block radius. In other words, Music Row looked like any other old residential neighborhood in the south with little or no indication that hits were being written or recorded behind those doors. There were no neon lights or billboards or flashing signs to indicate that this was ground zero of the country music industry. Just old houses lined up beside each other on a few average looking city streets, and besides, we had heard that there was a division within the ranks of the business. Rumor had it that the old guard who ruled the country music hit machine since its inception had it out for the new young upstarts who were now slowly infiltrating the music scene in Nashville.

Established artists like Waylon Jennings, Tompall Glaser and Willie Nelson were starting to embrace a new harder sound than the same old formula hits that had been the staple of Music City. Artists were starting to use their own bands on sessions instead of the standard line up of "A" team session players who appeared on just about every hit that came out of Music Row. There was a revolution brewing when we hit town and we were advised to be careful about sticking our nose in where it didn't belong and to steer clear of certain places on the row. In other words, we were "not" welcome.

Johnny Cash was bigger than the Nashville Music Machine. Nobody could intimidate him and he did whatever the hell he felt like with regard to his new hit ABC Network Show. Instead of catering to the old guard and filling his weekly guest line up with the usual over exposed country music artists, or old tired acts from the Grand Ol' Opry, Cash brought in the biggest names in pop music. John had his hand on the pulse of what was going on in the country and he embraced the music and the spirit of the younger generation refusing to cater to the established order of Music City. It was a tense time and you could feel it in the wind as you moved through the artists, the writers and the musicians who worked on the Johnny Cash Show.

One Friday night, Thad and I braved yet another winter snowstorm and went to the Grand Ol' Opry to watch the old-time radio show in action. The Saturday night WSM Opry radio broadcast, then held at the legendary Ryman Auditorium in downtown Nashville, consisted of a series of 20-minute shows, each sponsored by various products such as Goo-Goo Clusters or Martha White Flour and each show hosted by a Grand Ol' Opry star who performed his, or her, hits as well featured a special guest who also performed their old hits. The amazing thing about watching it all happen was that every show had a completely different line up of musicians and singers who scrambled all over the stage between shows during the commercials barely making it to their positions by the time the next show started. It was complete, organized chaos.

All the big stars of the Opry hosted their own shows. "The Tex Ritter Show" sponsored by Goo Goo Candy Clusters. Or the Bill Monroe and his Bluegrass Boys show brought to you by Martha White Self-Rising Flour. Behind each star the sponsor would provide a huge canvas backdrop featuring their product's logo which was clearly visible to everyone seated in the Ryman. Just like personnel, the backdrops would also change every twenty minutes. You couldn't help but feel the energy as announcer Grant Turner introduced each show and the Opry square dancers hit the stage backed by some amazing fiddle music. Thad and I watched from the balcony and picked out some of the musicians we had heard about back in California such as Leon Rhodes, the great guitarist for Ernest Tubb, or steel guitar legends such as Wendell Myrick and Curly Chalker. It was a sight to behold for a couple of skinny rock and rollers from Hollywood.

We recorded our segment on the Cash Show with Linda a few nights later before a packed audience at Vanderbilt University. She sang an Emmitt Rhodes song called "She's A Very Lovely Woman" and the performance was a typical slam dunk for Linda. The crowd loved her. As for me, I couldn't help wondering how I wound up in this strange universe I once thought only existed in my dreams back in Hometown.

There I was standing onstage in Nashville Tennessee being introduced to the crowd by Johnny Cash and having three huge television cameras looking directly up at me. This was now my reality. A place I would stay in for the rest of my life.

While we were taping the Cash Show, Linda and James Taylor were invited to sing backup on one of the tracks Neil Young was recording just down the street at Quadrophonic Studios. There was a terrible blizzard but they made it to the studio just in time to lend their voices to a little song Neil had recently written, called "Heart of Gold." Neil would preview that song on our show. Today, over 40 years later, I'll hear "Heart of Gold" playing in the super market or restaurant and smile, remembering the amazing time we all spent while guesting on the Johnny Cash Show during that wonderful snowy week in Nashville, Tennessee 1970.

Another stand out show we did that year was the Bobby Darin Show taped live up in Toronto Canada. Bobby Darin had always been one of my idols as a kid and to now be working alongside of him was another dream come true. Darin was at a crossroads in his career at the time of our appearance. He had changed his musical direction radically from a pop crooner to a folk-rock artist. The changes didn't sit well with his management who wanted to keep him in a tuxedo, a hairpiece and on a Las Vegas stage. So, Bobby made concessions and divided his overall style in half, performing his hits as well as showcasing his new venture into folk rock. It was a gutsy move. I was in the makeup room backstage getting fixed up for the show when I glanced over to my left and saw this guy in the next chair getting made up. He was bald with a mustache and kind of resembled Paul Stookey of Peter Paul & Mary. Suddenly, he turned my way and said

"Hey, are you in Linda's band?"

I answered "Yeah, I am. I'm John Beland, her guitar player."

He extended his arm my way and shook my hand saying "Cool, man. I'm Bobby." I couldn't believe this was the legendary Bobby Darin! He looked thin and a bit frail, as well as the bald head and droopy black mustache.

"Hi Bobby. Man, it's a real honor to work with you. I've been a big fan of yours for years."
Darin was gracious and thanked me. Then he really surprised the hell out of me.

"Listen John, you're playing the acoustic guitar on Linda's song "Long Long Time" right?"

Yeah, I sure am" I answered.

"Well dig this" he continued. "For the intro I was thinking of joining you. Just you and I on the guitars as I introduce her. Once she starts singing I'll back out and let you finish the song. Would that be cool with you"? I thought to myself, "are you fucking kidding me? Play guitar alongside of Bobby Darin?"

"Sure, that would be really great.' I replied in my most professional demeanor.

"Terrific" Darin said. "After you get finished in makeup come on over to my dressing room and bring your guitar so we can go over the chords"

"You bet." I said. "I'll be right over." "I was jumping out of my skin with excitement. I idolized Bobby Darin and now we were actually going to do a music segment together. I jumped out of my makeup chair and bolted to our dressing room to retrieve my acoustic guitar. Naturally, I boasted to the band what I was doing as I grabbed my guitar and headed over to Bobby's dressing room. Darin was sitting in a chair with his guitar trying to figure out the chords to "Long Long Time".

"Hey Bobby" I said as I poked my nose through the door.

"Hi John, come on in, brother".

He still had a makeup towel around his neck but I noticed the mustache was now gone. I sat down next to him and pulled out my guitar. Bobby asked;

"Hey man, what are damned chords to this intro?" I played the intro on my guitar and made sure he could see my fingers clearly.

"It's like this Bobby" I said as I picked the intro. It only took him a second to figure it out and soon we were playing it together, and it sounded beautiful!

"OK, man" he said with a smile" I think I got it. "This is going to be a lot of fun. I'll see ya on stage, and thanks a lot for teaching it to me."

"My pleasure" and we shook hands.

There was a live studio audience and a big band backing Darin up.

When the opening segment was ready to be taped, I rushed to the side of the stage to watch him in action. To my shock, the guy with the frail body, bald head and mustache was morphed into the classic Bobby Darin everybody knew and loved. He looked slim in his tuxedo and much younger with his hairpiece. He joked to the audience, doing impressions and adlibs. Then it was time for the opening number, a medley of his hits. And man, when that big band started up and Bobby Darin grabbed that hand microphone and started singing "Mack The Knife" the transformation was astounding! He looked every bit the giant star he was. He did flawless versions of his big hits like "Splish Splash" "Queen of The Hop" "Dream Lover" and my favorite "Beyond the Sea". What a thrill to watch this powerhouse work.

During a break between the opening segment and our spot with Linda, I made my way backstage to hook up with Bobby for the opening piece to "Long Long Time". Unfortunately, the producers wanted Bobby to sit alone on a stool picking his guitar as he introduced Linda. So, I did my part with him just off camera. Still, it was a real thrill to play guitar with him, if only for a few bars.

I was very sad to hear of his death shortly afterwards. For years he had been fighting off a weak heart, to the point of having to rely on an oxygen tank backstage when performing. To his credit Bobby landed two country folk hits on the pop charts, "If I was a Carpenter" and "Simple Song of Freedom". He could do it all. What a talent.

13 SESSIONS, TV, AND THE BYRDS

We went back to LA for a little time off between tours. For me that meant a chance to catch up on session work and there was always plenty of it over at Dan and Lois's office. Because of my workload with Linda and Swampwater there wasn't much time to go back and visit with them like the old days. When I did it was always fun to catch up on their various projects. Dan kept using me for session work on everything from demos, new artists to television and radio commercials. One in particular was for the new Mazda automobile. We recorded a Johnny Cash style track with myself on the Telecaster and none other than my guitar idol the great James Burton on acoustic guitar. I was petrified to be sitting directly in front of James for the date. I had learned everything I knew from listening to his solos on Ricky Nelson's old recordings. I would buy any album that featured his playing just to learn new licks of his. Now, I was hired to play lead guitar on a session where he played rhythm! But James was a pro and a lovely guy and after a while I felt quite at ease working alongside of him. The commercial we played on for Mazda went on to win a coveted "Cleo" award, which is the Grammy equivalent for outstanding commercials of the year.

In the studio Hollywood 1970

I also played Dobro and guitar on yet another Woody Guthrie tribute album produced by Rodney Dillard. On this particular session I played behind the great songwriter Hoyte Axton, who wrote a number of hits including "Greenback Dollar" for the Kingston Trio and "Joy to the World" for Three Dog Night. It was surreal working on a session with Hoyte, as he was the very first artist I had seen performing at the Troubadour.

Another session that year was for James Taylor's sister Katie. Originally Clarence White was booked to play electric guitar but he was unable to do it because the Byrds had picked up some extra dates on the road. So, instead he had me sub for him. I played guitar along with Bernie Leadon, Russ Kunkle on drums and Lee Sklar on bass, as well as the great singer/songwriter Carol King on piano. It was a very cool album to be on and I was flattered, and thankful Clarence got it for me.

During one of our breaks from the touring, Thad, Gib and I started hanging out with Clarence White at a house in north Hollywood they dubbed "The Byrd's House". It was a hangout for the band where they could kick back and relax between gigs. When I first went there I noticed Roger McGuinn's iconic Rickenbacker 12 string guitar perched on a stand in the living room. It was plugged into a little Fender Champ amplifier. Everyone was sitting around rather stoned and off into their own world while I inched my way closer to McGuinn's guitar. I sat down next to it and without thinking picked it up and started to play a little bit on it. Naturally, all I played was Byrds songs, namely Roger's original licks from "Tambourine Man" to "Turn Turn Turn." I knew those licks up and down and couldn't resist the chance to play them on the exact guitar that played on the records. I didn't think anybody could hear me so I played the guitar for the next 15 minutes, hearing that sound that so inspired me back in Hometown years earlier.

The next morning Clarence called me on the phone.

"Hey John" came the dead pan voice. "Clarence here"

"Hey man" I cheerfully responded. "What's up?"

"Did you piss off Roger last night"? He asked.

"What?" I responded in shock. "What are you talking about?"

"Well, it seems like he heard you messing around on his guitar last night and thought you were making fun of him because all you played were old Byrds licks."

I was horrified!

"Oh man, Clarence! It was anything but that!" I explained. "I was inspired by his playing and couldn't help but play those licks on the guitar he used on those records. I certainly didn't want him to feel as if I was mocking him!"
Clarence laughed his ass off and said "OK don't worry. Roger's real sensitive and he probably got all paranoid when he heard "Mr. Tambourine" being played by someone else. Here's his phone number. You might want to call him and explain it to him yourself"

"Jesus, thanks Clarence. I'll call him now" I promised.

Clarence was still laughing when we hung up.

I immediately called Roger up.

"Hi Roger" I nervously started. "This is John Beland from Swampwater.

"Oh, Hi John" came the calm friendly voice on the other line.

"Listen Roger, I think there's been a misunderstanding that I wanted to clear up with you" I said.

"A misunderstanding?" Roger asked.

"Yeah" I answered back. "I didn't mean to make you think I was making fun of you by playing your 12 string at the house the other night. Man, your playing inspired me when I first started out in music back in Chicago. I couldn't resist playing your guitar and couldn't help playing those signature licks that I listened to so many times. I hope I haven't offended you and if I did I'm really sorry, man."

Roger was very cool and said "Oh, that's cool John. Thanks a lot for saying that. Yeah, I was kind of thinking that you were poking fun. Man, there's no problem with us. Tell Linda I said hi."

With that he hung up while I breathed a big sigh of relief. But that wasn't the only time I couldn't resist playing an iconic guitar. Linda was booked on the Mike Douglas Show one afternoon and this particular show was to be taped at The University of Southern California in Irving, California to a live audience of college kids. The lineup for the show was solid. Linda and Swampwater (we even got equal billing with Linda), Rick Nelson and the Stone Canyon Band, who's bassist, Randy Meisner, would go on to form the Eagles two years later, comedian George Carlin and the one and only Chuck Berry.

We performed outdoors on the campus at USC and all the acts shared the limited equipment available. During a break in rehearsals I was heading off to get something to eat when I noticed "it". Like the quest for the Holy Grail there "it" stood in all its glory perched on a guitar stand, Chuck Berry's *actual red Gibson Stereo guitar*. "Holy, shit" I thought. " There it is, Excalibur!"

This was one chance in a million and I was going to grab it. I looked around and the stage area was empty. Not a soul around, including Chuck Berry. I carefully picked the guitar up and held it in my lap. I wondered what my buddy Carmen would say if he could see me holding it. I took another look around. The coast was clear, so I knocked off a series of classic Chuck Berry riffs starting with "Johnny B Goode" and then "Maybelline." I was surprised how heavy Chuck's strings were. They almost seemed like bass guitar strings. Nevertheless, I played every Chuck Berry song I knew before I quietly and carefully placed the guitar back on its stand. Nobody knew that I played Chuck's legendary guitar. But I sure as hell did!

The Mike Douglas Show was fun to do. The college kids made for a great lively audience. Mike Douglas was a very nice guy but clearly out of his element with this young audience. The once big band singer seemed so square next to his hip guests. He even attempted so sing the Beatles song "Hey Jude" and that came off like the Hindenburg's final landing. But I have to give him credit for reaching out to newer hip rock and roll artists rather than the usual daytime afternoon talk shows that featured the usual boring aging Hollywood film stars and old tired big band crooners.

Doing the Mike Douglas Show gave me the opportunity to finally meet my hero, the one and only Ricky Nelson. I caught him during a break as he was tuning up his guitar.

"Hi Rick" I said "Hope I'm not bothering you. I'm John Beland, Linda's lead guitarist."

Rick couldn't have been nicer, just like the TV Show he appeared on in with his folks.
"Hi John" he answered with a warm smile. "How's it going?"

"Going great. I just wanted to say hi. I've been a huge fan of yours and great admirer of your records. I probably have listened to everything you've recorded ten times over."

"Hey, thanks a lot, man" Rick said in an almost embarrassed tone.

"My style of playing is a direct result of listening to James Burton's playing on your records. Just wanted to tell you how much you inspired me, Rick." I said as we shook hands.

I felt a strong connection with Rick from that first day I met him, as if I had known him all my life. He was gracious and very humble when it came to compliments. I felt as if our paths would cross again. Little did I know!

One day I got a phone message. Larry Murray wanted to meet up with myself and Swampwater at his home in the Hollywood Hills. He said he had a deal that might interest us. Larry's home was just above the famed Magic Castle Magician's club on Franklin Avenue. He lived in a small charming old cottage with his lovely wife Lorrette. It was a magical little house not far from the Hollywood Bowl.

The four of us arrived at Larry's, all curious on what kind of "deal" he had in mind.

"Hey guys" Larry started out. "I think Swampwater is a killer band. How would you feel about my producing an album on you for RCA Records?

"Are you joking?" I asked in amazement.

"I'm serious, John" my partner Ken Mansfield and I want to do an album on you guys.
Who is Ken Mansfield?" we asked.

It turned out that Ken Mansfield was a heavy hitting top record executive in LA who once headed up the USA branch of the Beatles Apple Records Division for Capitol Records. He was very tight with John, Paul, George and Ringo as well as a lot of other top names in pop music. In fact, George Harrison was Ken's best man at his recent wedding. Larry and Ken had joined forces and started their own production company called Hometown Productions. Ken was also president of Andy Williams' new pop label Barnaby Records. Having finished our deal with Starday King we jumped at the chance of doing a new album, and this time in Hollywood instead of way out in New Mexico. And this time for a major record label!

The Greek Theatre with Linda and Swampwater 1970

14 CHANGES IN THE WIND

Soon we were back in the studio starting work on our first album for RCA Records. It was a great thrill to be working at the famed RCA recording Studios in Hollywood, the very place where the Rolling Stones recorded "Satisfaction" and where John Lennon and Harry Nillson recorded, as well as all the Monkees records. Even Elvis himself had a secret office on the top floor. The shingle on the door to that office simply read "Hollywood Tours."

One late night as we were recording in the big studio, I went out to the hallway for a cup of coffee. As I was pouring myself a cup I heard Elvis music coming from one of the smaller studio rooms. I figured they were probably editing some tapes for another Elvis album. I decided to stick my nose in and take a peak. To my shock, I looked inside the door and there was Elvis and his band rehearsing! "Holy shit" I said out loud, and ran to our studio to tell Thad, Gib, Stan and Larry. Needless to say we all deserted our session and ran over to watch the rehearsals. But like schoolboys we were called back to our studio to resume recording. Elvis was as fit as a fiddle and looked fabulous. There he was, the King right in the next room rehearsing for his Las Vegas return.

Later, in the wee morning hours when we were leaving RCA and going to our cars, we saw a helicopter take off from the top of the RCA building. There, high in the clouds was Elvis heading back to his home in Bel-Air just down the strip. The sun was coming up on Sunset Blvd as his chopper flew off towards the ocean. A fitting way for the king of rock & roll to be taken home.

We returned to Nashville a month later to finish our album at RCA's studio on Music Row. This was a thrill for us because we were able to employ the services of two legendary Nashville steel guitarists, Jimmy Day and Curly Chalker. Day showed up to the session drunk as a skunk. He managed to play on one track before falling off of his seat, crashing to the floor. As a replacement we quickly called in the great steel guitar ace Curly Chalker, who showed up with his thumb in a cast.

"Jesus" I asked Thad. "What's the deal with steel players down here?"

But Chalker paid little attention to his broken thumb. He simply taped a pick to it and laid down some of the prettiest steel guitar that any of us had ever heard. As we finished for the day, the engineers went out to the main room and prepared the studio for the next session, a Jerry Reed, Chet Atkins project. We watched through the producer's booth as Reed, Chet and their band set up in a circle. But something appeared strange to me.

Recording at RCA Studios in Nashville 1970

"Hey Thad" I remarked. "Isn't that somebody laying on the floor next to Chet Atkins?"

We looked a bit closer.

"I'll say" laughed Thad. "It's Jimmy Day!
I guess that after he had fallen off his stool while recording for us, nobody bothered to come and collect him.

Following our Nashville sessions we headed back to L.A to re-join Linda for a series of concerts with folk artist Arlo Guthrie, son of the famed songwriter Woody. Arlo was hot that year riding on the wings of his big hit Alice's Restaurant as well as the film by the same name. We did a series of concerts up and down the coast of Southern California.

Although Linda opened the show and Arlo was the headliner, both acts joined forces together at the end of each show with Swampwater backing not only Linda but Arlo too. It was a great deal of fun and comradery. Arlo was a joy to tour with. He had a cool sense of humor and a deep love for music which we all shared. The concerts were recorded for what was to be a live album that is until the promoters torpedoed the recordings by announcing to the press that Arlo and Linda would be taping the shows for a live album. As a result, every stoned-out freak in the crowd found out where the microphones were and simply screamed into them throughout the shows. The entire "live" album recordings were useless. The project was scrubbed.

After the tour we all went home and back to our semi-normal lives. I had been corresponding with Susan Faulkner from Mother Blue's house in Chicago for quite a while and we both decided I would fly her out to California to come stay with me. I had never lived with a woman before but at the time everybody seemed to be moving in together so I thought I'd give it a try. Susan arrived not long afterwards and settled in with Jerry and I at our house on Whitley Avenue. We had a lot of fun together and enjoyed each other's company a lot. It was kind of cool to share a bed together every night and I'm not talking about sleeping.

Hell, we were basically still kids who really stood little chance of turning a live-in situation into a lifelong partnership. We lived from day to day. Susan was a great seamstress and loved embroidering designs on my jean shirts and pants for on stage. I really enjoyed her company and for a while things seemed perfect. That is until one day when Susan informed me that she was pregnant. When she told me the news I was jumping for joy. I had wanted a child, possibly more than she did. We agreed that the right thing for us to do was to get married and not let anyone know about the baby until we were a "legal" couple. I called my parents and Susan phoned hers informing them of the upcoming wedding. Naturally, the news didn't quite go over well with her parents. Marrying a rock guitarist in Hollywood wasn't exactly their dream plan for their daughter. My folks weren't thrilled either, fearing that getting married would hurt my career which I had worked so hard for. But regardless, Susan Faulkner and I were married in 1971 at the Little Chappell in Hollywood. Each of our parents as well as the Daltons came to the wedding. My dad was standing next to her father during the service. Quietly Susan's father whispered, "Clarence, I give it a year."

We had a party after the ceremony back at our house. Everyone seemed to be having a good time drinking wine and playing music. Throughout the party I kept hearing the doorbell ring constantly.

"Mom, can you get the door, please?" I asked.

A minute later after she returned I asked "Mom, who was at the door?"
"Oh, just some hippie with a damned banjo. I sent him away" she answered.

I didn't think much about it until 5 minutes later when I suddenly jumped up and ran to the door. There standing on the front porch holding a banjo and wearing a confused look on his face was none other than Arlo Guthrie! I couldn't help but laugh my ass off when I showed Arlo inside and introduced him to my mother.

"Mom, this is Arlo Guthrie". All my embarrassed mother could get out was "Oh my God."

I guess even Arlo had a great time at the party because the next morning I spotted him slipping out of the maid-of-honor's bedroom.

Arlo and I rehearsing for Hollywood Bowl" 1970

15 NEW BOSS, NEW DEAL AND A NEW BABY

Arlo took a real liking to all of Linda's band members. We felt as if we had known him for years. So, it was no surprise when I received a call from Arlo's manager Albert Grossman (also Bob Dylan's manager) about playing behind some of the greatest legends in the folk world at the Hollywood Bowl for what was being called "A Tribute to Woody" concert. This tribute to Arlo's dad, Woody Guthrie, would be held in two separate concerts on the east coast and west. The east coast portion of the show would be held at New York's famed Carnegie Hall. The backing band would be none other than The Band and they would provide the music for guest artists such as Judy Collins, Pete Seeger Tom Paxton and other legendary folk singers, and last but not least, making his first live public appearance since his near fatal motorcycle accident, the one and only Bob Dylan. The narration for that particular show would be handled by the great film actor, Robert Ryan.

For the west coast Hollywood Bowl show, I was hired to play Dobro and electric guitar along with my Swampwater bandmates Gib Guilbeau on fiddle and Stan Pratt on drums. Joining us would be Flying Burrito Brothers bassist Chris Ethridge and on mandolin the great Ry Cooder. Also on board was Arlo's guitarist, the wonderful John Pilla. The guest line up was a who's who of contemporary folk music, Joan Baez, Pete Seeger, Rambling Jack Elliott, Odetta, Ritchie Havens and Country Joe McDonald. The narration would be handled by the terrific film actor Will Geer, from the popular Waltons television show. The rehearsals were held on the top floor of the Continental Hyatt House on Sunset Strip. We started very early each morning and needless to say the coffee never stopped brewing.

One morning I had a terrific wake up call. I was sitting in a folding chair holding my Telecaster and studying the music charts in front of me when all of a sudden, a bikini clad Joan Baez came strolling in and gave me a "good morning kiss" right on my forehead. Hell, who needs coffee to wake up when you have that happen to you? All of the artists were very pleasant to work with. I found that many of the seasoned artists were quite eccentric and required a bit more attention to minor details than others. While Ritchie Havens took his time and meticulously went over every detail of the arrangement to his number, Country Joe McDonald just slapped on his guitar and roared through

John Beland

his tune at the speed of light. The one problem case, however, came from one of folk music's grand legends, the highly respected singer songwriter Pete Seeger. Pete was a stickler for traditional acoustic folk music and seemed to have a wild hair up his ass about electric instruments. One day as we were getting ready to rehearse a number, Seeger suddenly stopped everyone cold in their tracks and said in a stern voice "Does anyone hear that constant buzzing? Am I the only one who hears this irritating sound?" I didn't have a clue what he was ranting about and paid little attention. I was more interested in my chances of seeing Joan Baez in a bikini once again.

"That buzz that damned buzz is horrible" Seeger continued to rant. Finally, he walks my way straight up to my amplifier. "There it is!" he shouts, as if he has discovered gold. He looks at me and says "Son, can't you hear that horrible (and then he starts mimicking the sound)
BUZZZZZZZZZZZZZZZZZZZZ !"

His face is right in mine and I hadn't a clue what to do. A sound tech came to my rescue and told Pete that the buzz was unavoidable due to the fluorescent electric lights up on the hotel ceiling.

"Seeger pouted off, grumbling "Well let's see if we can do something about it."

"Boy" I thought "There goes a living legend, even if he is a cranky old cuss."

The concert was amazing. The band and I set up to the right of the Hollywood Bowl stage. I was on a stool with my Dobro and to my surprise the actor Peter Fonda was perched on a stool right next to me!

"What's he doing here?" I thought.

It turned out that this production used two narrators, actors Will Geer (Grandpa from the Waltons) and Peter Fonda.

"Very cool" I thought. I loved "Easy Rider" and Fonda was a very nice fellow even if he appeared a little dazed in the eyes! One by one the acts came forth, each singing their own versions of Woody Guthrie classics. Some were mesmerizing, and it was hard to stay concentrated on the music when witnessing such powerful performances. As Will Geer was narrating on the far side of the stage, the rest of us were blacked out. I smelled something funny and familiar coming from my right side and spotted Peter Fonda puffing away on a joint, right there on the Hollywood Bowl stage in the middle of the performance!

It was time for Fonda to do his narration so he nudged me on the shoulder and simply said, "Hey man, hold this for a minute."

Suddenly, I'm there in the shadows a foot from a spotlight as Peter Fonda who's reading one of Woody's poems to the Hollywood Bowl audience and I'm nervously holding his lit joint!

"This is terrific" I thought. I could just envision the show being stopped as the LAPD runs onstage, throws me to the ground and cuffs me for Marijuana possession! Some "Tribute to Woody Guthrie"!

Fortunately for me that didn't happen and when Fonda's bit was over and the spotlight moved, he simply took the joint back and resumed puffing away.

Both concerts were recorded and are now in the Library of Congress, something I am deeply honored to have participated in.

Arlo, my buddy Jerry Tate, and I onstage at the Hollywood Bowl soundcheck

Around that same time, I was hired to play Dobro for two great artists who were being featured on yet another Woody Guthrie tribute album. The first one was the great Peter Yarrow, from the world-famous trio Peter, Paul & Mary. We were recording the Guthrie song "Deportee" the same song I had backed Joan Baez up on at the Bowl concert. Peter was in a weird mood that night because the drummer was giving him a lot of problems and he was also drunk. Beer cans littered his drum booth and it looked as if he was going to topple over any second. The drummer was playing very hard and Yarrow wanted the exact opposite feel. He wanted the song to be soft and folkie but the drummer had other ideas. Finally, Peter came up to me as I was sitting in my chair arranging my notes.

"John, could you do me a favor and explain to the drummer what the feel for this song is? I think we're going to have problems with him."

"Sure, Peter" I answered. "I'll talk to him."

I walked over to the drum booth and explained to the drummer what the feel of the song should be.

"I'm playing the right fucking feel!" came his loud and pissed off response.

He continued "I'm playing it just like the fucking Byrds did it!"

I had to clue him in that "Deportee" was written and recorded by Woody Guthrie 20 years before the Byrds ever heard it! I went on to tell him that it was originally intended as a folk song, and that's the feel Peter was looking for.

"Well shit" he answered while he popped open another beer. "I wish somebody would have told me that. No problem. Let's do this."

And that's just what we did and the session came off just as Peter had intended.

The other artist I recorded with for the same project was famous singer songwriter Hoyt Axton, who penned such big hits as "Joy to the World" "Greenback Dollar" and many more. I was looking forward to this session because Hoyt was the first artist I had seen perform at the Troubadour during those first days I hit the streets of Hollywood. This session was an over dub date. The music track and Hoyt's vocal had already been recorded and by the time I arrived at the studio, Hoyt was far away in China performing. Rodney Dillard, from the Dillards, was producing the session. I really liked Rodney. He was a great musician and easy-going guy to work for, although at times he could get a bit nervous and excited. I sat in my chair alone in the main room of the studio listening to the track on my headphones. I couldn't hear Hoyt's vocal, so I asked Rodney to give me more of it. I could see Rodney lean close to his engineer explaining what I had asked for. I couldn't hear anything because they were in a soundproof booth. But I could see their movements. I just sat alone in silence waiting to run through the song again. Rodney ran the track for me and again there was no vocal.

"Hey Rodney" I said on my microphone "I'm not getting any of Hoyt's vocal. I have to hear it to know where I should play."

Now I could see Rodney more animated as he talked to his engineer. Then all of a sudden, I heard a big "What?" come through the glass soundproof booth. Rodney's hands were up in the air and he was obviously directing his panic towards his engineer. Finally, Rodney got up and came into the main room where I was sitting.

"Man, John you're not going to believe it. My engineer accidentally erased Hoyt's vocal! What an idiot! I don't know what to do."

I thought for a moment and said "Hey Rodney, no problem. I recorded this song before so I think I know where the vocal comes in and out. I'll play some Dobro fills where I think they should go." And that's just what I did. Hoyt eventually did his vocal over again and the parts I played on worked fine.

It was inevitable. Arlo wanted to hire us away from Linda. He was going on a major tour and wanted Swampwater to be his band. He offered us a few hundred dollars more than Linda paid us so we turned in our notice. There were no hard feelings and she wished us well. I felt a little sad leaving her, but at the same time excited about working for Arlo who was extremely popular that year. It turned out that we didn't have to worry about Linda for long. With the help of producer / boyfriend John Boylan she put together a new band consisting of drummer Don Henley from a band called Shilo, Bernie Leadon from The Flying Burrito Brothers, Glen Frey from Longbranch & Pennywhistle, and Randy Meisner from Rick Nelson's Stone Canyon Band. They didn't have a name at that time because they really weren't a full band, just individual players. But in the coming months they would come together as a unit, calling themselves The Eagles, while Linda's fame would continue to go through the roof. Linda will always remain the greatest singer I ever worked with.

As for us, we hit the concert trail with Arlo Guthrie. The venues were mostly all beautiful concert halls. Swampwater and Arlo fit together perfectly and we had a ball. The concerts were a lot tamer than Linda's. For the most part the crowds were a listening audience. Occasionally, you would hear a scream or two in the audience, but basically everyone was quiet and caught up in Arlo's great stories as well as his terrific music.

Along the way we stopped off in Chicago to play a popular club called The Quiet Knight. It was a famous place in the Windy City that featured some of the best names in contemporary folk and pop music of the day. One afternoon we were doing a sound check at the Quiet Knight when this short little guy, nearly the size of a midget, comes walking in carrying a guitar case that seemed bigger than he was. When he got closer to the stage I recognized him through the beard and the long hair, it was singer / songwriter Stevie Goodman, Thad's and my old friend from back at Mother Blue's a few years earlier. Stevie was a beautiful little guy with a smile that could make you feel he was your best friend. We hugged and talked about the days in Old Town at Mother Blues. I told him I had married Suzie Cream Cheese from Blue's house and he couldn't believe it. Actually, it was Stevie who first introduced me to her when One Man's Family had first hit town. Arlo and Stevie were great friends and on this afternoon, we were going to learn a new song of Stevie's that he had just written. We sat around him as he played it for us.

"Riding on the City of New Orleans. Illinois Central Monday morning rail."
It was a killer tune and we started to work it up right there at the Quiet Knight.

"Good morning America how are you? Don't you know me? I'm your native son. I am the train they call the City of New Orleans and I'll be gone 500 miles before the day is done."

We worked up an arrangement of "*City Of New Orleans*" and started to include it in our concert shows from that day forward. The song would go on to become Arlo's biggest hit and as well as one of the most popular songs in pop and country music history. As big as Stevie Goodman's smile was, it masked a hard reality. He had MS. Although he fought a brave fight, traveling to and from Chicago to New York for treatments, the disease would claim his life in a few years. Such a huge talent for such a little guy whose heart was bigger than a mountain. The world lost a great song writer when he died, much too soon.

We traveled to New York to play the prestigious Carnegie Hall. We were all thrilled to be performing at this highly respected venue whose stage had been graced by some of the most iconic names from all walks of the entertainment industry. There's an old saying that goes "New York City is the greatest place to be when you're working, and the worst place to be if you're not." How true! But in our case we were working right at the top. It doesn't get bigger than Carnegie Hall. Walking into the backstage area of Carnegie Hall is like walking into history. The sense of greatness and success totally surrounds you. I had to call my parents up. I found a pay phone backstage.

"Hi mom" I said with a burst of energy.

"Hi honey! Where are you?" She answered, calling my dad over to the phone in a loud whisper.

"I'm in New York City, Mom. Guess where I'm playing tonight?"

"I have no idea" she responded. "You're always playing

somewhere"

"I'm playing Carnegie Hall this evening. I guess we made it, mom."

I felt a huge lump in my throat during the short but seemingly eternal silence that followed. I knew she and dad were overwhelmed. All that we had been through: my nights on the street, begging for money, stealing food, being ridiculed by my Grandmother, my aunt and uncle, watching the fire go out of my father's spirit when we hit such hard times. Now, here I was just minutes before stepping onstage at the most prestigious venue in show business.

"We're very proud of you, Jack" came my dad's trembling voice.

That's all I needed to hear. I couldn't help crying although I fought it like a champ. I remember my grandma Foley and my Aunt Elaine telling my father that I would end up a "failure" like him. Their words were burned into my soul. Now they could eat them. A "failure"? My father was my hero, and because of his willingness to allow me to catch a dream. I was now playing at Carnegie Hall.

"We made it, Dad" I said with my eyes filled in tears.

"We love you, son. Go out there and kill 'em" came the reply.

Show time approached. From behind the curtain I could hear the house music being played through the PA and the muted rumble of the crowd getting to their seats. I checked my Dobro and strapped my guitar on, waiting nervously for the lights to lower and the curtain to rise. I thought about all those movies I watched as a kid, where Judy Garland sings at Carnegie Hall to an audience of Tuxedos and evening gowns. Now I was in that movie, preparing to see an audience of the highest caliber. Then the lights dimmed, the crowd silenced and the curtain rose to not only polite, warm applause but to screaming long haired fans in tie-die shirts and jeans. One clown even yelled out "Rock and Roll, Motherfucker!" Well, it wasn't quite Judy Garland's version but it was still Carnegie Hall.

On December 3rd 1971 Arlo and Swampwater played the Los

Angeles Convention center. It was an important gig and everyone was on their toes to do a great show. At the same time Susan was ready to have our baby any day now. During her pregnancy she had become angry and very difficult to live with, constantly throwing fits in front of friends and creating embarrassing moments at an alarming frequency. So it wasn't a surprise that on the way to the LA concert she started screaming that she was having the baby. She had already given us so many false alarms that it was hard to take her seriously.

However, we left her and Thad's wife Jeanie at the hospital in Culver City on the way to the show. We would pick them back up on the way home. When I got to the backstage entrance of the Auditorium I received a phone call. It was from Jeanie Maxwell. "Congratulations, Daddy. You have a baby girl." I couldn't believe it! This time Susan was telling the truth. I had a beautiful new baby daughter who we named Sarah Daniel Beland, named after Dan Dalton. When Arlo announced Sarah's birth to the audience the crowd went crazy and I gladly took a bow! Afterwards, we went to the hospital and I saw my daughter for the first time. She was so tiny and beautiful that it took my breath away. She was yet another blessing in my life and I held her close to my cheek thanking God for her. Beautiful Sarah was my first child and I was walking on a cloud.

My wife Susan, daughter Sarah, friend Jerry Tate and actor Danny Bonaduci

16 POETRY IN MOTION …
MOVING ON WITH JOHNNY TILLOTSON

Swampwater's second album didn't sell. RCA wasn't behind it and I could see why. It was weak and not nearly as fresh and original as the little album we recorded with John Wagner for Starday-King in New Mexico. Larry Murray's production left a lot to be desired. Bad editing, weak engineering and no direction. Larry lacked the skills of top experienced producers like Wagner and Dan Dalton. Producing requires knowledge of the latest technology and the ability to control a session and know how to pick out flaws and make substantial contributions. Larry had none of that. He was a fun guy and talented songwriter but in essence had no business behind the board.

RCA allowed us to record three more songs before deciding to drop us from the label. We went into the studio with great sidemen such as Flying Burrito Brothers' steel ace, Sneaky Pete and rock and roll's top sax player the great Jim Horn. But it wasn't enough. At RCA's request, we even did a short promo tour of high schools up and down southern California along with ex-Monkee, Mike Nesmith who had just embarked on a solo run. Mike was a great guy and he appeared onstage with just his guitar, no band. The reception to both acts was lukewarm at best.

The writing was on the wall, in my eyes. The rest of the guys in the band wanted to continue on but I couldn't see the point. Country rock just wasn't making it to radio. It filled up clubs, halls and festivals but didn't sell records. We had the talent and the material to score hits but we lacked skilled production. With Larry behind the board we were dead in the water. I was frustrated and felt that it was time to move on. At that very same time I got a call from Kenny Hodges from One Man's Family.

"Hey John, how are ya, buddy?" came the old familiar voice of my dear friend and former bandmate.

"Hey Kenny!" I replied. "I'm doing ok, I guess. Not much happening with Swampwater, though. Trying to figure out what I should do."

Kenny then answered "That's why I'm calling. Remember when I introduced you to my friend from Florida, Johnny Tillotson when we were rehearsing in Topanga Canyon?"

"Yea" I replied. "I remember. He was a great guy. I always liked his records."

"That's good because he's looking for a guitarist to be his music director and I suggested you. He jumped at the idea and the gigs yours if you want it."

I was thrilled! This meant a steady check and a future.

Swampwater was finished as far as I was concerned and I sadly handed in my notice to the guys. I wished them well and we parted as friends. We were a pioneering band that should have struck pay dirt. But RCA had their sights on another band similar to ours called Pure Prairie League, who did manage to score big with an acoustic guitar laced number called "Amy." Soon after we were dropped from RCA another band emerged with the same similar sound Swampwater had, harmonies and rockin' telecasters. Even their guitar riffs were like ours. They signed to a new label called Asylum Records, started by industry mogul, David Geffin. The band had even backed Linda Ronstadt like we once had. We knew the guys well and had worked with them individually and were well aware of their talent as singers. They would call themselves the Eagles and would change the whole playing field with regard to acoustic country rock acts. Swampwater, unfortunately would fall through the cracks. It was time for me to move on.

Johnny Tillotson was born in Palatka, Florida and got his start in the 1950's singing on a local television program in Jacksonville called the Toby Dowdy Show. Cadence Records owner Archie Blyer, who was responsible for the success of the Everly Brothers and Andy Williams, took notice of Johnny and signed him to the country division of his label. Although he recorded his records in Nashville, Tennessee and used the top country session players of the day, Johnny's records ended up becoming top 10 pop smashes and soon he was a major rock and roll star with hits like "Poetry In Motion" "It Keeps Right On A Hurtin" "Heartaches By The Number" "Send Me The Pillow That You Dream On" "Dreamy Eyes" "Without You" "Talk Back

Trembling Lips" to name a few. Johnny was all over TV and radio even long after his hits stopped. Through the sensible advice of his longtime manager Mel Shane, Johnny learned early that the run of hits wouldn't last forever and that he should concentrate on performing, namely in Las Vegas, to sustain the non-hit portion of his career. It was sound advice and by the time I hooked up with Johnny he was already a well-established star, not only in Vegas but in dinner theaters and clubs throughout the world.

I met Johnny at his home in Encino, California. It was a beautiful house in a very upscale part of the Valley where many celebrities resided. Johnny met me at the door with a warm smile and a handshake, inviting me in to meet his lovely wife Lou. From the minute I met Johnny I felt a connection between us. He was by far and away one of the nicest artists I had met. We sat down and talked about my gigs with Linda and Arlo. Johnny listened intently to every word of every story coming out of my mouth. He seemed keenly interested in learning all about me with a sincerity that was rather surprising.

Johnny Tillotson and I in an ad for Randall Amps 1972

"John", he began, "I'm so thrilled that we're going to work together. I've heard so much about you that I feel I know you already". Johnny filled me in on the details of his career as well as the gigs before us. He didn't take a band on the road because it was too expensive. Instead, the local promoters would furnish a rhythm section, namely a local drummer, a bass player, a keyboardist along with me playing guitar. It would be my job to rehearse the band in the early afternoon of the gig and have them ready by show time. I would handle all the charts and direct the musicians during Johnny's performance. When we played more important venues like Las Vegas I would help him put a great band of LA players together for that engagement. The gig paid $500.00 a week with a $20.00 a day food allowance. We would travel together, just him and me, no road crew.

"That sounds good to me Johnny. Count me in" I said.

"Fabulous" he shouted with a big smile and a warm hand shake. I liked Tillotson. He was a character, full of energy and experience and I took to him instantly. I had the feeling we would make a great team.

Our first gig was at the Sahara Hotel in Las Vegas. For that engagement we put a band together consisting of a rhythm section of top players from Oklahoma City, where Johnny performed quite regularly. For backing vocals, he hired two sisters, Debbie and Patsy Clinger, who were studio vocalists and had sung on tons of records and TV shows in Hollywood. And they were stunningly gorgeous too!

We had some very cool stage outfits designed by Bill Balloo the famed costume designer in Hollywood. They were denim western style shirts and jeans all tailor made for us and looked very sharp.

We rehearsed the show for a week, going over every song in detail. The band was exceptionally good and the girl's vocals were flawless. For the final rehearsal at the Sahara, Johnny brought in his good friend, the infamous Italian no bullshit music conductor for Elvis Presley, Joe Guercio. As a favor to Johnny he agreed to come over and straighten out any rough parts in the show.

Guercio was right out of a movie with his macho demeanor, dark black hair, black goatee and silver rimmed sunglasses, big rings on his fingers and a gold TCB chain around his neck. The TCB was Elvis's trademark meaning "Taking Care of Business." Joe also wore a huge flashy Elvis style belt around his waist. Nothing was subtle or humble about Joe Guercio. In Vegas he was "the" man and walked through a casino as if he owned it. Everyone kissed his ass. If Joe said the sun was polka dot you can bet it certainly was in the eyes of those who bowed at his feet. Joe had a razor-sharp tongue and wasn't afraid to chew musicians out who didn't play the proper way, especially those he felt he could intimidate by his status as Elvis's conductor. However, I never let him bother me in the slightest. I had worked for bigger names than his and besides I gave him no excuse to be on my back. I was a seasoned session player by now and very important to Johnny and Guercio knew it. Tillotson had filled him in about me well in advance, so by the time we finally met, Joe was a pussy cat to me. In fact, we became good friends and would work together on many recording projects in the future.

Las Vegas in 1972 was still in its Rat Pack era and was still very much a desert oasis. The little Italian lounges remained there and many of Sinatra's friends continued to perform in the main rooms and lounges along the Strip like Dean Martin, Sammy Davis Jr, Shecky Green, Don Rickles, Jerry Vale, Al Martino, Joey Bishop, Buddy Hacket, Debbie Reynolds, Phyllis Diller, they were all there as big as ever. I was also surprised to see a lot of old music acts I had presumed had vanished, still alive and well working the main room lounges like, Little Anthony & The Imperials, Chubby Checker, Fabian, The Ink Spots, The Mills Brothers, Bobby Rydell and of course the ever popular "Mr. Vegas" of the Strip, Wayne Newton.

Johnny and I backstage at the Hilton Hotel in Las Vegas 1973

Las Vegas was a wild place to experience during that first week I arrived. It never closed. In the casinos people moved here and there like ants on a hill and the sound of slot machines paying off was continuous. You could walk into a lounge at any hour of the day and see a show for free. Food was cheap and it was easy to lose track of time once you were swallowed up in everything. Myself and the rest of the band stayed at a nice motor court on the strip while Johnny stayed at the Sahara. I preferred the motor court because it was easier access to the stores and you didn't have to fight crowds every time you left your room.

The Strip was pretty wide open back then. Not at all like today where it resembles a Disneyland theme park. You could get from one point to another with ease and not have to fight traffic or navigate through countless malls and theme rooms. It was still the town of "Ocean's Eleven". You could breathe a bit and stretch your arms out. I loved it and really enjoyed playing there.

Johnny was fabulous on stage. He had the charm and the vocal chops and was always a crowd favorite. He sang pitch perfect and carried himself with absolutely no sign of ego. Everyone loved the guy. The shows went off without a hitch night after night. It was a bit of an adjustment doing such late performances, especially the 2am shows. But in Las Vegas you tended to lose track of time anyway.

I met Johnny's Las Vegas publicist Joan Guertin who did a nice write up in the local news on my joining forces with Johnny. There was something "happening" every day and night in Vegas. Much more exciting than the grind of touring one-night stands with Linda and Arlo. And the money was much better as well.

After Vegas, Susan, Sarah and I, along with Jerry Tate, moved into a great old house a block over on Grace Street in the Hollywood Hills. It was a Spanish style home built in the 1920's with a big yard and avocado trees taller than the roof. It was a terrific place but Susan still wasn't happy. She complained about everything constantly and when I would have to go on the road she would make an issue out of it. At times she became unbearable with her mood swings and temper fits. I couldn't wait to get back on the road again, even though I hated leaving Sarah behind.

One time, actor Cliff Robertson was at the house meeting with myself and a few musicians who were set to play on his new film "JW COOP". We were discussing the film and the music involved when

Susan walked in and shouted "How much longer are you guys going to be here?" It was an embarrassing scene and slowly but surely everyone slithered out the door. I was furious. Jerry was busy working at Paramount doing sound for the Partridge Family television show. Some days he would bring home visitors to our house. One was young Danny Bonaducci, who played the wise cracking kid brother bass player in the series, loved coming over to our house because he could smoke cigarettes and drink beer without getting busted. He was a good kid but in certain ways a lot older than he appeared to be.

Johnny and I hit the road playing dates throughout the heartland and the south. We would fly into some little rural airport to be met by the promoter who would always have nothing but the most positive things to say, even though 80% of it was bullshit. We would check into the local hotel, grab a quick bite to eat and head to the club for rehearsal. Most of the time the bands I had to work with were average at best and it was a test of patience to whip them up into a professional unit. I had to work up an entire hour and a half show in one afternoon and it wasn't easy. Many times the musicians just couldn't read charts and it seemed like forever teaching them the material.

Johnny would always send a show tape in advance weeks before we arrived. But just about every time we arrived at our destination and asked the promoter if the band had received the tapes, the answer was usually "not yet" or "the tapes just arrived today." It was nerve racking but I'll be damned if we didn't pull it off every goddamned night. Between Johnny's talent and my musicianship, we covered any flaws the band was making and delivered a terrific show all the time. We were great together. We traveled endless miles playing in towns I never knew existed. Through it all he and I became very close friends and faced each situation with experience, determination, professional attitudes and lots of humor.

Traveling with Johnny was an education in more than one way. He had a gold mine of knowledge when it came to the country music scene in Nashville. John had so much experience that it was fascinating listening to his stories and hearing all about his adventures in the business. What I learned from working with him could never be measured. He taught me a universe of show business knowledge ranging from the ins and outs of country music to performing onstage as well as on television. Johnny knew the business like the back of his hand.

Another subject he mastered in was the wonderful world of the opposite sex. Johnny knew it all and sometimes he could even make "me" blush! Over the years being a teenage idol, he had accumulated quite a bit of wisdom when it came to women. He seemed to know everything about how to please them. At times on long drives or in air flights he would describe encounters he had with various women like a pathologist describing an autopsy. Every physical detail would roll off his tongue and into my ears to the point of making me cringe. Playing for Johnny was like taking up sex education as a major. Women adored him and he adored them, always pandering to them in the most blatantly charming way. For example, he would spot a pretty flight attendant and flatter her until she didn't know what hit her and then, he would turn to me and say loud enough for her to hear: "John Beland, doesn't Ms Beverly have amazing bone structure"? I was always embarrassed to be roped into John's conquests but I couldn't help but laugh my ass off watching him operate. He was amazing.

Working with Johnny allowed me to see the country in a way I had never seen before. Although he had many pop hits, his fan base was in country music and as a result many of our gigs were in the Heartland as well as the Deep South, where he still maintained a strong fan base. Quite often we would be invited to home cooked dinners out on someone's farm where we would meet the most wonderful people, all salt of the earth rural folks who were true blue country music fans, going out of their way to make Johnny and I feel welcome into their homes. In a way, it reminded me of my early years back in Hometown. Sometimes we would do radio interviews in these small town venues and I would get a chance to see and meet program directors and disc jockeys who operated out of the same old buildings and houses they did in the early 1930's. Most the folks who operated these "mom & pop" stations treated John and I with courtesy and kindness and really made us feel at home. It was a far cry from the phony manic pop radio and college stations I had been to with Linda and Arlo. This was Middle America where God and Country still set the pace for those who lived there. One interesting place Johnny and I performed was in the town of Waldorf, Maryland, just outside Washington DC. The entire town was basically set along an interstate highway and featured gigantic Las Vegas style showrooms featuring old rock and roll performers like Fats Domino, Ronnie Dove and Jay & The Americans.

Johnny and I at Bob Woods Music in Oklahoma pickin' and grinning 1973

As it turns out, these showrooms were actually gambling casinos built when gaming was legal in the area. Now, since gambling was outlawed, they became dinner theaters and venues for oldies acts from the 50's and 60's. Two rooms in particular were very popular with the locals. One was a former car dealership featuring a giant glass Indian tepee around the main stage area. The club was called The Wigwam and John & I played there in 1972. The other club, just down the street, was called The Thunderbird Club and it also featured oldies acts from the 50's and 60's but of a higher quality of talent than the Wigwam. Where the Thunderbird featured acts like Paul Revere & The Raiders, Ricky Nelson and Jay and the Americans, the Wigwam presented acts like Billy Joe Royal, Johnny Tillotson, Ronnie Dove, Dave "Happy Organ" Baby Cortez.

Waldorf was a surreal place. Cars whipped by it on their way to and from Baltimore and DC. The showrooms stood there like monoliths during the day, neon signs announcing who was playing and parking lots seemingly deserted. It was no more than a speed bump, remnants of a once thriving gambling mecca now existing off old rock acts from days past. One day while we were in Waldorf for a one-nighter, Johnny stopped by my room.

"John, I have a good friend coming to the show tonight and I want you to meet him. I've told him about your songwriting and solo work and I think he might be interested in helping you out. His name is Sean Downey." I was surprised and thrilled that Johnny thought so much of me as to bring my name up to a friend of his.

"That's great, JT" I said. "But what does Sean do?"

"Well" Johnny began after pausing to think "He does a variety of things. He's involved in politics and knows everyone in Washington. His father was a famous radio star named Morton Downey, who was just as popular as Bing Crosby in the 30's and 40's and his mother Constance Bennett was a famous movie star." I was impressed.

"I've known Sean for many years and he's a very colorful character" said Johnny. "You'll meet him tonight."

That afternoon Johnny and I rehearsed the band the promoter had furnished for that night's gig. To our relief, these musicians were surprisingly good considering the poor quality of players we generally were faced with. Not having our own steady band was a challenge. We constantly had to settle for average musicians, most being local guys who played part time and worked normal 9 to 5 gigs during the day. It was always a crap shoot and at times very nerve racking when faced with having to put together an entire show in a relatively short time with very poor players. However, these guys were great and played the music charts with ease. What a relief! Now we could look forward to a great show that evening. Come show time the once empty parking lot of the Wigwam Club was now jam packed for tonight's performance. Johnny could still pack them in. Backstage he and I were going over last-minute details in his dressing room when the door flew open and there stood a tall, sharp dressed man with styled black hair, perfectly capped white teeth and a dark tan that looked as if he had just stepped right out of a Coppertone Tanning commercial. He was flanked by two gorgeous women, one blonde and one red head both clinging to each of his arms.

"Hi ya, JT !" he bellowed out in a big loud radio announcer's voice.

"Sean, it's great to see you" answered an excited Johnny.

"How the hell are ya, pal?" Downey asked while pumping Tillotson's hand up and down like he was drilling for oil.

Immediately Johnny threw Downey's two female companions one of his hallmark teenage idol smiles as Sean introduced the girls to the star of the night.

"Sean, I want to meet the man I was telling you about, my guitarist John Edward Beland" Johnny boasted. Johnny loved calling me John Edward and always introduced me by my full name.

"Hi ya, pal" Downey chimed with that huge perfect smile "Johnny's been telling me some great things about you. I want to talk with you after the show ok"?   Before I could answer this bigger than life character, he was out the door dragging his two bombshells behind him. "Have a great show, JT" he roared, and out the door he went.

"Whew" I exclaimed. "That was Sean Downey?"

Tillotson laughed and said "That's him. He's a real character but an important one. He knows everyone in politics and just about everyone in the record business. I've known Sean for a lot of years and he can help you with your career. Don't let the outrageous personality fool you. I think he's going to make you an offer."

I was a bit suspicious of Downey, but I trusted Johnny completely so I went along with everything, curious about where it all was going to lead to." Little did I know that this same Sean Downey would transform himself into the number one national TV shock talk show host Morton Downey Jr over a decade later.

We did another killer show that night. Johnny charmed and sang his way through hit after hit to a packed club of delighted rock and roll fans. I had to hand it to him, he was a master onstage. He knew just when to smile at the exact right time or when to look as sincere as your best friend. People loved the guy, and he knew it. After the show Downey came roaring back to Johnny's dressing room. "Jesus Christ, can this guy get any better?" he bellowed out. "Great show, Johnny. And holy cow, how about this kid guitarist you found? Just incredible!" Downey then took me off to the side. "Listen, pal, let's meet tomorrow after you get up. I'll pick you up at noon and we'll have lunch together. I want to talk to you about something that might interest you." Before I could answer Downey was out the door with his two female friends and Johnny in tow. I gathered up my guitar and charts and drove back to our hotel with the promoter, who kept babbling on and on all during the drive back, but all I could do was wonder what this guy Sean Downey had in mind for me. I'd find out soon enough.

As promised, Sean picked me up the next day at noon in his brand-new Lincoln Continental. He was all smiles as I got into his car.

"Good morning, John. How the hell are ya, pal?"

"Doing fine, Sean. This is a beautiful car you've got here" I said.

"Yeah, well the wife likes it" he dismissed. "Let's head into D.C and I'll show you around"

With that we took off for Washington DC about 45 minutes away from Waldorf. All along the way Sean told me about his life. It was really an amazing story. Downey grew up in Hollywood, the son of two very high-profile entertainment stars of the 30's and 40's, the Irish hit tenor Morton Downey and the highly popular film star, Constance Bennett. When he was a little kid, Spencer Tracy bounced him on his lap. Dinner guests at the Downey residence included the who's who of the entertainment business and Sean grew up surrounded by the Hollywood elite. As he grew up he tried his hand at singing and then moved on to become a rock and roll disc jockey. Finally, he settled for politics and became a lobbyist in Washington DC where he was very close friends with the Kennedy's and other high profile names in the Democratic Party. Downey was a "jack of all trades" so to speak. He had an overbearing Irish personality and took command in every room he walked in. Everybody was his "pal" and he could work a room like Segovia could play a guitar.

Downey took me on a fast tour of the city, pointing out the White House, the Capital, and the Watergate Building. I was fascinated by it, even though I suspected that it was all boring to Sean. We ended up at a fancy restaurant in nearby Georgetown where Sean got us the best table in the house. All through lunch people were stopping by our table saying hello and shaking Downey's hand as if he was the president.

"Phony sons of bitches" he would smile and say to me, under his breath, as they walked away. That congressman's wife is fucking everybody in Washington" he'd tell me in a loud whisper. I tried hard not to bust out laughing. "It's all bullshit down here, my friend. Just like the record business. You just have to learn how to navigate through it" he said never breaking his perfectly expensive smile. "Listen JB" he said in a dead serious voice while downing a glass of Champagne. "Johnny played me your demo tape and it's tremendous. I want to handle you. I have solid ties in New York with Scepter Records and feel positive we can land you an album deal there." I was all ears, to say the least. "Let me talk to my friend Florence Greenberg who owns Scepter and see what I can do. Meanwhile, keep writing these great songs. I'll advance you any money you may need for the demos. I also want to publish any original material you come up with and get you an advance for that. How does all this sound to you?"

Are you kidding me? It was impossible to say anything but "YES" to this guy. There I was, dining in one of the finest restaurants in Washington, surrounded by politicians and high profile faces I recognized from TV. Waiters catering to my every need and feeling every bit like the star Downey expected me to become. Being offered a recording and publishing deal, a management contract and a shot at the brass ring as a solo artist, no band, no backup job, a solo career of my very own.

"It sounds great to me, Sean" I answered back, with a big shit ass grin on my face. We shook hands and talked about the future.

For legal reasons, Downey couldn't manage me. Instead, he talked it over with Johnny and they decided to approach Tillotson's manager, Mel Shayne, about taking me on. Mel was legendary in the business. He navigated Johnny's career when the hits were coming as well as when the hits stopped. Although Johnny's hits had ended, he became huge on the live circuit, performing solid in Vegas as well as dinner theaters and clubs across the country. Not only that, Johnny was very popular with American servicemen overseas, and that is just where we were headed. Johnny was booked for a string of one-night appearances at military bases throughout Germany. Following that he was set for a tour of the UK on a package deal with the great Del Shannon ("Runaway") and Bobby Vee ("Rubber Ball"). And the most exciting thing was, I would be going along with him as music director and lead guitarist, my first trip to Europe. "Could anything be better than 1972" I asked myself?

When Johnny and I returned to Hollywood, I immediately went into the studio and recorded a song I had written called "Banjo Man", a pop ballad with a Beatles, Bee Gees influence. I did a basic track using John Ware, from Mike Nesmith's band, on drums, studio bassist Joe Lamano and my friend arranger and pianist Paul Parrish on piano. It sounded great and I envisioned adding strings to it once Downey secured a deal with Scepter Records. I made a rough mix of the session and packed it away to take with me on the Germany / UK tour the following week. It was great to be behind the board and producing my own music for the first time. I had usually been the aggressive creative member in the studio with Swampwater but any and all of my suggestions still had to be filtered out through other producers. This meant a lot of compromise as well as frustration. In the case of Swampwater's 2nd album for RCA, we were produced by Larry Murray whose production skills were very limited and nowhere near the caliber of Dan Dalton, whom I had studied under in the 60's and greatly admired.

Being the youngest in the room was a handicap as well when I would record for Larry. Most of the time I was spoken down to like a step child being lectured. I resented that treatment, especially coming from a producer whose own skills and commercial track record left a lot to be desired in my eyes.

But now I was running the show and I used all the skills I had learned from producers like Dan Dalton and John Wanger and put them to good use and to my own advantage. I felt in my element as a producer and more than qualified to handle my own sessions. It was nice to answer to only myself, for once.

In the winter of 1973 Johnny Tillotson and I flew to Germany for a series of shows at various Armed Forces bases throughout the country. For me it was a real thrill to be traveling over the Atlantic Ocean, my very own US passport in hand headed to my first foreign country and performing for G.I.'s from the Army, Marines and the Air force. This was the closest I ever came to any military experience in my life! It was also my first time in Germany, or any other country outside of the USA. For the tour Johnny and I were supplied with a road manager and a personal driver. The band was made up of military personnel and they were terrific musicians, if a little bit on the straight, conservative side. They guys were country musicians and ran their band like a well-trained combat unit. In some cases, where we had to play two shows at two different bases on the same night, Johnny and I would jump into the limo and be taken to the next gig while the band cleared and packed up the gear, loaded up the band and made it to the next venue…before we did! Once there, they set the gear, including my amp and guitar, back up and by the time Johnny and I arrived they were already onstage playing a warm up set to the crowd! Incredible. Like I said, the guys were terrific. They treated me like I was somebody of a much higher rank which lasted only one gig when I nearly begged them to simply call me John and to loosen up! We became great friends after that. Considering I had hair long over my shoulders, it was quite cool to be accepted into their circle.

I recall that the guys had an expression when hitting the stage. They would all say "charge" as if we were headed into battle. And sometimes it appeared that we were, in fact! One night while we were in the middle of a show at an Army base, someone threw a full beer can up on the bandstand that knocked our bass player out. With precision timing, Johnny and I were immediately escorted to a private room while the rest of the band grabbed mic stands and "charged" into the crowd and after the fool who threw the can. We played quite a lot of military clubs. The Air force club gigs were the best. Those guys were the elite of the military and their clubs were always the most expensive high-class gigs on the tour. Audiences were dressed to the hilt and very well behaved during our performances. We were always supplied with great dressing rooms and gourmet style dinners before show time. The Army bases could be rough. The clubs were a bit more down scale than the Air force rooms. The crowds could be much looser and wilder too. The food was average fare and our dressing rooms were usually the local Colonel's office. One time I remember Johnny and were getting ready to have our dinner and we noticed that BBQ was on the evening's menu. The black cook happened to come over to our table to say hello and I asked him how good the BBQ was.

In the coolest laid-back tone bordering on singing, he simple said "Mister Beland, this BBQ is so good you'll want to fuck it." And I'm here to tell you, it was!

While in Germany, Johnny and I stayed at local B&B style hotels in little villages. Everything was small, the rooms, the closets, the beds and in most cases you used a communal bathroom. Hardly anyone around us spoke any English, including the owners of the hotels. We communicated using my cartooning skills. When we would eat breakfast, I would simply draw a picture of a chicken and an egg for the cook. Then I would point to the egg and hit it with my fist. That's how I ordered scrambled eggs for us, much to the disdain of the cook.

Some of our gigs were in remote training areas where the soldiers were on what they called "reforging maneuvers." For these shows we played in a tent for an audience of GI's all dressed in combat gear. And they were always the greatest crowds to play for. I always wondered where these kids were headed. They were always so polite and respectful despite the seriousness of their job. I always hoped that they were never in harm's way and that every one of them made it home safely.

It was at this time that I learned about how to keep up with the grueling schedules of the road. Like many rock and rollers of his time, Johnny fueled his days and nights with various pills. I first noticed when I stopped by his room and saw them all lined up perfectly on the dresser, all in various colors and shapes. There were pills to get up, pills to watch your weight, pills before dinner and pills before and after show time. And there were pills to help you come down after a show and be able to relax on the long drives back to the hotel. These latter pills were called Placidyland they were large green gel-like pills that knocked you on your ass. Johnny shared them with me on this first trip to Germany. What we would do is take the Placidyldirectly after the last song, as we were hopping in the limo for the drive home. Midway on the ride they would kick in and you would be in a drunk like state totally at the mercy of our driver. By the time we reached the hotel and our rooms it only took us minutes to fall into a much-needed rest. Without Placidylit would have taken hours to get comfortable enough to fall asleep especially after a full night of performing. Most times we wouldn't even get back to the hotel until 5 or 6am. We never abused ourselves on Placidyland never took them for amusement.

They were strictly used when working. Still, I had to laugh when Johnny told me all about the New York doctor who made a livelihood out of shooting up the teen idols of the day with shots of vitamins and speed at a time when drugs were not even considered a part of late 50's and early 60's rock and roll. The scene back then was no different than what came later when drugs became such a fixture in the business. Only back then it was all hush hush.

As the weeks and months went on, Johnny and I became very close friends and I looked up to him like an older brother. I really grew to love the guy. He took advantage of every available opportunity to help further my career and never asked for anything in return. He became a real role model to me. It seemed that every day was a new learning experience when it came to working with Tillotson. He may have been a cute ladies guy with a string of teenage hits, but just below all that was a chiseled veteran of a thousand gigs and a million miles of touring. He was an expert on nearly every aspect of show business and never seemed to mind sharing his knowledge and experience with me. Since it was just Johnny and I alone together out in the big world, we were like a team. I never once felt as if I was working for someone, rather working "with" someone who I considered my closest friend.

17 "LET ME TAKE YOU DOWN"
LONDON, ROCK & ROLL AND SIGNING
WITH THE BEATLES.

After an exhausting 3-week tour of Military bases throughout Germany, Johnny and I flew across the channel to England. I was thrilled that I was going to perform in the very country of my childhood heroes, from Robin Hood, Sherlock Holmes to the Rolling Stones and of course, the Beatles. I felt as if I was going to Disneyland for the first time as I peered out the jet window. As we descended, the clouds broke and I could see the rooftops of London below, looking exactly like the Peter Pan books I read as a kid. There it was, home of the fab four. It was all I could do to keep my excitement contained as our jet touched down at Heathrow Airport. We were met outside Heathrow by our English road manager Phil Luderman, a tall John Cleese-like crazy, wonderful character who instantly appealed to me. Far from being low on energy he scooped us up and drove us into London to meet with Johnny's UK agent Henry Sellers. Smack into swinging London's Piccadilly Circus we drove and it was a sight to behold! People everywhere were dressed in both respectable and conventional business attire or decked out in the latest colorful Carnaby Street fashions. It was wonderful and exciting to look out the car window and see historic buildings, beautiful parks and an endless stream of hip, cool, beautiful people walking here, there and everywhere.

"Mr. Beland" Phil suddenly blurted out to me. "Do you fancy ice cream?"

Scratching my head, I answered "Sure, Phil. Of course, I do"

Then to my surprise Phil slams on the brakes and calls over to one of the most beautiful women I had ever seen in my life, with long blond hair and legs for days barely covered by a short mini-skirt. She wore pink granny glasses and stood there on the curb looking at us, while licking an ice cream cone!

"Hallo Luv" Phil called out from the window. My American guitar playing friend, John, fancy's a lick of your ice cream cone. He just arrived after a terribly long flight from overseas, the poor boy. Would you mind?"

I was in shock as she ran to the car while Phil reached over and rolled down my window. Tillotson was in stitches. The girl reached in with her ice cream cone as I took a nice lick and thanked her.

"Thank you, sweet" Phil purred back to her, and off into traffic we tore back again.

I was too busy looking out the back window at the most beautiful girl I had ever met to pay much attention to Johnny's loud laughter. "Welcome to London, boys" Phil shouted out as he cranked up the car radio to Spencer Davis's "Gimme Some Lovin" blasting at volume 11 as we sped off through the streets of London headed to Henry Sellers office.

Henry Sellers was a top agent in England who handled a variety of rock and roll acts from America. He started out his career as a song plugger for Leeds Music in London. After that he went to work for one of the largest booking agencies in the UK and was instrumental in booking the Beatles first major tour in England in 1963. In 1970 he struck out on his own and started the Henry Sellers Agency and quickly established himself booking acts like Neil Sedaka, Chuck Berry, Peggy Lee, Jackie Wilson, Johnny Ray, The Drifters, Benny King and of course, Johnny Tillotson. Like our tour manager Phil, Henry was full of energy and positive news. Everything out of his mouth was "no worries." That is until I asked him whether our British rhythm section received the show tape we sent from America. "No" Henry answered with a concerned look. "I don't recall receiving anything like that." This was typical and always a major problem because it meant more work for myself and Johnny. Now, like so many times in America, we had to whip up an entire band only a day before our opening night, and with no advanced tapes for the musicians!. Suddenly, our excitement of playing in the UK dampened with the prospect of having to work our asses off with additional rehearsals for our band. No worries.

Back at the hotel Johnny asked me if I still had a copy of my demo recording of "Banjo Man." I told him I did have it but why did he want to know? Johnny said, "Well, I have a dear friend who used to do publicity work for me back in the early years when I first toured England. His name is Tony King and he's now the manager of Apple Records, the Beatles new label. If you don't mind I can call him and possibly set up an appointment for you to play him the tape. That is, if it's ok with you."

"OK with me?" Are you kidding? The Beatles? Absolutely it's "OK!"

While Johnny called Tony on the phone, I ran to my room to make sure I still had the tape. I couldn't believe that I was going to play it for the manager of the Beatles record company. The enormity of this was almost too much. The Beatles had been the biggest influence in my music from the first time I saw them on the Jack Parr show, where he played a short clip of them singing and made wise cracks throughout the film. Nobody in the USA had ever heard of the Beatles before. I was riveted. That clip was like a religious experience for me and literally started me on my journey into music. Now, here I was in London about to go down to the Beatles office and play them my songs. I was petrified, to say the least." There's an old saying "Be careful what you wish for, for it may come true." This certainly applied to me.

"It's all set, John Beland" Johnny beamed as he poked his head in my room. "I spoke to Tony and he would be very pleased to meet with you tomorrow and listen to your demo. You need to be there at 10am". I stood there frozen with my knees knocking. Tillotson smiled and assured me that Tony was a standup guy and that the whole experience would turn out just fine. "Just be yourself, John. I know Tony is going to be impressed."

That night I looked out my hotel window and stared at the street below and the rooftops of the old buildings around me and wondered how I ever arrived here. It was only yesterday when I stared down the railroad tracks that split Hometown in two and wondered, imagined what life was like beyond the point where the trains faded into the horizon. All the nights I lay in my bed with that cheap transistor radio playing in my ear, listening to WLS and getting lost in the fantasy of life as a recording artist. I mean, it was only meant to be just a dream, never to come true. Now, here I was on the eve of playing my own songs for the Beatles, right here in London far beyond where those trains faded away from sight. Far beyond my imagination. It was a lot to think about as I tossed and turned in my bed, trying desperately to get some sleep. Tomorrow was going to be a big day.

The hotel wakeup call came at 8am and I sprang to my feet. I met Johnny downstairs for breakfast and he gave me the address of Apple Records. I simply had to give it to the cabbie and I would be there in a matter of minutes.

"John Edward, I know you're going to knock Tony out" Johnny assured me between sips of orange juice.

"I have all the faith in the world in you."

His assurance meant the world to me, even if it had little impact on my nervous system.

I hailed down a cab, one of those old classic black ones I remembered from the old post war films I used to watch as a kid.

"Apple Records, please" I told the driver and gave him the address, although he didn't need it. He, and half of London, certainly knew where the Beatles record company was. All along the way, through the busy streets the driver chatted away but I was deaf to his words. I was trying to collect myself and maintain some small piece of coolness for my big meeting with Tony King.

Apple head Tony King between John Lennon and Sir Elton John

When I arrived at 3 Savile Row it suddenly dawned on me that this was the very building where the Beatles gave their historic rooftop concert. I stood on the curb and looked straight up towards the roof, imagining what it must have been like on that famous cold January day in 1969 when they gave their last live performance at the very top of the building I was about to enter. The outside of Apple Records was all white, like a wedding cake. The four stone steps leading up to the door were flanked by a large iron fence. I remember thinking that I was opening the very door the Beatles had so many times passed through. It was surreal. Inside I was greeted by a beautiful receptionist who cheerfully led me to the elevator that would take me up to Tony King's office. All along the walls were gold records and photos of the Beatles. It was very intimidating and part of me wanted to run right out the door and head back to the relative safety of my hotel room. Instead, up the elevator went. The doors opened into Tony's office where he warmly greeted me and instantly made me feel relaxed and comfortable.

"Hello John, hello" said the tall, thin warm mannered smiling Tony King. "Do come in and sit down" and he led me to a comfortable brown leather chair in front of his desk. "Can I get you anything? Tea, coffee, juice, soda?" I requested a cup of coffee and Tony called his secretary and relayed the order.

We chatted for quite a spell about Johnny and how we each thought the world of him. Not once did I feel I was under any time schedule or had to be out of the office soon. Tony seemed to have all the time in the world for me. He was a true gentleman and I enjoyed his company.

"Johnny says you have a terrific recording. Can we take a listen?"

I handed Tony the cassette and told him the background of the track. It was only a basic track, unfinished. I also informed him that I wrote and produced it myself.

"Very good then" he said. "Let's take a listen!"

With that he hit "play" and out came the track over his incredible sound system. It sounded better than I ever could have hoped for. It was very Beatles influenced and that was evident to Tony, who sat back in his chair with his eyes closed taking the whole song in. When it was over he played it again, louder. And when that was over he played I yet another time even louder. When he finished playing "Banjo Man" for the third time, he hit the stop button and looked at me and simply said. "This is terrific." I was thrilled and relieved as he looked at me with a smile and asked "So you wrote AND produced this?" I nodded with a huge grin on my face. "Here's what I would like to do" he then said in a very serious voice. "Three of the boys (Beatles) are out of the country. However, Ringo is due back in today. Let me play this for him and get back to you. Can I hold onto this?" I answered, "Hold onto it? I'll be happy to gift wrap it for you, Tony!" He laughed and rose from his chair extending his hand. "Great, John. I will get together with Ringo and get back to you immediately. This is terrific, simply terrific and I can't wait to play it for him." With that we shook hands and I headed toward the elevator.

"And John, please give Johnny my warmest regards and thanks" he said as the elevator doors closed.

"Yeah, yeah, yeah!" I shouted from the back seat of my taxi.

I was riding on a cloud. I actually got to play my music for the Beatles label and they liked it! I had no expectations on whether or not things would go any further. All I knew was that my music was played for the Beatles and I was as happy as could be with just that experience.

When I got back to our hotel I ran up to John's room and told him all about the meeting. He was thrilled.

"John Edward" he said to me in a serious voice "I believe in you and I know Ringo is going to love this every bit as much as the rest of us." With that he threw me the biggest grin his face could make. I could have thanked him, but words failed me and with Johnny, it wasn't necessary. He knew how I felt.

The next morning Johnny and I and our ever faithful tour manager Phil headed to the rehearsal hall to meet and work with our British back-up group, the "John McFlaire Band". It was a dingy little rehearsal hall on the edge of town where you had to think twice before strolling around the neighborhood at night. The studio had three rooms and I could hear the other acts blasting away as John and I walked down the hall to our rehearsal space. Inside the guys all greeted us warmly and were so nice to us that I felt as if I had known them forever. It was a good size band from Birmingham, and they were top players. If I had any worries about the band not getting the rehearsal tape, they were dashed once we started playing. These guys were top of the line and rehearsals went smooth as clockwork. Johnny's show was going to kick ass! During a break Johnny told the guys all about my meeting with Apple. The guys were genuinely excited for me and shook my hand with congratulations and good luck wishes. After rehearsals, Johnny and I went back to our hotel feeling a sense of relief and total confidence in the John McFlaire Band. What a load off our shoulders.

The next morning the phone rang. It was 8am and I was barely awake when I grabbed it and in a half dead tone mumbled

"Hello?"

"Is this John Beland?" the female voice on the other end asked. "Uh, yea. Who the heck is this?"

"Please hold for Tony King."

I immediately sat up in bed.

"Good morning, John" came the familiar voice. "I have a request from Ringo I think will interest you. He says he would like to know if you would be interested in joining the Apple family. Congratulations. He loves the tape!" I was stunned and speechless as Tony continued. "Can you possibly meet with us in a few days to go over the contracts and discuss the project?"

I explained to Tony that I would have to call my agent in the USA and see if he could fly out here. "No worries, John. Call us as soon as you can make arrangements and once again, welcome aboard."

I jumped out of bed and ran down the hall to Tillotson's room. I banged on his door till he answered, half asleep as well.

"JT...we did it! Ringo loved the tape. I'm in!"

Original solo album for Apple and eventually Scepter Records 1973

Johnny let out a loud "whoo hooo" and we gave each other a warm hug. I was now an artist on the Beatles record company. This was big and I knew it would shake things up with my family and friends back in California and Hometown. My head was spinning like a top and my heart was racing with the speed of a near sonic boom. What a way to wake up.

18 A THOUSAND TOWNS A THOUSAND SHOWS

As rewarding and incredible as the Apple offer was, it presented a few major problems. Namely, Sean Downey had already secured a verbal deal for me with New York based Scepter Records while I was in England. Unbeknown to me, Downey had already met with Scepter owner Florence Greenberg and played her my tape. She loved it and they shook hands for an album deal. All that was needed was my signature.

"Are you fucking kidding me" screamed Downey over the phone. He was angry. "I've already made a verbal commitment with Florence Greenberg and Scepter. I can't back out of it now! Who the hell told you to go meet with another label while you were in England? I'm over here in the USA busting my ass getting you a record deal here!" Downey was livid, but I was adamant. "Sean, settle down and listen" I said in a calm voice. "This is a deal with the fucking Beatles. Do you understand? The damn publicity value alone is worth it! I want this deal and we have to take it. I need you here in London in two days to negotiate the terms with Tony. Can you make it over?"

There was silence on the line. Sean was steamed but he knew I was 100% right. This deal was too important to pass up.

"Let me see what I can do. Florence is going to chew my ass out with this. Maybe I can smooth things out. I'll get back to you after I make arrangements here." Instead of "goodbye" he just yelled out a loud "FUCK!" and hung up.

A couple days later Sean had arrived in London and we all met in Tony's office at Apple, Johnny as well. Sean was all smiles despite the change of events and together with Tony they hammered out a record deal for me. The deal allowed me to produce my own product, which at the time was very rare for a new artist signed to a label. However, the Beatles had started Apple on the premise that all artists should be in control of their own music, a noble undertaking. For years the band had watched millions of dollars slip through their hands as a result of men in suits sticking their hands in the Beatles pockets and ripping them off of publishing, record royalties and merchandising. They were determined to not let Apple artists be victims the same catastrophes.

Another reason why I admired the Beatles so much. The deal also allowed me to record in any EMI recording studio in the world. However, I chose to stick to the studio where I recorded the original track that landed me the Apple deal, Golden West Studios in Hollywood. One final part of the deal was much to my benefit. The contract stated that should Apple or their parent company EMI fall into any litigation causing a halt or a freeze on any recording in progress, I could get my masters back and seek another deal elsewhere. This clause would prove it's worth in the not too distant future.

That night Tony and some of the Apple staff held a dinner for me at an exclusive "members only" restaurant in the heart of London that the Beatles frequented quite often. Sean, Johnny and I were treated to an amazing dinner, served by gorgeous waitresses dressed in sexy gay 90's attire, short skirts, stockings and garters with half their cleavage on display for the very satisfied clientele, including yours truly. Ringo was to join us but had to leave London at last minute's notice. I was disappointed he couldn't be there, but much as I was thankful to him and admired him tremendously I had my sights on one of the sexy brunette hostesses who, as luck would have it, had her eyes set on me. By the end of the night we "officially" consummated my solo deal back at my hotel.

The entire experience was beyond my imagination. My first trip to London and immediately I find myself signed by the Beatles. What would my friends all say? What would by parents think or my Aunt Elaine and Grandma Foley who warned my father only a few years prior that I would end up a "loser and failure", like him? It was too much to digest so I just rolled with it, something I practiced throughout my career when finding myself in an amazing moment. Just like surfing. Keep your balance and hold on for the ride. But I couldn't help but think "We showed 'em, pop!"

A couple days later Johnny and I performed in Birmingham England on the bill with Bobby Vee and Del Shannon, two rock and roll artists I greatly admired. We played at an old theater that must have been well over a half century old, and the place was packed to the rafters. The John McFlaire band performed flawlessly, probably because we were playing in their own hometown. Kids were screaming, and the joint was rocking just like one of those old rock &b roll films from the 50's.

Bobby Vee came out with his guitar strapped around him and

launched into hit after hit, "Rubber Ball" "Take Good Care Of My Baby" "Run To Him" "The Night Has A Thousand Eyes" and more. Each tune raised a huge scream from the fans pressed around the front of the stage. Bobby's performance was flawless and the crowd ate him up.   Next up came the balls to the wall sound of the great Del Shannon. Del played the first rocking chord to his great hit "Runaway" over and over as he strolled out with a Telecaster around him and a big old white cowboy hat. When he opened his mouth and sang the first line, out boomed that one of a kind signature voice, totally unaffected by the years that had come and gone. The place went crazy! He never let up as the hits, one after another, tore into the crowd "Hats Off To Larry" "Little Town Flirt" "Searchin" and many more. Del even sang an amazing version of Roy Orbison's "Crying" that sent shivers down everyone's spine.

Finally, Johnny came out and I plugged in with the John McFlaire band. Johnny looked fabulous and the crowd screamed and shouted like they had for Bobby and Del. I conducted the band, drums, bass, 2 guitars, keyboards and three sax players and we launched into Johnny's big hits "Poetry In Motion" "Talk Back Trembling Lips" "Heartaches By The Number" "Dreamy Eyes" Keeps Right On A Hurtin" and more. The response was tremendous. These rock and rollers were still respected and loved every bit as much as when they were topping the charts 10 years earlier. Such were the British fans, who's respect for their rock and roll legends far surpassed that of the fickle record buying public back home in the USA. Half way through the show John introduced the members of the John McFlaire band to thunderous hometown applause. Then he introduced me.

"Ladies and gentleman I want to introduce my music director and one of the finest guitarists in the business who has played for Linda Ronstadt and Arlo Guthrie and many others. But not only that, just a few days ago he became the latest artist to be signed to the Beatles record label Apple Records. Please give it up for the great John Edward Beland"

The place went crazy, much to my embarrassment. But to add to that, from the wings stepped Bobby Vee and Del Shannon each with a pitcher of beer and put their arms around me, leading the audience in a toast and three cheers to me. I will never forget that night as long as

I live.

From Birmingham we bid goodbye and good luck to Del and Bobby and pressed on to other towns and smaller venues. What a thrill it was to have shared a stage with those mega talented guys and it was mind blowing to have worked with them after enjoying their records when I was a kid back in Hometown. Sadly, in the years to come Del Shannon would put a gun to his head and commit suicide and later Bobby Vee would fall victim to Alzheimer's disease. But I will always remember Del and Bobby for that incredible night we played together in Birmingham on my first trip to England. That's how I will always see them in my mind, rocking and rolling onstage to a half crazed adoring audience.

John and I traveled north to Liverpool where I had the chance to see the place where it all began for the Beatles. It was a big seaport town and everything in it seemed without color. Like an old black and white photo from years past. It was old and rough and not the kind of place where you would want to walk around alone after dark. It was hard to imagine that The Beatles ever made it out of there, let alone conquer the world of popular music.

We played in what used to be a Chinese restaurant now converted into a supper club called Wookie Hollow. It was the strangest place I had ever played. Decor from the previous ownership still could be seen all around the room, including a small-scale bridge that crossed over a little babbling brook. Straight out of the Flower Drum Song! Performers had to walk across the bridge to reach the stage much to the delight of the audience. However, it was a very dangerous maneuver because when show time rolled around and the houselights turned off, the only way to navigate through the dark was a blinding spotlight that hit the performer smack dab in the eyes. Needless to say, when Johnny was introduced he slipped when walking over the bridge and had to be taken to the hospital. Some entrance!

We soldiered on, playing a number of Workingman's Clubs throughout the U.K. Most of the venues were the same as the previous. Variety shows usually featuring a comic MC, a magic act and an international headliner. At one place we shared our dressing room with a bird act. Scores of white parrots cackling away as Johnny and I sat by our makeup table, laughing at the insanity of it all. One time we shared the bill with a wrestling match. A ring was set up right on the floor in front of the stage where a referee and two big old boys went 6 rounds.

When it was over, the stage hands simply tore down the ring and set up for the next act ... the Johnny Tillotson show! Cities and towns flew by us in a blur. Every night a new venue and new surroundings but the same old drill. By the tours' end we were more than ready to head back to the USA. But we had one more gig to do before we left Jolly Ol England, the famed Speakeasy Club in the heart of London.

The Speakeasy, known as the "Speak" to locals, was nothing more than a small beer and restaurant joint in the heart of London. However, it was a late meeting place for the music industry as well as one of the top hang outs for the biggest stars in British Rock. Every night you could walk in and spot your favorite rock and roll artist and their entourage piled into booths drunk out of their minds roaring the night away to some of the best live music in the UK. Some of the acts that played the "Speak" were none other than the Beatles, Deep Purple, David Bowie, Jimi Hendrix and Bob Marley, to name a few. Now we were scheduled to play our last UK gig there before heading back to the US. The Speakeasy had a stage the size of a postage stamp and all the musicians were squeezed in like being in an elevator. Furthermore, the crowd was a rough lot. Drunken industry people pissed out of their heads, as loud as a jumbo jet aircraft at full throttle. The night we played, I noticed Paul and Linda McCartney sitting with some of the members from Wings. I didn't dare walk over and introduce myself, fearing to get eaten alive by the rock elite and the hangers-on surrounding McCartney's table. But there he was, holding court while we prepared to play.

I was a bit dumbfounded that Johnny would be booked at the Speakeasy in the first place knowing that the history of the club was centered on a more hardcore rock crowd. But we gave it to them anyway and Johnny did a good show to a surprisingly good reception. A funny thing happened mid-way through the show ...a drunken Wings guitarist Henry McCullough walked up to the stage and started talking incoherently on the microphone. Everyone in the room knew who he was except poor old Johnny, who turned to Henry and said over the mic "And who may you be, sir?" McCullough grabbed Tillotson's mic and yelled into it "JESUS!" Johnny, never one to miss a beat, simply took the mic from Henry's hand and announced "Ladies and gentlemen....please give a warm Speakeasy welcome to Jesus Christ." The audience howled!

The next morning Johnny and I were driven to the airport by our faithful road manager Phil Luderman. It had been a terrific tour with great turnouts at every venue we played. Phil gave us both warm hugs with wishes for a safe flight home but a speedy return to the UK. With that, we boarded our flight and took off towards home. All during the takeoff I stared out the window lost in thought, trying to absorb it all. It had been surreal, this first tour of England. I went there without any expectations beyond playing guitar behind Johnny and now I was coming home with a recording contract in my hand signed by the Beatles. Was it all a dream? Would I soon be waking up in my bed back in Hometown hearing my mother shouting at me to get dressed for school? Would I still be standing on those railroad tracks that split Hometown in half wondering what faraway places and adventures lay just down the line? I watched as London disappeared into the clouds and we broke through to a clear starry night sky with a bright, full moon. We were headed home. Soaring through the night, higher than I ever could have imagined.

19 WINS AND LOSSES.

We arrived in LA sometime in the middle of the night. Both Johnny and I were glad to be back after a grueling tour of both Germany and the UK. First, we took a cab back to my house where I knew Susan would jump at the news about signing with the Beatles. I couldn't wait to tell her. I had confided in Johnny that my marriage was in shambles and that Susan wasn't happy. John said "John Edward, when she gets this news I bet things will turn around for you both. This is a great way to restart your relationship with news like this." I believed him, too! How in the world could you not jump for joy over hearing what had happened? We both were excited as our cab turned down my street and found its way to my house in the Hollywood Hills.

All the lights were on. The front door was wide open. It was 3am in the morning. Something wasn't right as Johnny and I slowly approached the front door to my house. "Susan?" I called out. No response.

We entered the living room and found it empty of furniture. The same with the other rooms. Susan and Sarah were both gone. No note was left behind. The only clue to her leaving with another man was a single cowboy boot we found in the bedroom and it wasn't my size. Had it just been Susan leaving me I would have just picked up the pieces and moved on. But there was a child in all of this, our daughter. I was determined to find out where they were and get my daughter back. I now had the financial means to do it and that's just what I would set out to do in the coming weeks. But for now, Johnny and I stood in the empty living room where there once lived my family.

"John Beland" Johnny said in a soft tone. "If there's something I've learned from the many women I have been with over the years it's one thing, and that is *I don't know a thing about women!!*"

One morning I received a call from my former Swampwater bandmate, Thad Maxwell. The news was devastating. Clarence White, our dear friend and arguably one of the greatest guitarists in country rock, was killed by a drunk driver while loading his amplifier following a jam session with Gib Guilbeau in Palmdale, California. I was stunned as Thad passed along the funeral details. Clarence had become a great friend and many times had loaned me his Dobro and amp to use when he was away on tour with the Byrds. Everyone in Hollywood loved him and the news of his death shocked the town. The funeral was held in Palmdale and everyone from the music business was there from Kris Kristofferson and his wife Rita Coolidge to Bernie Leadon from the Eagles and Roger McGuinn, Gene Parsons and Skip Batten from the Byrds. During the service in the chapel Gram Parsons showed up flanked by two groupies. I found it a bit disrespectful that he made his entrance right in the middle of the service. At the gravesite everyone gathered around Clarence's family and sang the old hymn "Farther Along." It was hard to believe he was gone, so young with such a future in front of him. I remember looking over at a fragile Gram Parsons thinking "He's probably next." And, sadly, I was right.

My buddy Jerry Tate and I found a great old Spanish style house just off Hollywood Blvd and soon after Susan had left me, Jerry and I moved back in together. He was now working at Ryder Sound in Hollywood and busy doing sound for both television and films. We were two bachelors with great jobs, living the good life right in the center of Hollywood. Needless to say, there was a steady flow of females coming and going through our front door, literally. In our living room was parked Jerry's beautiful custom Harley chopper which was occasionally rented out to the studios for TV shows. Next to Jerry's chopper stood my beautiful baby grand piano. What a combination he and I were. When I would get a call for a session, I would hop on Jerry's bike and together we would roar down the Strip to whatever studio I was booked at. It was a great feeling to be so independent and successful at our age. We were living the dream and not shackled down to some mundane boring day gig nor to any demanding dramatic relationship. We were young, free and bullet proof and Hollywood was our oyster.

Between tours with Johnny, I was getting increasingly busy doing session work. Back then, most of the commercial recording studios in Hollywood were all within minutes of each other. So, it was easy to do more than one call a day. I had an answering service called Arlen's who booked my dates. They handled all the top session guys and I was now a part of their roster. All of my guitars (12) were now housed at a cartage company called Royal cartage. When I would be booked for a recording date I would simply call Royal and give them the information on where and when the session was booked. They would make sure my guitars were delivered to the studio and set up just prior to the date. Afterwards they would pack everything up and cart them to the next session.

A certain near fatal session that stands out in my memory was for the great Oscar, Grammy Award winning producer Quincy Jones. One day I received a call from Quincy's office and the gentleman on the other line asked if I would be available to play Dobro for a film date that Quincy was producing. He had seen me play a while back at the Hollywood Bowl and was so impressed by the sound of the Dobro he incorporated it into the film score he had written for this new film, called "Honky."

"Would you be available tomorrow for the session, John?" Quincy's assistant asked.

"Absolutely" I answered.

I was thrilled to get the call and really looked forward to working with such a giant in the music business.

"One thing I have to ask you before I go" the assistant said to me. "Can you read music?"

Oh oh, I thought. If I told the truth that I didn't know how to read a single note of written music I would miss a golden opportunity and a nice fat feather in my resume. But then I thought, "How hard could this session be if I'm just playing a Dobro? I can fake it. My ears had never let me down yet."

"Oh, sure I can read. You bet!" I answered in a confident voice.

"OK, that's terrific, John. Mr. Jones will expect you at Goldwyn Studios at 8pm tomorrow."

"I'll be there" I answered in my most contained voice.

I was jumping up and down when I told Jerry the news. This was big for any session player. I couldn't wait to get to the studio in the next day. Then it hit me. What if Quincy Jones hands me sheet music and I have to play exact written notation? Now I was sweating and getting nervous. How humiliating would it be if Quincy Jones yelled at me in front of the musicians and threw me off the date! Now what was I going to do?

"Ah, you'll pull it off like always, JB" Jerry said in a calm "matter of fact" tone. "I hear he's a very cool guy."

The next evening I hopped on the back seat of Jerry's chopper and we headed down Sunset Strip to Samuel Goldwyn Studios. I notified Royal cartage to deliver my Dobro ahead of time so it would be waiting for me when I arrived at the date. I was still pretty nervous about the possible mess I had gotten myself into. Seems I have always had the terrible habit of jumping in the door as soon as opportunity knocked, and many times without thinking first.

We arrived at Goldwyn Studios and walked in while Quincy Jones was conducting one of the many great pieces he had written for the film. I was terrified when I noticed that all of the musicians were reading thick pages of written sheet music. Man, I was quickly sinking like the Titanic.

After the piece was recorded and the musicians were changing around and the engineers were setting up for my part, I walked over to Quincy Jones, Dobro in hand. I felt that I had to be honest and just suffer the consequences.

Quincy was on the conductor's podium when I made my way over to him and introduced myself.

"Mr. Jones?" I said. "My name is John Beland and I'm here to play some Dobro for you."

A warm smile crossed his lips as he shook my hand. "Hey, John. Thanks for coming over and playing for me. I love the sound of that instrument. Man, I think it's going to be perfect for this next scene."

I swallowed and spoke. "Well, Mr. Jones, I have to confess to you that I can't read music notation. But I have a great ear and can play anything you throw my way."

I waited for what seemed like an eternity as Quincy gave it some thought.

Then, he smiled and said "Man, don't sweat it, John. Here's what I want. When I point to you, I need you to give me a train whistle kind of lick. You got something like that?"

I was beaming. "Yes sir. Something like this?" And I played a train style lick on the Dobro for him.
Quincy slapped his hands and said "That's it! Do that every time I give you the cue, ok?"
"Yes sir" I answered.

"Thank you Guarding Angels, once again" I whispered as I made my way into the orchestra.

The band and I were positioned in front of a huge screen where the scene was to be played while we lay down the music. Only the conductor could see the scene being shown because our backs were to it. I sat between the guitar player and the banjo player and got ready for the take. The scene is where two rednecks are chasing a very beautiful young black girl through a cornfield somewhere in the Deep South. The name of the song was called "Train Whistle" and it was in a fast bluegrass style, sung by a vocal group of three male and three female singers. It was all recorded live. No room for errors.

The signal bell rang and the time click began. Quincy raised his baton and bang, we were off! Banjo's played, drums and bass laid down a solid bluegrass beat as the singers belted out the song. Just as the singers sang the title words "Train Whistle" Quincy pointed my way and I let out a moaning bluesy train effect on my Dobro. He smiled from the podium and winked his eye at me. I'll never forget it! At the end of the session, we all watched the scene complete with our music. It was incredible to witness. This was the life I had always wanted and working with Quincy Jones was beyond my wildest dreams.

"Great job, thanks a million, John. I loved what you did" he said as I headed out the soundstage door.

"It was my honor, Mr Jones." He just smile and shook my hand

John Beland

and simply said "Quincy."

When Jerry met me outside the studio I told him what had happened. As he fired up his chopper and we got ready to head out to the Troubadour, Jerry laughed and said, "JB, you lucky bastard."

A few years later Quincy Jones would team up with pop icon Michael Jackson to record the biggest selling album of all time "Thriller." What a history. And what a session!

I had a solo album to produce and I got to work on it immediately after Jerry and I moved into the new house. I booked time at Golden West Studios in Hollywood, on Selma Avenue. It was a small studio in an alley way not far from Hollywood Blvd. It had a great sound and so I started to book the first sessions. However, just before I went in to start recording the first tracks, we received a telegram from Tony King at Apple Records in London. The album was put on hold, along with projects from all Apple artists, due to a major lawsuit between the Beatles, EMI and Allan Klein. I was shattered and called Sean Downey immediately.

"Don't worry, Johnny" he said in that cocky attitude. "I got Apple to give us back the contract and masters and I was able to salvage our original offer from Scepter Records in New York. Fuck the Beatles, my friend."

"Easy for you to say" I said to myself.

We could have waited out the lawsuit but that could have taken years. Instead, Tony gave us our release and wished me well. It was disappointing, but not the end of the world in the slightest.

While Sean negotiated the new deal with Scepter, Johnny and I hit the road again. This time we would travel all over the south and Midwest, performing in supper clubs as well as hosting a few telethons for Cerebral Palsy. It seemed our travels would take us to every small town and big city imaginable. We played venues in places like Waterloo Iowa, Cape Geraldo Missouri, Waldorf, Maryland, Oklahoma City and on and on. As always, Johnny used house bands with me on guitar. It was nerve racking and a lot of work to whip local

178

musicians into a strong backing unit for Johnny's show and it had to be done the day of our performance. Most of it all went by in a blur. Towns and gigs all looked the same as Johnny and I went through the motions, traveling, rehearsing, sleeping etc. Occasionally, we would be invited out to someone's farm for a home-cooked dinner in our honor. Those moments were priceless, right out of a Norman Rockwell painting. For the most part, I discovered that people could be so kind and generous without the slightest hint of expecting anything in return but friendship. I strengthened my deep affection and love for the rural heart of America. These were solid, church going, God fearing, salt of the earth people far and away removed from the glamour and glitter of our world back in Hollywood. Many of them had grown up with Johnny's records and were more than happy to welcome him and me into their homes to meet their families and neighbors and to share supper with us. It was a throwback to my years growing up in Hometown, when neighbors cared for each other and could be relied on during hard times and you never had to lock your doors if you were away. It was a way of life which I grew up in but which I never really appreciated until I did these gigs with Johnny Tillotson. I realized that regardless of my lifestyle back in Hollywood, I would always be one of them, a Midwest boy with roots planted firmly in the heartland of America. In a way, this explained my deep love for country music. Back then, country music was the music of these folks, the common man, the hardworking man, the farmer, the trucker, good folks who loved their country and respected it shamelessly, to the point of being labeled "rednecks." They were the ones who lost their kids in Vietnam and were proud to have made the sacrifice. They were amazing people to be with and although I was a long-haired Hollywood musician, I knew them and would always be one of them. And as Johnny and I sat at their table, many times outside a farm house or beside the barn, or near the crops, I felt honored to be in their company, breaking bread and sharing their life, if only for one day.

Many times, Johnny and I would visit local small-town radio stations while passing through the heartland. A lot of these stations still looked as if they were in the 1930's and many of them still had the same employees running it as they did 30 years prior. Some stations were located inside very old buildings in the downtown areas of these decaying Midwest towns. Once inside, you could smell the age of the building in the air and see it in the old wooden furniture in the reception areas. It was a trip back in time, long before stations were automated or broadcast by satellite. Everything was run by real people. The disc jockeys were always friendly and totally thrilled to have a star like Johnny drop by and at every interview Johnny would include me at the microphone. That's how I first began learning about how to conduct myself on the radio ... by watching the master, Johnny Tillotson. Many of the interviews we did were at very early morning hours, when the farmers were up and milking the cows. Sometimes our interview would be sandwiched between the "beef and hog prices" for the day. It was brutal to do these early shows especially the morning after a show when we didn't get to bed until after 3am. But they were important and Johnny knew it. I have to hand it to him, he always walked into those stations as if everyone in the building was a relative. He knew all their names and family member's names. He handled each visit like a master politician. And they loved him for it!

20 MUSIC ROW, LAS VEGAS AND CROSSING THE HEARTLAND

Although many consider Johnny a pop singer, his roots and career were planted firmly in Nashville Tennessee where he recorded all his hits using the top A-Team players of the day. His publisher's office was there as well and it seemed as if Johnny personally knew every single recording star, producer, publisher and musician on Music Row. Being with Johnny, one on one, for so long was like being locked inside the Country Music Hall Of Fame. He was a wealth of knowledge about country music and he taught me just about everything he knew.

At the time, Johnny was signed to CBS Records and produced by the legendary hit producer Billy Sherrill. I was privileged to attend Johnny's production meetings with Billy at CBS Records on Music Row and got a firsthand look at how country records were made, from the initial selection of songs to the final recording date. It was something to see.

Billy Sherrill was a pleasant enough guy but could be a hard ass, ruthless record executive as well. For example, when we walked into Billy's CBS office directly above the studio, I noticed that none other than the very popular singing star Tanya Tucker sitting in the reception area all by herself not paying any attention to us. Billy's secretary led us directly into his office. Sherrill met us at the door and was very pleasant in a low slow southern way. After Johnny introduced us I asked Billy, "Is that Tanya Tucker in your reception area?" "Yep, and she can just sit out there and do some thinking today. You see, after we recorded her first big hits, she and her daddy manager, decided to take a more "lucrative" deal with another company. After that, her hits suddenly stopped. Now she wants to come back to us. So she's out in the hall thinking things over." It was a cold bit of news to hear, but I dropped the subject quickly.

Johnny told Billy that I had written a great song called "Willow County Request Line" and he felt it was a hit and wanted it included on his next session.

"Let's hear it" Billy said and handed me a Martin guitar he had next to his desk. After I played it for him Billy looked at Johnny and said "That's a keeper. We'll do it." That was that.

Furthermore, Billy asked me if I would like to play guitar on the session!

Are you kidding, I thought? "Sure Billy, I'd love to."

"Good. I'll put you on acoustic guitar along with Jimmy Capps and Ray Eddington. I like your feel on the guitar. I think we need that on the session." I was thrilled to be asked to play with Jimmy and Ray, two of the top session A-Team guitarists in Country Music! Three songs were selected but the third one hadn't even been written yet! No problem, Billy and Johnny went out later on Billy's boat and wrote it! Such was the way of Nashville.

The next day Johnny and I went to CBS Studios for his session. All the musicians were piled into what seemed like a small studio for such a famous track record. The band was a who's-who of Nashville's "A" Team elite. On drums was the great Buddy Harmon. On steel guitar was the legendary Pete Drake, who had played on Dylan's Nashville Skyline album. On guitars were Jimmy Capps, Ray Eddington and myself and being led to the piano by his wife, was none other than the famed blind session master keyboardist Pig Robbins, himself. Also, next to Johnny was the famous vocal session group, "The Nashville Edition" on harmonies. Wow, what a line up!

All the musicians treated me as an equal. It was a terrific feeling to play with these Hall Of Fame players who had picked on countless hits from Pasty Cline to George Jones.

The amazing thing about CBS Studios and Billy's production was that once you recorded a take the engineer would play it back through old "Voice of the Theater" speakers out on the floor. Today everyone hears it in the control room. Furthermore, when it was played back to us, it sounded like the final record! What a totally incredible experience.

While in Nashville I had some free time, so I demoed a few new songs I had written over at Pete Drakes studio on Music Row. I hired a drummer and bass player and recorded three new tunes. My engineer, Scotty, was a great guy. He really made me feel at home and did everything he could to help the songs shine. I felt as if I knew Scotty all my life. He seemed so familiar. It wasn't until I was packing up to go home that I found out why. I knew him simply as Scotty, but the world of rock and roll knew him as the one and only original guitarist for Elvis Presley, the legendary guitar god, Scotty Moore! I couldn't believe that the engineer I had been working with side by side for three hours was the same guy I had worshiped as a kid and watched so many times when Elvis appeared on television. Talk about a small world!

After Johnny's sessions for CBS we headed out of town for Cape Geraldo, Missouri where Johnny was booked to host the local Cerebral Palsy Telethon television show. The telethons were always a weird experience because the guests were mostly familiar TV faces from soap operas or sitcoms with a few old torch singers and actors from the early 50's era. Many of them were so consumed in their image that at times it was embarrassing to watch them play the big star role to the hilt. The actors always wanted to sing and for the most part were always terrible. They would show up at rehearsals with their lead sheets and charts as if they were appearing on the Ed Sullivan Show. Usually we used a local band to handle the music and often they were extremely limited in their ability. I was the music director and conductor who had to sort out all the complicated music charts the acts would bring to the show. The charts were originally written for big bands, not for the local high school combo I had to work with for the next 24 hours. It was a constant battle with the over-ego stars to get them to simplify their number. When they didn't get their way they would huff and puff and make out that everyone in the studio was unprofessional, everyone but them, of course. Many of them would want to do Broadway show tunes and big dance numbers and had to be reminded that this was local TV and not the Jerry Lewis Labor Day Telethon out of Hollywood. Most of these "has been" stars didn't give a rat's ass about the kids, who were the single reason they had the Telethon in the first place. They were only interested in parading their mediocre talent on TV and strutting their aging images in front of anyone who would pay the slightest attention.

I did manage to meet personalities who were terrific and did a hell of a job raising money for such a worthy cause. Buck Taylor, who played the blacksmith "Newly" on Gunsmoke, was a fabulous person. He was a warm and friendly guy who I really admired. Buck was a great character actor like his famous father Dub Taylor, who played sidekick to just about every cowboy hero in the 30's and 40's you could name. Another great guy was Anson Williams from the TV show "Happy

Days." He couldn't sing to save his ass, but he knew it and worked hard to raise money and keep the phones ringing. He was a kind friendly guy and as down to Earth as you can get. We did quite a few of these Telethons together and ended up sharing cab rides to the airport together quite often. Another fun guy to work with was the late Ted Knight who played the over blown egomaniac TV newsman Ted Baxter on the Mary Tyler Moore Show. Ted was always on and hilarious to be around. He was a big hit with the audience.

I handled the music the best I could but the telethons were draining. For me, it broke my heart to see these helpless victims of this terrible disease struggling to maintain their dignity. Theirs was a hard-long road to walk down while the rest of us lived in our Hollywood glass bubbled lives. Watching them was a true test of one's faith. There but for the grace of God.

Johnny and I hit the road again playing supper clubs throughout the country. The only thing that seemed to break up the monotony of it all was one thing, women. And there were plenty for the taking. In Augusta, Georgia I fell head over heels for a lovely olive skinned black haired beauty named Toni Myers. She certainly taught me more about sex than I ever imagine existed. In Baltimore I was smitten by one of the loveliest girls I had ever seen. Her name was Donna Goldsboro and she was a living breathing angel who smelled like a field of strawberries in bed. In Orlando I wound up with the gorgeous, sensual long brown-haired southern beauty, Faye Nibblet who was so sexy she could stop traffic. I loved sex and I loved being with beautiful women. Still do. It was an escape from the grind and a refuge from the out of sync feeling you experienced by living from one town to another. It was good to be held, loved, and screwed senseless at the end of a show, away from the crowds, away from the clubs. If not for those moments of escape and intimacy one would go crazy.

A funny thing that happened in one major Oklahoma town. It was at a very popular hotel Johnny and I were performing at. I was picked up and seduced by a very beautiful, sexy female assistant district attorney who took me upstairs and screwed me every which way but loose. She even had a loaded pistol under her pillow. Anyway, we tore up the hotel room between Johnny's shows. Sometime into our lovemaking I noticed I was late for the second show. I panicked and jumped into my clothes and ran to the elevator and down the hallway to the showroom. Johnny and the band were already onstage playing the first song. I snuck out on the bandstand after the opening song and to my shock, Johnny, the band and the entire audience gave me a huge round of applause. It seemed that JT had informed the crowd of my whereabouts and activities between shows. To my horror, as soon as I inconspicuously tried to sneak on stage I was greeted by thunderous applause from the audience! Tillotson stood there with a huge grin on his face. That's what happens when you play with the law.

Though Johnny and I covered the country playing supper clubs and telethons in nearly every state imaginable, our most important gig was Las Vegas. The town was like no other. It truly "never slept" and unlike the boring grind of touring supper clubs, Vegas was always hopping with excitement 24 hours a day. Johnny and I headed back to Las Vegas to work the Sahara Hotel lounge. As usual we had a hell of band, including the great drummer John Ware from Mike Nesmith's First National Band and the ace pianist Alex DelZoppo from the legendary group, Sweetwater. Furthermore, we were joined onstage by Nashville vocalists Sandy Rucker and Diane Sherrill, both incredibly talented and beautiful. It was a great line up. While in Vegas I continued to work on my solo album, this time at Las Vegas Sound Recorders, a great 24 track studio not far off the Strip. My engineer was Brent Maher, a creative, inventive guy who was a joy to work with. In the years to come Brent would move to Nashville and become one of the top producers in country music, discovering an unknown mother and daughter singing act called, The Judds and scoring hit after hit as their producer. But at the time of my album sessions, Brent was a staff engineer mostly recording boring local commercials and an occasional Vegas lounge act or two. With me, he found a young act he could get creative with. We were a great team and I always looked forward to using my day time in the studio rather than floating all day in a hotel pool like most of the Vegas musicians in town. Many years later Brent and I would team up again, this time in Nashville with the Burrito Brothers, Gib Guilbeau and I. Brent would produce our last hit "It's Almost Saturday Night" for Epic / Curb Records.

During our run at the Sahara, I became good friends with none other than the infamous Joe Guercio. Joe had heard some songs of mine that Johnny had played him and Guercio was impressed. He knew I wasn't just another musician in the band and that my musical horizons extended far beyond Johnny Tillotson and even further than that of your ordinary touring guitarist. I was now an in-demand session player with an impressive song writing resume as well. Furthermore, I was a singer and recording artist who, by this time, had already recorded for Starday-King, Ranwood, RCA, Apple and now Scepter Records. Joe invited me to his home where I had dinner with him and his lovely wife, Corky. Guercio lived just off the Strip in a beautiful home fit for his stature as Elvis's conductor. All around were photos, memorabilia and souvenirs from his many gigs with the King of Rock & Roll. It was impressive alright.

After dinner, Joe and I sat down in his music room and he asked me if I would be interested working in the studio with him. He was going to take Johnny in and produce a couple sides on him for CBS in the hopes that the label would consider him to take over Johnny's recording from Billy Sherrill, who was growing cold on Tillotson. Of course, I was interested in working with Joe. Who wouldn't be? He was the boss in Las Vegas as far as all the musicians on the Strip were concerned. But I suspected there was more to Joe's asking me to work with him than just a demo session with Johnny.

The sessions didn't produce anything worthwhile. As good as Guercio was conducting orchestras he was out of his element in the recording studio. However, the experience did give me a chance to cement a relationship with Joe that would prove very fruitful in the coming year.

Whenever we worked Vegas there was always a lot of down time. Hours were all out the window and you basically found yourself bored to death after the shows. But one night I happened to stumble upon a small lounge at the Bonanza Hotel, where a duo called Chris & Ron were appearing. Ron was your average lounge singer / musician, good looking guy who was all smiles with a reasonably good voice. But Chris was another story. She was one of the most beautiful creatures I had ever seen in my life. Beautiful long brown hair and sexy bedroom eyes, with a body to kill for, she was something straight out of a dream. I had presumed she and Ron were husband and wife, but my waitress informed me they were brother and sister. Thank you, Jesus!

Between breaks I managed to make my way to Ron & Chris's table and introduced myself to them. Ron was warm and friendly and seemed very excited to meet me. However, my motives were pretty self-serving as the only focus of my attentions was the beautiful sultry sister of his sitting across the table. When Chris's eyes met mine, there was an instant electricity jolt between us. And throughout the night we couldn't keep our eyes off each other. Even though her brother went on and on about music and the acts I had worked with, I couldn't hear a word he was saying. I was on another planet, alone with his beautiful singing sister. I stayed until they finished their show, transfixed on Chris as if I was witnessing the return of Jesus himself. Chris had a warm smile, charming personality and beautiful eyes that poured over you like a tsunami. I wanted her as bad as anything or anyone I had ever wanted before in my life. As luck would have it, Ron and Chris were clients of Johnny Tillotson's Las Vegas publicist Joan Guertin. As one of their guests at the table, Joan quickly picked up on the connection between Chris and I and helped us arrange some "alone" time at an out of the way hotel called the Bali Hai off the Strip. It seemed that Chris's brother was always around her and impossible to get rid of. But with Joan's help, Chris and I finally found a night to ourselves, an unforgettable night.

To that point in my life I had never had a woman so tender and loving in my arms than Chris. She was the most beautiful and passionate woman I had ever been with and I fell for her like a ton of bricks. I was in love, big time and it certainly seemed as if the feeling was mutual. It was all very romantic. I was the well-known young guitarist at the Sahara Hotel while just down the street she was the sultry beautiful lounge singer that every guy in the club wanted. We were both single and head over heels in love with each other. The possibilities were there for us. They seemed endless.

One night, following another show at the Sahara I was paged over the hotel system. When I picked up the phone I heard Joan Guertin's voice.

"John, there has been an accident. Chris is in the hospital. She has taken an overdose."

I was frozen. Behind me the sound of slot machines and crap tables roared away but I was deaf to it. All I could think about was Chris. Was she alive? What the hell happened?

"Joan, why did she do this? Is she ok?" I asked in a desperate voice.

"She's ok. Ron is with her now. John, there is something you need to know and are bound to find out about."

I was feeling numb and sensed more bad news was about to hit me.

"What is it, Joan?" I asked.

"Honey, Chris is not Ron's sister. She is his wife."

"What? You're joking, right Joan?" I asked

"John, Ron and Chris billed themselves as brother and sister just for show purposes. But their marriage was always rocky. I know that Chris truly loves you."

"Loves me?" I exploded! "She lied to me! She's been married all along while I've been telling her I loved her."

I slammed the receiver down and stood there in the casino, dumfounded. Like Vegas itself, Chris was just an illusion, not real. It was time to dust myself off and move on.

I never forgot her, though. For decades I often thought about her and even tried to find her, with no luck. As hurt as I was I still loved her deeply. I would continue to work Las Vegas in the years to come and every time my flight would touch down I would wonder and remember. I never saw her again but it certainly wasn't because of any lack of trying. I searched for her everywhere but to no avail. In the years that passed I learned that she had been looking for me as well. But our paths never did cross again. Little did I know she was always right down the street from me, working as an operator at the Golden Nugget Casino and then as a singer in a Vegas lounge band. So close. So far away.

21 THE BIG APPLE AND SAYING GOODBYE

I traveled to New York to finish my album and to meet with Scepter Records founder Florence Greenberg. Scepter's offices were at 254 West 54th Street in the heart of Manhattan. I showed up at the label on a cold winter's afternoon. It was an old office building that reminded me of the kind of publishing companies I used to solicit my songs to at the Taft Building back during those very early years in Hollywood. I was greeted by Florence's secretary, a cute little red head named Janet Revere who made me feel at home instantly. Janet fixed me up with a cup of coffee and notified Florence that I was there.

Scepter was an old label with a long history. It was started by a New York housewife named Florence Greenberg who discovered the Shirelles for her little independent record company Tiara Records. The vocal trio landed a local hit with "I Met Him On A Monday" and with $4,000.00 from the profits she sold Tiara and started Scepter Records. Scepter would become one of the leading independent record labels of the 60's who's roster of artists included Dionne Warwick, BJ Thomas, The Shirells and many more hit acts of the decade. Florence was a blunt woman and wasn't one to beat around the bush. She was tough as nails and I liked her and I believe she felt the same way about me, so much so that she even took me out to dinner at New York City's famed 21 Club. When we arrived at the 21 Club for dinner they tried to seat us at a table near the kitchen door, which Florence called "Alaska." She raised a fit and immediately the head waiter sat us at a more appropriate table. I was a bit embarrassed because I showed up without a dinner jacket and had to be escorted to the gentlemen's room where the waiter fitted me with a club jacket. Not very cool on my part.

I liked Janet Revere, a lot. She was very cool, pretty and intelligent and obviously very important to the running of the label. Just from listening to her on the phone, I could tell that she was much more than a secretary or your average receptionist. I asked her out on a date and we hit it off immediately. It was great to be with someone who was so in tune with the record business and shared the same passion I had for music. She also kept a caring eye out for me while I was producing my own sessions for Scepter at their New York Studio. I was surprised at how Scepter allowed me the freedom to choose whoever I wanted on the dates and without the slightest intervention or final say. For the sessions I hired the top New York players who worked with my hero Paul Simon such as the keyboard wizard Bobby James and the famous session drummer Grady Tate as well as the great studio bassist, Bobby Edwards. It was fantastic to work with these incredible players who treated me with respect and kindness and never once displayed any attitude to an unknown record producer like myself.

Recording in New York was a total rush and completely different than L.A or Nashville. It was intense and you had to be able to be assertive and stand your ground when handling top players like these guys. Also, it was important to make sure your engineer respected you as well. Being timid or laid back like in Hollywood would get you chewed up and spit out. I wasn't about to let that happen to me and I ran my sessions with a firm hand making sure everyone knew that I had my studio shit together, which I certainly did.

Over the weeks Janet and I became very close and stayed in close touch long after I returned to California. She was a dear friend whose company I always enjoyed being around. And she watched out for me too, letting me know of any "behind closed doors" business dealings at the label which may or may not have affected me. I always knew where I stood with the label and with my manager Sean Downey, thanks to Janet who kept and eye and an ear open on my behalf. What a dear. We remain dear friends to this day.

Johnny and I continued to work all over the planet from Germany to Waldorf, Maryland. It was starting to become a grind right out of a scene from the Bill Murray film, "Groundhog Day." It was also becoming clear that Johnny's label CBS wasn't thrilled to have him on the roster any longer. By this time, 1973, his hits were a distant memory and his appearances were just a series of the same old supper clubs and military venues with an occasional Vegas stint or telethon in some rural farm belt. The new songs he recorded for CBS failed to make the charts and the label was seriously considering dropping him. Although he never let on that anything was wrong, I knew Johnny worried about his career as a recording artist. By now pop music had radically changed from his era and country music radio seemed skeptical of taking a once teen idol as a serious country music force.

In light of this, Johnny's work only increased and now we were gone more than ever. It became surreal. We were still using local house bands and I was getting tired trying to whip average musicians into a solid backing unit, all in one day. Some of the gigs were simply ridiculous. One time as we were flying into Lincoln, Nebraska I asked Johnny where we were playing.

"Oh, it's a surprise, John Beland" he said with a mischievous smile on his lips and twinkle in his eye. I suspected something was about to happen that I may not be too thrilled about. Then, as we touched down at the Lincoln Airport, I noticed a marching band and cheerleaders on the tarmac with a huge banner that I couldn't quite make out clearly. But it soon it became apparent as the plane door opened and we stood at the top of the stairs. There, stretched across 10 yards and held high in the air, was a big red banner that read "SHAKEY'S PIZZA WELCOMES JOHNNY TILLOTSON." I stood at the top of the plane's stairs frozen trying to keep my jaw from falling onto the ground. As the marching band kept playing and the crowd kept applauding and cheering, Johnny turned to me and shouted, "John Beland, now don't laugh but Shakey's is trying out a new promotional campaign to include bringing top talent to their restaurants. We're kind of a test run for the company." At that moment Johnny was met by the owner of Shakey's and some local dignitaries, while I was left behind, standing by the plane, alone and dumbfounded, watching the marching band and the welcoming committee whisk Johnny away in a waiting limo. I was taken to the gig in a station wagon.

At the restaurant, a stage had been assembled with a small sound system geared more for a high school hop than an artist of Johnny's reputation and caliber. On my arrival I was met by the owner who introduced me to the musicians who would back us that night. They were 3 kids fresh out of high school, all were scared shitless and looked as if they were going to lose their bodily functions at any minute. Fortunately, this time they had received the show tape in advance and had rehearsed on their own prior to our arrival. But although they had rehearsed the show the band was still very weak. I instructed the three nervous players to keep their eyes on me and nobody else at all times. I would give all the cues and guide them through the show, but it was vital that they gave me their undivided attention throughout the performance and not watch or listen to anything Johnny did onstage. They assured me they would. That night Shakey's Pizza in Lincoln, Nebraska was packed to the rafters with people from miles around, all clamoring for a table close to the stage to see hit artist Johnny Tillotson in person. I was quite shocked at the turn out but felt nervous about the band and their ability to do the job. Johnny, as always, acted as if everything would be perfect without a care in the world. Easy for him to say. I was the guy at the steering wheel of this ride. Surprisingly enough, the show went off without a hitch and the crowd went absolutely wild over Tillotson's performance. However, one funny thing did occur during the show. While Johnny was singing his big hit ballad "It keeps Right On A Hurtin" his voice was over taken by the following announcement through the public address system. "Smith & Johnson party, two large cheese and anchovies. Your order is ready"

22 BACK WITH THE SILVER TONGUE DEVIL

When I got back to Hollywood, fresh from Johnny's latest run, I had a message waiting for me on my answering service. It was from none other than Kris Kristofferson calling from backstage at the Sonny & Cher Show at CBS Studios. He asked me to call him back as soon as possible and left his number. "Wow" I thought. "What's this all about?" By this time Kris Kristofferson was now a household name and a major star not only in music, but in motion pictures. He was on the cover of every magazine you could imagine, and his celebrity had exploded worldwide. To add to that, he married none other than the Delta Lady herself, the sexy sultry voiced singer Rita Coolidge and the two were now performing and recording together as a duo. I immediately called Kris who answered in a very upbeat positive tone.

"Hi Kris" I said. "John Beland here. How the hell are ya?"

"Hey man" came the familiar gravelly voice I had come to know so well.

"I got your message. Just made it back home this afternoon. What's up?"

"Well," Kris replied "My guitarist Stephen Bruton just turned in his notice and we need somebody to take his place. What are you doing these days?"

I explained to Kris that I was still working with Johnny but was growing bored with the same old routine.

"Listen, Hoss. Why don't you come on board? I think I can finally afford pay you a hell of a lot more than I did back at the Troubadour."

Opportunity was knocking. Hell, it was banging on my door and I knew I couldn't turn down working for the biggest name in the business at the time. I knew it would hurt Johnny, but I had my own career to think about and just couldn't continue going around in circles like I had been with him. I loved Johnny like a brother but I couldn't refuse such an offer from Kris.

"Yeah man, I'll do it" I told Kris. "I have to give Johnny a 2-week notice. Would that be cool for you?"

Kris understood completely. "Sure thing, Hoss. We'll look forward to seeing you in two weeks."

I was excited about the new gig but dreaded telling Johnny that I was leaving. He had done so much for me and I was eternally grateful. But just as he had to look after his own career, I had to do the same. It was time to leave and hopefully we would remain the best of friends regardless.

I held off telling Johnny about the Kristofferson gig for a few days because he wanted me to accompany him to San Diego where the CBS Records Convention was taking place. Johnny was going to meet with producer and A&R head Billy Sherrill and he wanted to play Billy another one of my newer songs called "Sad Country Love Song". Johnny believed with all his heart that it was a hit tune and that as soon as Billy heard it, he would feel the same. This was a crucial meeting for Johnny because his last single record for CBS failed to do anything. If Billy believed in "Sad Country Love Song", Johnny would get another chance at CBS and very possibly score a much needed hit. We drove down to San Diego, a little over two hours from Los Angeles and all the way there Johnny played the cassette demo of "Sad Country Love Song", each time saying that he was "sure" it would be a smash hit. He was very positive and it felt like old times. Johnny joked and told stories and discussed his plans for the year. I hadn't seen him pumped up like this in a long time. When we reached San Diego we immediately met with Billy Sherrill at his hotel suite. It was a strange scene because the room was filled with a number of people we didn't know, as well as a few we did, including a very drunk CBS star, Charlie Rich. Rich had just come off of his own "comeback" hit "Behind Closed Doors" and was strutting around the room like the cock of the walk. I found him arrogant and a total redneck. Sherrill was holding court when we arrived.

"Hi Johnny" Billy said in that slow, southern drawl. He was slouched in a big leather chair with a drink in his hand, and it wasn't lemonade.

"Everybody" Billy announced. "You all know Johnny Tillotson. And this is his guitar player John Beland."

Nobody seemed exactly thrilled.

"Johnny, I hear you have a hit song for me."

Johnny was all smiles as I pulled out my guitar and got ready to back Johnny up on "Sad Country Love Song."

"Billy" Johnny said "I believe with everything in me that this is the song we've been looking for. John Beland wrote it."

Billy didn't seem too impressed that I had anything to do with the song. He just leaned back in his chair and said, "Let's hear it." The room got real quiet as Johnny sang the song. He did a great job too. It sounded like a hit record to me after hearing his rendition of it. It was a slow ballad about a good love gone bad, lost love, the kind of stuff country hits are made of.
When we finished Billy took a drink and said, "Nice song". I could tell he wasn't thrilled with it.

"Johnny, I'm sorry to have to tell you this" Billy said, "But we're clearing a lot of our roster at the label and I'm afraid we're going to have to let you go."

Johnny's face turned to stone at the news. It was a cold thing Sherrill did and he did it in front of a room full of people as well. I was angry as hell as I put my guitar back in its case.

"I'm sorry, Johnny" Billy halfheartedly said. "I wish you all the best, you know that buddy."

With that we left the room. Instead of knocking Billy over with a potential hit song, Johnny had driven two hours to San Diego only to get kicked off the label. He was devastated. There wasn't much to say on the way home. I drove. What made the story even sadder was the fact that the following year, singer Thom Bresh would have a top ten hit with "Sad Country Love Song." Johnny was right. The song "was" a hit, unfortunately not for him.

I had witnessed the cut-throat, backstabbing side of the record business first hand. It was cold and bloody. After that experience I'd keep my eyes and ears open and never turn my back on strangers who patted it. Johnny was a sweetheart of a guy who didn't deserve the humiliation that Billy Sherrill put him through. I felt horrible for Johnny and although I admired his talent for producing gold records, I despised Billy Sherrill for what he did to my dear friend.

As it turned out, a week later Johnny didn't take the Kristofferson news well, either. In fact, he was extremely hurt to the point of looking like a jilted lover. He offered me a raise but it was too late. My mind had been made up. I wished him my best and we shook hands, but I could tell he was hurt deeply. Over the past few years he had relied and counted on me to be there for him through thick and thin. We had shared endless miles and countless stages together and had been closer than brothers. He took the news hard but I had to move on. It was time.

Kris Kristofferson and I onstage 1974

Immediately after Johnny's gig had ended I started rehearsing at Studio Instrument Rentals in Hollywood with Kris, Rita and the band. It was a fabulous band made up of Memphis session aces drummer Sammy Creason and organ player Mike Uttley. There was also Nashville songwriter, pianist Donnie Fritz and bassist Terry Paul. Exiting guitarist Stephen Bruton stayed on for a few gigs until I knew the show well enough to do it on my own. Also on board was a songwriter and drinking buddy of Kris's, Bobby Nuewirth, a real colorful, loud hanger-on whose claim to fame was being Bob Dylan's wise-ass sidekick in the documentary film "Don't Look Back" as well as co-writer of the Janice Joplin hit "Mercedes Benz". Kris's road manager Cleave was a big tall guy with a pony tail and as warm and gentle a guy you would ever want to meet. He certainly had his hands full keeping this lot corralled.

As good as the band was, things were quite loose. Kris had to be "followed" rather than trusted to stick to a regimented set arrangement. But the band managed to pull off every song and fit quite nicely behind Kristofferson's loose musicianship. Nuewirth did a couple of his songs in the show and they too were loose thanks to the alcohol he and Kris downed throughout the rehearsals. But all in all, everyone in the band treated me terrific and we quickly became good friends and tight bandmates.

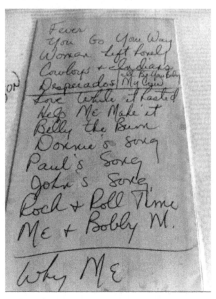

Kris' original hand written set list from 1974

Rita Coolidge was an enigma of sorts. On one hand she could be friendly enough but on the other hand she seemed unapproachable and not the kind of person who made you feel all warm and fuzzy. I never was able to read her and thus kept my distance. She was talented no doubt, but a bit non-emotional kind of singer; nothing close to the caliber of Linda Ronstadt. I found her style rather boring and her personality pretty much the same. Some of the tours we embarked on would just be with Kris as a solo, while other tours would be booked as the duet with both Kris and Rita sharing the bill. The two had just recorded a duet album together and were making the rounds on all the national TV shows promoting it. To be frank, they sounded very rough and unexciting thanks in a big way to Kris's limited vocal skills. Rita was the real singer of the two and carried the duet musically. Kris always looked embarrassed to be singing with her on television. It was cringing to watch. I couldn't understand why he was putting himself in that uncomfortable position. He certainly didn't need it. His solo career was shooting through the sky like a meteor. But fans didn't seem to care. Kris and Rita were the new "hip couple" on the music scene and it didn't matter what they sounded like, people still filled up halls to see them perform, although I couldn't understand why. Individually, they each had respectable solo careers with a solid fan base but together they seemed like a silly media hype to capitalize off their celebrity instead of the content of their work as a legit duo.

I was thrilled to have landed the gig with Kris and Rita. The pay was much higher than any gig previously and the visibility factor was very high profile. With the money I earned from Kris's gig, I bought a few more guitars to add to my arsenal. I bought a 1956 Fender Telecaster, a beautiful black Gibson Everly Brothers acoustic guitar and a 1958 Fender Strat. I also had 3 new guitar flight trunks made with my name stenciled underneath Kris and Rita's. This was big time. Most of the major producers and studio musicians both in LA and Nashville were now aware that I was Kristofferson's new guitarist and that meant more session work for me when we were between tours.

Kristofferson's Kid Punk Guitarist

Although Kris Kristofferson introduces him on stage as "our kid-punk guitar player," John Beland is too old to be considered a kid (he's 24) and much too sensitive to be called a punk. Ole Kris, however, remembers the young singer-songwriter when he was a 17 year old punk kid and probably the only guitar picker in Los Angeles with enough balls to go on stage at the Troubadour with an unknown country singer named Kristofferson.

"I had just run away from home and I was playing guitar for nothing behind different people at the Monday night 'hoots' Larry Murray would put on at the Troubadour. One night, Larry said, 'there's this friend of mine who just came out from Nashville and he wants to play a coupla tunes. Why dont'cha play guitar behind him?' So I got together with Kris and he showed me these songs like "For The Good Times" and "Me And Bobby McGee" and I said, you know, wow! He had real short hair back then, slicked back;

and we got up on the stage and we bombed. The people hated it, they didn't want to hear country music. This was the first time Kris had ever stepped on stage."

Shortly after the Troubadour fiasco, Beland joined a country-rock group called Swampwater which toured the world backing-up Linda

Ronstadt, Arlo Guthrie and Johnny Tillotson. They recorded one album on Standay-King and another on RCA (under the name of Swampfire) before various conflicts caused the group to splinter. By that time Kristofferson had become a household word and John Beland was back on the road with the "Silver Tongued Devil."

"The greatest thing about Kris is he doesn't pull any star trips. I can look at him the way I did when I first met him and he was sleeping on the back seats of cars in L.A. . . . and you know he's like Hank Williams — the dude is a legend and I really enjoy being a part of it."

When he's not working the concert circuit with Kris, Beland spends his time at home in L.A. working on his own material. Scepter Records recently released his first solo album, John Edward Beland, an impressive, if a bit over-produced, collection of John's refreshing and enchanting styles. Stand out tracks may be the

tender "Banjo Man," the plaintive "Goodbye," or the rousing "Back On The Road Again;" but the highlight of the set is John's moving "Song For Hank Williams" — "oh can't you hear a lonesome cry/from the steel guitar as he takes just one last ride/how about it neighbors? Let's bring him back one more time/lord, it's so hard to say goodbye."

Beland used a snatch of "Lovesick Blues" as an intro for "Song To Hank Williams" and amidst the scratches and hisses of a seemingly ancient recording, you'd swear that was Hank himself singing, It's not.

"You'll never guess who it is," laughed Beland. "Originally, we were going to use Hank's recording but Johnny Tillotson dropped by the studio and said he could do a pretty good Hank Williams imitation. When he started singing Hank Williams, it just blew us out. He sounded more like Hank Williams than Hank Williams did."—ALVIN COOLEY

Feature story in Zoo World Magazine 1974

At the same time, my album, simply titled "John Edward Beland" was finally released on Scepter Records to positive reviews. In fact, Kris even let me perform two songs off the album as part of his show. One of the great things about Kristofferson was that he was always willing to showcase one of his band members whenever he could. Like a proud parent showing off one of his kids. In a way he was much like Johnny Tillotson. Kris also mentioned me as often as possible in his own interviews which led to a few features on me in various rock magazines. The press dubbed me "Kristofferson's Punk Kid Guitarist" which I found a bit cool, but at the same time a bit embarrassing with the guys in the band.

One of the early gigs I did with Kris was the first Willie Nelson Picnic in Dripping Springs, Texas. We were on the bill with Waylon Jennings, John Prine, Doug Sahm and Tom T. Hall. I had pictured Texas as all rednecks and cowboys and conservative right wingers, but boy did I get a rude awakening. The audience was a sea of long haired stoned-out, t-shirted, blue jeaned, wild college kids hooting and hollering passing joints and flashing tits. There must have been over 20 thousand of them (fans, not tits). It was as crazy as crazy could get but it was terrific. I took my position on the outdoor stage and prepared to start the show with Kris when this little guy in a big baggy jean shirt walked up and set his old Baldwin Amplifier right next to mine. He began playing along with me on the shittiest looking beat up old guitar I had ever seen. I looked down at him as if to say, "Who the heck are you?" but before I could, he simply smiled and said "Hi, I'm Willie."

Happy times back with Kris, at first

It was quite amazing to witness the transformation of Kris from the struggling singer / songwriter to Kris Kristofferson the actor and Grammy Award winning star. Fans and all sorts of weird characters tried to barnacle themselves to him wherever we played. But despite his huge success he was still "Kris" who remained a good soul and very humble guy. However, the scale of his sudden star status caused him to struggle with a few demons. First and foremost, he was very insecure about his performing. He would constantly apologize to the audience and at times even offer to refund their ticket money, much to the horror of the concert promoters. The audiences didn't give a damn about how good or bad Kris was. They loved him and shouted out to him their approval and loyalty at every show. Still, he felt very insecure and it didn't help when he tried to drown those insecurities in a sea of Jack Daniels before each show.

One of my jobs was to tune Kris's old Martin guitar just prior to the show. However, when Kris would hit the stage drunk he would accidentally bang his guitar into a microphone stand causing it to lose tuning and when it became obvious his guitar was way out of tune he would make a comment into the microphone about my inability to tune a guitar. I would be pissed off the entire night, having been humiliated on stage and blamed for his drunken actions. Many times, I thought about quitting but Kris would always call me up in my room after the show and apologize saying "Man, I'm sorry I was an asshole, Hoss. That was the fucking whiskey talking and I apologize."

I let it roll and told Kris that I was ok. But the same scene replayed repeatedly throughout our touring and it became a real problem for me. I didn't want to quit Kris but I felt as if I was being pushed to throw my guitar down and storm offstage. It was getting unbearable.

The other demon he seemed to be battling was his embarrassment at being labeled "The New Dylan". Kris, a huge Dylan admirer, was very self-conscious about the enormity of his new success, especially when it came to facing his old writing mentors back in Nashville who had influenced him and was still great friends with. I believe he felt unworthy of all the attention while his role models and fellow writing friends back on Music Row were still struggling in their own careers. It was hard for him to face them now knowing how much they had impacted him only a few years earlier. I know he felt as if he didn't deserve this new fame when his closest friends, who were such a big part of his inspiration and influence as a songwriter, were still relatively unknown to the general public. This was a real hard pill for a humble man like Kris to swallow. It's important to remember the enormity of Kris's success at this stage in 1974. He was on the cover of every magazine in the country. Rolling Stone was comparing him to Dylan and other country artists were now landing career making number one songs, all written by him. He was on every television and award shows as well as staring in top grossing movies such as "Alice Doesn't Live Here Anymore" and "Cisco Pike.". He was huge, and it swept him up like a giant tidal wave.

All of this only added additional fuel to his ever-growing drinking problems. And it didn't help that Bobby Nuewirth tagged long like a court jester influencing Kris to get drunk and stupid as if we were all going to a Frat party. Nuewirth was a pain in the ass. He was a loud, obnoxious rattling can who always had a smart ass comment for everything. He only did a few songs in the show but when he did he mirrored Kris's drunken performances with his slurred singing and out of tune guitar playing. And to make matters worse, the rest of us had to back him up every night, much to the disgust of everyone in the band.

Both Kris and Bobby would start their drinking early in the day and by show time they were both shit faced. Sometimes, Kris was alright and did a great show. But too many times he did a poor performance and put the band in a terrible position of having to stand up there behind him while he apologized for "OUR" shitty show. "OUR SHITTY SHOW?" The band was never drunk or stoned for any show. We played straight and did our best to keep Kris on course for 90 minutes every night. Whenever he included us in his apologies to the audience, we would be incredibly pissed off. It was Kris and Nuewirth who hit the stage drunk most nights not us, the band.

It hurt me to see Kris torturing himself night after night in front of 5 or 6 thousand adoring fans. Somebody would yell out "We love you, Kris" but he would ignore them and slur his way through each song, sometimes changing the lyrics to a few of his most classic songs like "Help Me Make It Through The Night" singing "It's the shits to sleep alone. Help me fake it through the night."

Every other word from his lips would be "Fuck" or "Shit" and it never occurred to him that younger people, church going people, clergy and others might be in the audience taking offense to his drunken behavior and foul mouth. It was hard to watch from where I stood.

The gigs started to get very bizarre, as well. One night we would be playing to a full house of country rock fans in t-shirts and jeans and another night we would be somewhere in the deep south playing to a straight red neck crowd where the first few rows consisted of sick patients in hospital beds, some connected to IV's all there to see the writer of the smash Gospel hit, "Why Me."

When Rita would join us, it would be like traveling and performing with a ticking bomb by your side. As much as they loved each other, they would fight when Kris would get drunk and many times onstage, heard only by the band. Sometimes Rita would whisper to Kris that he was out of pitch and that would be all it would take for him to simply walk off the stage and let her finish the show. We, the band, would hear all the squabbling and digs between them onstage but the audience was totally unaware. Kris would swear at Rita during an applause and the next thing you knew they were nose to nose at the microphone singing a romantic song to each other. Kris never seemed happy when she came out with us and her bland demeanor certainly didn't brighten up the situation either.

That same year we traveled to Nashville to record an album with Kris which was to be produced by legendary Nashville producer Fred Foster, whose credits included many of the classic Roy Orbison hits. I was really looking forward to it, being a big fan of his production skills. The sessions were held at Monument Studios just off Music Row. As I set my amp up in the studio, I noticed an unusual amount of people in the control booth for a session. I had no idea what Fred Foster looked like, but I presumed that he was somewhere in the midst of the overcrowded control room. Kris came out to the main floor and played us the first song; just himself and his acoustic guitar. Slowly the band molded and shaped it until it seemed ready for a take. Kris went into a vocal booth to guide us with a scratch vocal as we laid down a track. When we finished what felt like THE perfect track it was played back to us through speakers in the main room. Back then the musicians never went into the producers control room to listen back. We remained on the main floor while the track was piped to us outside. I listened and had an idea for a guitar hook, so I got up and walked towards the control room to tell Fred about it. But before I could reach the famous producer I was intercepted by his assistant who advised me not to "bother" Fred during the session.

"I'm on the date" I firmly explained to the flunky.

"No matter" came his slow southern drawl response. "Fred will let you know when he's ready to hear any ideas."

I stood there with my jaw opened, scratching my head. Is this for real? I thought.

Foster never did get back to me. I continued to play take after take with the rest of the band until the session was over. All the while I wondered how a guy like Fred Foster, known for his amazing Roy Orbison productions, ever attained such a reputation. As far as I was concerned he offered absolutely nothing to the music we were laying down for Kris. In the coming days I found out that Kris was frustrated with Foster as well, and fired him. The songs we recorded at Monument were scrapped and the new sessions were books at famed engineer / producer Chips Moman's studio outside of Nashville.

Chips had a stellar record as a producer. He had produced an amazing 120 chart pop, country and soul hits including those by artists such as Waylon Jennings, Willie Nelson, Gary Stewart, Petula Clark and Tammy Wynette. He also produced "In The Ghetto" and "Suspicious Minds" for Elvis. Chips knew his stuff alright. We recorded at Chip's studio just outside of town. For these dates we were joined by none other than Byrds founder Roger McGuinn, singer-songwriter Larry Gatlin and, of course, Rita. It was a much-laid back setting but light years more comfortable and creative than back at Fred Foster's camp.

Kris was in fine form and very animated in the studio, a far cry from out on the road dealing with his demons. Roger McGuinn was a great guy to record with and we worked well together. He played acoustic 12 string while I played my Telecaster. After the session we all went to the famous Nashville BBQ restaurant, Charlie Nickens BBQ near downtown Nashville. It was a funky old place down by the rough part of town but it was a very popular place with the musicians in town. A funny thing happened while we were eating dinner one night after recording at Chip's. In the middle of dinner a telephone rang but it wasn't coming from any phone in the restaurant. Nobody could tell where the ringing was coming from until Roger lifted up his briefcase and opened it. As he did, the inside of the briefcase lit up with flickering lights. Roger reached inside and casually answered his telephone. You could have heard a pin drop in the restaurant as Roger chatted on his space age telephone. Mind you, this was years before anyone ever heard the word "cell phone."

Back to Los Angeles we traveled to tape the Sonny & Cher Show and to play the Troubadour for the week. It was fun returning to CBS Studios where I had first worked on the Glen Campbell Goodtime Hour. Sonny & Cher now had the top variety show and Kris and Rita were the guests. For the musical segment they put each of the band members on hay bales. Seems Hollywood never really quite knew what to do with country music performers other than to feature them on hay bales or sitting on a coral fence. Sonny was a bit of a cold guy and hardly spoke to any of us, but Cher was lovely and treated us warm and friendly. I was a bit surprised to see that she wasn't as tall as she appeared on TV next to Sonny. Looks can be deceiving. But one thing for certain, Cher was beautiful, even more so in person.

That week we headlined at the Troubadour. This time Kris didn't need the support of a Linda Ronstadt to draw people. They were lined up around the block to see him. I couldn't help but flash back to the night I first met Kris in the little upstairs dressing room reserved for opening acts. Back then he didn't have a pot to pee in and now he was a household name. Like many other careers, his started at the Troubadour as well, born from a 15-minute Monday night hootenanny performance. He had come a long way alright.

One funny thing I remember that night was that in the middle of Kris's set, someone threw a tomato onstage and hit Terry Paul's beautiful Hofner bass guitar. Suddenly the show came to a grinding halt as an enraged Terry wiped his bass and screamed out to the crowd "I make my living playing this bass!" The crowd was booing and rumbling and Kris grabbed his mic and said "Hey, listen. I like a salad like the next guy, but if I find out who threw this fucking tomato someone's gonna get their goddamned ass kicked."

23 A BAD DAY IN CUMMING, GEORGIA

We continued to tour the country playing sold out halls and clubs. In Shreveport, Louisiana we appeared at the legendary Louisiana Hayride, home of such country heroes of mine as Lefty Frizzell, Johnny Horton and of course an unknown singer from Memphis named Elvis Presley. For that gig Kris was in fine form and the audience ate him up. I watched him singing Bobby McGee and thinking "Damn, I'm witnessing history here."

In New York City we did a live CBS Country Music Special featuring Kris & Rita, Ann Murray and Mac Davis. It was great to see my old Ronstadt/Swampwater bandmate Thad Maxwell again. He was playing steel guitar in the Mac Davis band and it was like old times being together. In fact, old times meant old tricks and sure enough we played a few on each other. It seemed that Ann Murray needed a steel guitar to play behind her on her hit song "Danny's Song." She asked Thad, who was thrilled to do it, especially since he had only been playing the instrument for a year or so. Knowing that, I quietly un-tuned his strings just prior to air date. When Anne started up "Danny's song" Thad was horrified to find his steel completely out of tune. So instead of playing behind her, he just folded his hands and sat behind his instrument for the next two and a half minutes. In retaliation, just as we hit the air with Kris and Rita, I found out that my effects box wasn't responding to my foot. I reached down and opened it up only to find a note that said "Next time get a battery, asshole". No signature was required!

We returned to Hollywood where I was booked to play on Rita Coolidge's new album. I was surprised because she hadn't paid much attention to me in all the time we had toured together. But not being one to ponder an opportunity, I jumped at the chance. The sessions were produced by David Anderle, a great record man with a long impressive track record including producing Delaney & Bonnie, the Ozark Mountain Daredevils, Amy Grant and others. It was great to work alongside many fellow session players I had known for years such as Herb Pederson from the Dillards, and my old Swampwater bandmate Gib Guilbeau. We even recorded an old Swampwater song called "Mama Lou". So you can imagine my total surprise and frustration when my name was omitted on the albums credits. I was told it was a simple oversight but it only gave me an even "more" sour taste for working with Rita Coolidge.

On the other side of town I recorded again with Kris for his latest album "Spooky Lady Sideshow." This time I was hired for background vocals along with my buddy the great Herb Pederson. I had admired Herb's work since his days as the driving force behind the bluegrass / pop group, the Dillards. We shared the same musical tastes as well as the same sense of humor.

If that wasn't enough to keep me busy in the studio I was also booked on Bobby Nuewirth's solo album for A&M Records. As crazy as he was, Nuewirth was a good songwriter and knew just about everyone in the damn music business. For this album I was joined by a who's who of session giants such as Don Everly, Cass Elliot, Richie Furay, Chris Hillman, Ian Mathews, Richard Greene, Booker T. Jones, Timmy Schmit, Dusty Springfield and many more. The sessions were a lot of fun and Bobby was surprisingly terrific to work with. Again, he was a far cry from Kristofferson's loud mouth drunken court jester whom I had been touring with. I admired Bob's totally professional work on these sessions.

The long road continued. We shared the stage with acts like John Prine and Gordon Lightfoot as well as with a very drunk Charlie Rich. In California on the very day that Jim Croce's plane crashed, we had to fly in a helicopter to a remote location for an outdoor festival with Waylon Jennings, Commander Cody and Jerry Reed. Then it was up to Canada where a drunken Kris told the capacity auditorium audience that they could get a full refund considering the "shitty" show we were playing. This led to a physical fight backstage between Kris and the promoter.

In Waldorf, Maryland one of the country's top 4-star Generals showed up drunk out of his mind after spending a whiskey soaked afternoon with his old army buddy, Kris Kristofferson. Our road crew had to hide the General before the military police discovered him. In Nashville we were thrown out of the King of the Road Hotel after Kris threw a grapefruit at one of the housekeepers who had woken him up to clean his room. Then came Cumming, Georgia.

By now I had all I could take of Kris's drunken performances and the insults directed my way over the tuning of his guitar. One night we were in the middle of the show and again Kris laid into me about his guitar being out of tune and how I didn't do a very good job tuning it. All this over the microphone to thousands in attendance. After the show I walked up to our road manager Cleave and told him I quit. This time I was serious. The next morning Kris was having breakfast in the hotel coffee shop when he mentioned to Cleave that he felt bad about laying into me onstage the previous night.

"Shit" said Kris "I guess John *will* probably quit now."

Cleave looked up at him and said "Oh, so you already heard?"

"Heard what" asked Kris in a surprised tone.

"Well, yeah John quit after the show last night. He gave us two weeks' notice."

"That's news to me. Damn" mumbled Kris.

When we got home to LA I told my buddy Jerry that I had quit Kristofferson once and for all. My nerves were shot and I couldn't take any more drama scenes on the road. Jerry understood and was supportive, as any friend could be. However, Kris's office wasn't. I received a call from Kris's manager, Bert Block, who tried to talk me out of quitting by offering me a solo deal with Monument Records as well as a bit part in Kris's new film called "A Star Is Born" with Barbara Streisand. I still said, "thanks, but no thanks." It was time for Kris and me to go our separate ways. I agreed to do one more gig with him in order for my replacement, Billy Swan, to get familiar with the show. Billy had once played in Kris's early band and the two were great friends. In order to convince Billy to come back, Kris assured him that the times were much different than the old days when they were struggling. "It's different now, Billy" Kris was heard to say. "They respect us."

My last gig with Kris Kristofferson was in Cumming, Georgia. The show was billed as "Kris and Rita" but the actual booking was for Kris and Kris only. At the time of the gig, Kris's record "Why Me" was number one on not only the county and pop charts but on the Gospel charts as well. It was a staple in many churches throughout the country and popular with listeners who didn't know a single thing about who or what Kristofferson was. We were set to play a place called Lanierland Park in Cumming which was basically a tent in a big field.

When our two-car caravan came over the hill and we spotted the park, Cleave turned to Kris and begged him to reconsider playing the gig and instead turn the cars around and head straight out of town. "Let the lawyers hammer it all out" Cleave pleaded. But Kris wouldn't hear of it. He was already drunk and determined to do the show regardless of the outcome.

Cumming, Georgia was as deep into the Bible belt as one could imagine. Redneck and Bibles pretty much described the place when we arrived. The stage was nothing more than a flatbed truck with a tiny PA system meant for a high school combo. The area was packed with folks who looked as if they had just come back from church services. There they sat in the hot sun, fanning themselves and waiting patiently for the writer of "Why Me" and his lovely wife. Running the sound just to the right of the stage was a high school kid who was scared shitless. Kris had been known for chewing up professional sound men at our gigs so there was no telling what he would do with this young pup behind the soundboard. Kris's dressing room was a trailer behind the stage. The rest of us had already dressed back at our hotel in nearby Gainesville, Georgia.

From the very start, the PA started screeching bringing songs to a dead stop while the kid at the controls tried frantically to solve the problem. Kris would mumble a few profanities into the mic and we would start over. It was almost impossible to hear anything we were playing. Between songs fans started yelling out "Where's Rita?" Kris ignored them for a while but soon had enough. "Now listen" he announced. "Rita ain't here. She never was never meant to be here and won't be here today. The promoter has known this all along so bitch to him if you want to."

It started to get ugly. "We paid to see you and Rita, Kris" someone yelled out. People started booing and men from the audience started making their way to the back of the stage area.

"We love you, Kris" somebody yelled.

"Well, fuck it" Kris replied. "We came to do a goddamn show so let's fucking do it."

We started the next song and once again the PA howled.

"Who the fuck is running the PA"? Kris yelled into the microphone.

The booing got louder.

"Watch your mouth" someone yelled from the crowd.

Things were getting out of control and by the time we finished with the closing song "Bobby McGee" a mob headed straight to Kris's trailer. There was no parting applause from the crowd, only booing. While still on stage I nervously packed my guitar away, at the same time watching the backstage scene unfold from the corner of my eye. A little girl asked me for my autograph and I noticed that when I tried to sign my name my hand shook. Backstage the promoter banged on Kris's dressing room and shouted out that he had no reason to use such profanity at the park and reminded him that there were women and children who were subjected to all of it. More angry men gathered around the trailer door snarling and shouting at Kris, who noticed that some of them had guns showing inside their coats. The scene then turned violent. The mob had surrounded the trailer and started banging on the door until Kris opened it.

Someone shouted at Kris "You don't come down here and use that language in front of our families"!

Kris was shitfaced drunk and answered back "I'm sorry but things have been fucked up since we came here and…." Just then a hand reached up and grabbed Kris by the hair and pulled him down on the ground. Holy hell broke loose. Fists were flying everywhere.

From the stage I could hear the shouting and the screaming and see men running by me headed to Kris's dressing room. I thought we would surely all be lynched.

Finally, the sheriff arrived and we were put into cars and escorted out of the park and out of the hands of one angry redneck mob.

When we arrived back at our hotel in Gainesville, the sheriff took Kris to the side and offered some sound advice, Georgia style. "You should be alright from here on out, Mr. Kristofferson. But let me give you some words of advice." With that the sheriff moved a little closer to Kris's face so that his "advice" could be properly heard. "Mr. Kristofferson, don't ever come back here again."

That was my last gig with Kris Kristofferson, and for that matter Rita Coolidge. In the year that followed, Kris would go on to make the smash hit film "A Star Is Born" with Barbara Streisand. All the band had roles in the film, as Bert Block had promised me. Still, I had no regrets. Kris's music career never quite sustained itself after Cumming, Georgia and in a wise move he directed all his energy and focus on his acting career and with regard to his music career he pretty much faded away from all the attention and notoriety he received in 1974. His film career would continue to sustain over the coming decades to the point of him being more recognized for his acting than his music. He and Rita would soon split up and she too would eventually go back to making forgettable albums and playing occasional clubs and small venues. A far cry from the high visibility she received being one half of Kris and Rita. The party was over, but it certainly was one hell of a party.

24 TOGETHER AGAIN – BACK WITH TILLOTSON

I didn't have any trouble getting work after I left Kris and Rita. Immediately after returning to L.A from the Cumming, Georgia gig I received a call from Linda Ronstadt asking if I would be interested in coming back and playing guitar for her. She had just recorded a new single called "You're No Good" and was putting a new band together made up of some of the guys who played on the recording. I thought "great" and told her that I would love to come back.

Linda was playing the Palomino Club that night and invited me out to catch her and the band. I thought this would be a good chance for me to take out and impress a beautiful girl I had been dating named Mary Gottschalk. We had been set up on a blind date by a mutual friend and had immediately hit it off. She worked for a management company that handled actor Burt Reynolds and she had previously worked in London for a publicist named Tony Brainsby, whose clients included Paul McCartney.

Mary was originally from Bay St. Louis, Mississippi and had a wonderful southern charm to her delightful personality. She was funny and loved the same things I did, from music to films. She was also a knock out! Mary and I went to the Palomino Club to see Linda's show. The place was packed and we had a terrific time. I introduced Mary to Linda following her performance. It was great seeing Linda again and I told her that I looked forward to re- joining her band. "That's great, Beland" she said in that nasal voice of hers. "Rehearsals are Friday at Alley Rehearsal Hall in the Valley. See ya then!"

Jerry and I headed to Linda's band rehearsals on Friday afternoon. I looked forward to the gig and Jerry was equally excited, having had a crush on Linda ever since I first went to work for her in 1970. When we arrived at the rehearsal hall I noticed that Linda wasn't around. I asked her bass player Kenny Edwards where she was and he told me that she wouldn't be around for this rehearsal session. No problem. I took out my old Telecaster and realized I hadn't an amplifier because mine were still in storage with the rest of Kristofferson's gear all the way across town. Linda's other guitarist and pianist Andrew Gold had a number of small amps and I asked him if I could borrow one for the day until I could get mine back from Kris.

His answer was "no!"

He really didn't elaborate on it. He just made it clear that he didn't like to lend his amp to anyone.

"Hmm, ok" I thought. "This is going to be weird." I called the main office of the rehearsal hall and they delivered me an amp without a problem.

All through the rehearsal neither Kenny nor Andrew said much to me. They were quite serious and very into themselves. It was very uncomfortable, but I just chalked it up to getting familiar with each other on the first day. However, I was in for a shocker. When rehearsal was over and I was packing up, Andrew walked over to me and said "Hey man that was good today. We'll get back to you and let you know what we decide."

"What?"

"We have to listen to two more players before we make a decision. But we'll get back to you" came his smug comment.

"You mean this is an audition?" I asked in an almost joking manner.

"Yeah, man" came his response. "We'll let you know"

I paused and collected myself and then spoke.

"Hey Andrew. I'll give you my response now and you can pass it along to Linda. Find someone else. I don't audition for anyone, especially acts I have already worked with extensively"

With that Jerry and I left. I was blood red and too pissed off to call Linda myself. Instead, when I got home I called Johnny Tillotson and asked him if he wanted me back. He gladly did and in a few minutes, I had my old gig back.
Johnny and I flew to Canada for our first gig back together again.

It was great being with him. He was just like a big brother to me and I really appreciated our relationship, and missed it terribly. One morning while in Toronto, I received a phone call in my hotel room.

"Hey Beland. Linda here" came the familiar voice.

"Hi Linda. How ya doing?" I cautiously asked.

"Beland, listen. Are you coming back to work with us?"

I told her the whole rehearsal story and how I was insulted to be auditioning for her.

"Linda, no offense but Andrew and Kenny were assholes to me and I don't see how we could ever work together in a band." I'm sorry but I just went back to work for Tillotson and I'm staying here."

"But the guys loved your playing and want you in the band" she explained.

"I'm sorry, Linda. If you had told me in advance that I would have to audition for your gig I would have never accepted" I told her. "I know Kenny and Andrew can be a bit hard to get to know, but I think you guys would be great together" she said.

"I'm sorry, Linda. I hope it all goes great for you and the guys and thanks for calling me."
With that I said goodbye.

Linda went on to have her biggest record hit to date with "You're No Good" and it launched her to a super star status. Kenny Edwards and Andrew Gold went on to play on a string of hits for Linda which even led to a well-deserved Grammy for her. Sadly, Kenny and Andrew have passed on and Linda is now retired and battling Parkinson's disease. Time, it seems, auditions for no one. Soon, I was back in Las Vegas with Tillotson playing the Hilton Hotel. I loved being back in Vegas and Johnny was a hot draw in town.

While I was in town I returned to Las Vegas Recorders where I wrote and produced an ad for the Las Vegas Sun newspaper as well as the theme for a local TV sports show. I also appeared with Johnny on the Merv Griffin Show which was being taped at Caesar's Palace. It was a good feeling to be working with people who were not only professional but made you feel good and look forward to playing with each night, a far cry from the drama over at Kris's camp or with Linda's new band.

It was common practice to get into town a day before opening night just to get settled in the dressing rooms and make sure your stage clothes were hung up and that all was ready for the following evenings show. I loved getting to the Hilton a day early because it gave me a chance to watch the previous act's last night of performing from backstage. This particular week the legendary BB King was wrapping up a week's run and I didn't want to miss him. He was one of my biggest influences on guitar starting as far back as my earliest days back in Hometown. BB was a god to me and I now had the chance to watch him close up, from the wings of the Hilton stage. It was between shows and the dressing room area was dead quiet with absolutely no activity going on. I had decided to check in and get my stage clothes hung up when I noticed the door opened part way in BB's dressing room. I walked over to take a little peak when suddenly the door flew open and a huge black body guard stood there towering over me.

"Can I help you?" he said in a low no nonsense tone.

"Uh, well" I stammered "My name is John Beland and I'm lead guitarist for Johnny Tillotson. I was headed to my dressing room when I noticed the door was opened and….."

Just then a voice from behind the door called out to the bodyguard "Let John in, Bob. He's ok"

The door opened wider as the body guard led me into the room. There, sitting comfortable on a soft leather chair was none other than my idol, the one and only BB King and next to him perched on a stand was the Holy Grail of guitars, BB's red Gibson Stereo, Lucille.

"Hi John" said BB in a pleasant warm tone with a big smile on his face. "Sit down and relax. Do you drink Champagne?"   Although

I didn't drink at all I certainly wasn't about to refuse the greatest guitarist in the world. "Sure, BB. That would be great!" BB turned to his towering guard and ordered two glassed of bubbly for us.

"How long have you been playing for Johnny?" BB asked between sips.

"For a few years," I answered, constantly finding my gaze switching back and forth between BB and Lucille.

"What kind of guitar do you play, John?" he asked.

"I play a 58 Telecaster. I've always played a Tele."

BB noticed me staring at his iconic guitar. "Do want to play, Lucille?" he said with a big smile.
"Are you kidding me?" I shouted out.

"No, here ya go" and he reached over, picked her up and handed the "guitar of guitars" over to me. Just holding Lucille felt like a religious experience of sorts. I mean, this was the very guitar that made me want to become a musician. I looked up at BB and said "This is the first real lick I learned off your "Live at the Regal" album, BB. And I started playing. BB reached over to me and said, "That's good John, but you need to move your wrist a little to get that vibrato correct." With that he took my wrist as I was playing and moved it with his hand. Lo and behold, there was the BB Kind sound. I thought "Holy Christ, I'm getting a guitar lesson from BB King"

I asked BB if he would sign my Telecaster and he agreed. I ran down the hall to my dressing room and grabbed my old blonde tele and ran back to BB.

"Well, that's a beauty" he said as I handed it over to him. "You know, John, as much as I love the sound of Telecasters I never was able to wrap myself around them. But I sure love the tone they get." He then took a black ink marker and wrote on the face of my Telecaster and wrote "To John, stay with it, BB King."

"Thanks, so much BB. I'll never forget this"

BB laughed as he stood up

"No problem, John. It was nice to meet you and good luck with Johnny too. It's time for me to hit the stage, walk down there with me."

So I followed BB down the stairway to the backstage area. The band was already playing the warm up song and they were smoking. BB strapped Lucille on and looked at me and said, "Good luck, John" then strolled out onstage to thunderous applause. I watched from the wings as he plugged his chord in and hit the first few notes of "Every Day I Got the Blues". His playing was flawless and his singing was as soulful as I had ever heard. There he was, the likes of which we will never see or hear again. I was so blessed to have shared a few intimate moments with my hero whose music continues to inspire me to this day.

While in Las Vegas, Johnny was going through some personal issues. He had fallen for a Lido Show dancer named Karen Buchard, a tall beautiful sexy piece of work who towered over Tillotson like Godzilla over Tokyo harbor. The two were having a steamy affair and eventually John's wife Lucille found out about it, the very hard way. One-night John and Karen were together in his room when a knock came at the door. John called out "Who is it"?

The voice outside the door answered "Hi Honey, it's me, Lou. Open up!" Lucille, with the best of intentions, had decided to surprise her husband by flying to Vegas unannounced. The knock continued. "John, open up its me." John fumbled through his cloths while Karen covered herself up in bed. "John" called Lou "What are you doing?" A stammering Tillotson answered "Uh hold on. Just looking for a towel." An angry Lucille fired back "You don't need a damned towel for me. Open the door!" When Tillotson did, Lou found the 6 foot Lido dancer naked in her husband's bed. That was the end of the marriage!

A few days later as Johnny and I were boarding a flight to Augusta Georgia I asked him what Lou did when she discovered Karen in his bed.

"John Beland" answered Johnny in that familiar style of his "remember those karate lessons I paid for, for Lou?"

"Yea, I remember. What about them"? I asked.

Johnny lifted his shirt and lowered his jeans a little bit, revealing a huge black and blue mark on his torso. "Say no more".

Karen was a drag. A big drag. From the minute she got her hooks into Johnny she was running his life and his career. She would follow him around like Yoko Ono with John Lennon, constantly straightening out whatever clothes he was wearing and correcting him every time he opened his mouth. Furthermore, she started to suggest song ideas and band wardrobe ideas to him much to the disgust of the guys and girls in the band. The two of them would be seen at all the highbrow events in town, dining with this celebrity or that celebrity, parading each other around like poodles. It was about all I could stand until things finally came to head backstage at the Merv Griffin Show that we were about to tape. Johnny brought me along as his music director and I would join Merv's band in the orchestra section while Johnny performed. I was excited about the show because Johnny's new record was a song I had written called "Willow County Line." Doing it on Merv's show was great exposure as well as nice little bonus check for me.

However, backstage in the dressing room Karen and Johnny showed up carrying the stage outfit I wore as part of the band each show night. It was a stupid outfit that resembled a Davy Crocket style suit, designed by the famous Beverly Hills designer Bill Ballew. In the context of a live show and a full stage band, the outfits worked great. However, alone in the Merv Griffin Orchestra section, I would look like I complete fool. I refused to wear it and told Johnny so. Johnny said

"Well, Karen seems to think it would look very sharp on TV, John."

"Well, then tell her to wear it herself because I won't" was my response.

The final straw was when Johnny informed me that we would not be doing the new record. Instead, Karen had suggested that he sing the Eagles new huge hit "Take It Easy."

"Are you kidding me, John?" I answered back in shock!

"No, John Edward I'm not. Karen thinks it would be a good idea to do a song that everyone watching would recognize."

I looked over at Karen, all decked out as if she was going to a photo shoot.

"John, you're crazy not to do your new single on the show. You know better than that! Why in the hell would anyone be interested in you singing an Eagles hit?" I asked as if I was losing my mind.

"Well, we're going with "Take It easy" and that's that" came his stern response.

"Well, John. That's fine with me because after Vegas, I quit" came *my* stern response.

I couldn't believe that a show girl who's only experience in show business was wiggling her tits in front of a Vegas audience every night was now advising a 20-year veteran of hit records and TV what to do regarding his career. Nobody could be "that" incredible in the sack! I had had enough. I turned in my notice for the second and last time.

25 LET YOUR LOVE FLOW & FOND FAREWELLS

I was crazy about Mary and found myself missing her more and more each day we were apart. I had even written a song about her that Johnny had recorded called "Mississippi Lady." She was a perfect lover and a perfect friend and I was head over heels in love with her. It was only a matter of time before we decided to live together, so with a fond farewell to my faithful roommate Jerry, Mary and I soon moved to a great little bungalow she had found up in the Hollywood Hills at 2270 North Beachwood Drive. Villa Monterey was a magical place with an old Spanish hacienda architecture and a quiet courtyard with a lovely little fish pond in the center. There were 12 units and most of them were occupied by people in the media.

We quickly settled in and soon became part of a circle of friends we came to love and admire who were also a part of the music business. Larry Murray and his wife Laurette were our closest friends. Larry was now a staff writer for Johnny Cash as well as a successful record producer and songwriter whose tunes had been covered by The Byrds, Kris Kristofferson, Rita Coolidge, Tommy Cash as well as many artists overseas in countries such as Holland and Australia. I admired Larry greatly ever since I first saw him running the Troubadour Hoot Nights when I was still on the streets as a runaway. He took a liking to me back then and treated me like a kid brother. I learned a lot from him and as I grew more successful in the business our relationship became both personal and professional. I played on nearly every session Larry produced and we even became a great songwriting team as well. Mary and I loved Larry and his wife and spent many great times at their magical little cottage up in the hills just above the Hollywood Bowl. I called it Sycamore Hideaway.

It was up at the Sycamore house where I first met Australian rock legend, Brian Cadd. He was visiting the Murrays and Larry thought it would be a great idea to get us together. From the instant we met we became the best of friends, a friendship that I'm proud to say remains just as strong today, 40 plus years later. Brian was a keyboard wizard, a hell of a writer and a legendary performer to boot. In Australia he was considered a legend having become one of the first successful singer/songwriters in Australian rock and roll history. We immediately hit it off, both sharing the same musical tastes and sense of humor. We also began playing a lot of sessions together in the weeks to come and found that we made a great recording team in the studio. In the years to follow we would become the best of friends, recording throughout the world together as well as songwriting and performing.

Brian Cadd

The Sycamore house was a magical little hideaway and the home of many great picking sessions. Larry and Laurette's tiny living room hosted some of the best singer songwriters on the scene at the time, names such as Kris Kristofferson, Jackson Browne, and Jennifer Warren, country singer Johnny Darrell, folk singer Mary McCaslin and many more. So much talent walked through the front door that it made your jaw drop. It was a great watering hole for a few artists whose names would eventually become written in the stars.

Around this time, my father became sick. He had developed stomach cancer and didn't have long to live. I had never dealt with losing a parent, so right up to the end I always thought dad would recover. Not living with my parents, I wasn't subjected to the day to day anxiety my mother was facing in dealing with his illness. They had always been inseparable and the thought of one living without the other was unimaginable. I would fly up to Napa, California where they now lived and visit as often as I could. Each time I noticed dad getting thinner and more ill. But I couldn't even conceive of the idea he would

actually die. There was no way that could ever happen to dad. In light
of dad's deterioration and the fact that Mary and I loved each other
dearly, we decided to get married up in Napa. I had recently won
custody of my daughter Sarah and Mary was a tremendous mom for
her. It wasn't a surprise to anyone when we announced our plans to
get married. Jerry Tate, Larry, Laurette and Brian Cadd and his new
wife Linda all drove up for the ceremony. Larry was my best man. It
was a beautiful ceremony and I was so grateful to Mary for allowing us
to be married up in Napa so that my dad could be there. Mary was the
most unselfish person whoever walked the Earth and I was the luckiest
guy that ever walked the Earth as well.

Now that we were a family of three, we needed a bigger place.
In the same courtyard where we lived, a bigger unit was available. It
belonged to a very attractive blonde girl who I had seen and talked to
quite often down at the mailbox. She was British and very pleasant.
Her name was Christine. I figured she must have been the wife or
girlfriend of someone in a band because many nights the silence of the
quiet little courtyard used to be broken by loud voices coming from
her place, as if a band meeting was in progress. This went on for quite
a while but nobody in the building seemed to care. Anyway, Christine
was moving out and the landlord decided to take me on a tour of her
2-bedroom apartment while she was out of town. When I walked in I
noticed all kinds of photos of famous musicians on the wall and then
I spotted one of Christine playing a keyboard onstage at some huge
festival. I asked the landlord what band she was in.

"Oh, let me remember" he said, followed by a long pause. "I
believe they are called "Fleetwood Mac."

"You mean the girl at the mailbox was Christine McVee?" I asked
in astonishment.

"Yes, that's her" replied the landlord. "I think her band just got a
record deal and so she's moving to Beverly Hills. Do you and
Mary want her place?"

"Absolutely" I said. "We'll take it."

With that, Mary, Sarah and I moved into Christine McVee's place. It still makes me laugh when I think about the many nights the little courtyard would be filled with the voices of Fleetwood Mac's band meetings. Only in Hollywood!

One day I received a call from Neil Diamond's guitarist, Richard Bennett. Richard and I had played many sessions together and were great friends as well. Richard told me about a new act that he had recently recorded with for Warner Brothers Records. They were two brothers from Dade City, Florida named David and Howard Bellamy. David was a staff songwriter for producer Phil Gernhardt and Howard was a road manager for comedian Jim Stafford. Phil had recently put them together on a song he had found written by Larry Williams called "Let Your Love Flow" and the song was starting to get huge airplay all over the country. The Bellamy's were now looking to put a band together for their first major tour and Richard recommended me to Gernhardt.

Warner Brothers had pumped a lot of money into the Bellamy Brothers and I was offered a pretty fat pay check to take the gig. I took it on the promise of playing on their recordings as well as touring and Gerhardt accepted my terms. No audition was required. When I first met Howard and David Bellamy it was at a house they were renting not far from the Troubadour. I was struck at how laid back and unaffected they were, as well as their very funny sense of humor. I liked them both from that very first meeting. Both of the brothers were relatively shy guys and as green as the grass with regard to being major smash hit artists. They had never really appeared together in front of a serious audience and although they were quite funny and animated off stage, onstage they were frozen solid like deer in the headlights.

"Let Your Love Flow" became the biggest single pop hit of the year and big money poured into the Bellamy Brothers like Niagara Falls. I became their band leader and I was supplied with any kind of vintage guitar my heart desired. From 1950's Telecasters to beautiful Gibson acoustic guitars, I had them all. We rehearsed at the Paramount Pictures movie lot on one of the giant sound stages where Gerhardt and the top management brass and label execs could sit and watch us. There wasn't much to watch. Howard and David stood up onstage like two wooden statues with absolutely no banter between songs. As a live act, they certainly were a "diamond in the rough."

Onstage at the legendary Palomino Club in Los Angeles with the Bellamy Brothers 1975

One of our first gigs was opening act for pop singer/songwriter Mac Davis. Mac was starting to shake things up on radio after scoring his first two singles, "I Believe In Music" and "Stop And Smell The Roses" at number one throughout the country. I was thrilled to be on the bill with Mac because my old friend and bandmate Thad Maxwell was now playing in his band, as well as a few other players who I knew very well. We did a gig up in San Jose, California that was especially meaningful to me. My dad, mother and brothers and sister all came to the show. It was a very rare occasion for them to see me onstage in a concert setting. But what made it more special was the fact that my father was seriously ill with cancer and this would be the last time he would see me perform. Mac heard about my father from Thad and arranged to have my family sit at the side of the stage to get a close-up view of the show. He even supplied my brothers and sister with souvenir t-shirts and posters. And to top things off, when Mac came back onstage for an encore, he took my little brother Joe with him at center stage to take a bow. My parents were thrilled as they watched from the curtains.

I was so moved by Mac's kindness that I wrote him a letter and asked Thad to deliver it to him personally. In the letter I thanked him for making my dad so happy and for helping to take his mind off of his terrible illness, if only for one night. I told Mac that it meant the world to me and that if he ever needed a guitarist, I would play behind him anytime and anywhere for free. Thad told me later that Mac was very emotional when he read the letter. I'm glad because every word in it came from my heart.

A few weeks later I awoke from a strange dream. I dreamt that my father had come to me asking me to take care of my youngest brother Joey. It was so real it woke me up. Just then Mary came in the room with a serious look on her face and gave me the telephone. It was a call from my brother Jim. Dad had died. I couldn't believe it. I lay in the bed frozen in disbelief. The unimaginable had happened and it had hit me like a ton of bricks. He had passed away at home, quietly in his sleep. The world stopped. Time froze. The room grew cold and dark. I didn't want to get up. Mary held me in her arms but the pain was well beyond any kind of comfort. The loss was insurmountable.

I flew up to Napa for the funeral. When I arrived at mom's house she greeted me at the door and took me to the bedroom. We sat down on the bed and I fell apart. I blamed dad's death on my career, my carefree life and the seemingly easy money I was making. It was God's way of teaching me a lesson, I thought. Mom held me and assured me that I was terribly wrong and told me how proud he was of my success, proud beyond any words he could come up with.

I had idolized him. I had run away from home because I wanted to do something that would make him proud, instead of him being kicked around by my aunt and grandmother. I wanted my last name to be known so that he and mom could hold their heads up and never be looked down upon ever again. I didn't get into the music business for any ego reason, I got into it for spite. To show those who looked down at my parents that my name and my father's name meant something more than they could ever have imagined. I know the reasoning was wrong and over the top but that's how I felt. It's what fueled me and kept me going all of those nights on the street. He was my inspiration and it was he who took the heat from family members for letting me chase my career. He was the greatest man I ever knew and his loss was the greatest pain I had ever felt. I remembered the words Johnny Tillotson once told me on the day I found out dad was sick. "John Edward, you're going to find that the older we get, the more difficult life becomes."

We buried dad on a beautiful hill overlooking Napa, the place he and mom had come to love so much. It was peaceful on that hill. The kind of peace he deserved after working so long and so hard for his six kids and my mom. I would fly back to Hollywood the following day after his funeral leaving behind a big part of my heart up on that hill. Life would never be the same for me ever again.

Once home I went straight to work recording a new album with the Bellamy's. I enjoyed working with producer Phil Gernhardt who was one of the top producers in Hollywood at the time. He could be very intimidating to many musicians. He seldom smiled and always dressed in black … black hair, black sunglasses and a black pencil mustache. He resembled the villain in a cheap 1940's cowboy B movie. Phil also wore a gold Quaalude around his neck as well, but made sure nobody who played for him did any drugs on his watch. Gerhardt had golden ears and could hear a hit song through a brick wall but he could be as blunt as a baseball bat, as well. If he didn't like a particular guitar part he would simply listen and say "I hate that fucking guitar riff." For other players it would be a shattering experience but for me I never paid his outbursts any mind and simply threw more ideas at him till one stuck. Because I wasn't intimidated my him, he respected me and treated me as a valuable asset to the Bellamy organization.

I played guitar on the brothers' new album called "Plain & Fancy" which yielded a massive European hit called "Crossfire." Years later, Howard and David told me that my guitar part for "Crossfire" would inspire the guitar part for Bonnie Tyler's huge hit "It's A Heartache". Bonnie herself told the guys that little secret. I was more than happy to take credit for it, as well!

Unfortunately, "Crossfire" failed to do anything on the US charts and the Bellamy's now found themselves as "one hit wonders." This didn't stop them from touring, however. We played a few weeks in Las Vegas at the Golden Nugget showroom and became friends with the manager of the lounge, a sharp good looking young guy named Steve Wynn. Little did any of us know that he would go on to reinvent the town and become one of the most successful and richest businessmen in the world. But that was years to come. For now, Steve would hang with us backstage making sure we were comfortable and that everything ran smoothly.

After Vegas we hit the road as opening act for the Loggins and Messina "farewell tour". Kenny and Jim were terrific guys to tour with and onstage they were exceptional, especially the very animated Kenny Loggins who would hurl tambourines high into the air, spin around and catch them again while singing as the same time. They had a fabulous band and an incredible show and their road crew treated us great. Together we traveled across the southwest until we reached Chicago. There we were booked to play a club owned by some of the members of the band Chicago, called The Beginings.

The night before the gig we checked into the Holiday Inn and settled down for a good night's sleep. I was glad to be back in Chicago again, hoping to see old friends and possibly make a quick run out to Hometown for some Vito & Nick's Pizza after the show. The next morning a heavy knock on my door woke me up. I thought it was the maid, or perhaps one of the guys who, as a joke, took my "Do Not Disturb" sign off of my doorknob.

"Who is it?" I yelled out in an irritated tone.

"JB" came the familiar voice of our roadie Bobby Thompson, who we all called "Norton" because of his father being the famous comedian, Art Carney.

"Get up, brother. Bad news. The equipment truck has been stolen. Everything's gone!"
I ran to the door in a panic. "Bobby, are joking?"

But Bobby was not joking and it was evident from the look on his face. "It's all over, brother" he said as if he was also in a state of shock. "The cops are in the lobby making a report out right now. Looks like we're headed back home." And that's just what happened. With no gear, there was no band. Gigs were cancelled and we limped back to LA. I had lost more than 20 thousand dollars' worth of vintage guitars, mandolins and amplifiers. It was a disaster. But that wouldn't be the worst of it!

When we arrived home I was told that the Bellamy's would not be responsible for any of the gear that was stolen. There would be no compensation. How could this be? I tried to get Howard and David on the phone but they wouldn't face me. Instead, I was told by their management, the Scotti Brothers, that it was up to me to re-stock my guitar collection and that the boys were not financially responsible for the loss of any of my gear. I was as mad as I had ever been and not only gave my notice, but immediately called the Musicians' Union and informed them what had happened. The Union swung into action and called the Bellamy's management threatening to have them blacklisted unless I was compensated. Well, this certainly didn't sit well with the Bellamy's camp. Then, late one night I received a phone call from a very stoned Phil Gernhardt.

"John, Phil here" came the cryptic voice.

"Uh, hi Phil. What's up?" I cautiously asked.

Phil's voice was slurred, and he spoke slowly and mysteriously as if he was narrating a cheap detective thriller.

"John, John, John. What the hell are you doing, man?" Gernhardt whispered. "You can't go on with this lawsuit against the boys. You don't know who you're fucking with, man. These are heavy people. Do you know what I'm saying?"

"No, Phil. What *are* you saying?" I shot back.

"Look John, I like you. That's why I'm just saying that tomorrow when you get up be sure to check under your car before you start it."

I stood there frozen with the phone in my hand.

"What do you mean, Phil"?

"That's all I'm saying, John. You have a great career ahead of you. Don't fuck with these people. Think about dropping that lawsuit and come on back to the boys. They still want to work with you and I'll keep you busy in the studio. Just don't fuck up things and get yourself hurt."

And with that, Phil hung up.

I stood there with the dial tone ringing in my ear as Mary asked who the call was from. I was concerned for her and didn't want her upset. She was now pregnant with our first child and I didn't want anything to jeopardize her health. I sat her down and told her everything but reassured her that I would take measures to insure our safety. Mary was shaking but kept calm and cool and didn't get hysterical.

Immediately, I called up famed producer Jimmy Bowen, whom I had just started recording for on a steady basis as part of his stellar session band. Jimmy was also my publisher and we had recently just enjoyed two of my songs becoming top 10 hits for country artist Thom Bresh. Jimmy was as big as they get. He had produced "That's Life" for Frank Sinatra and even ran his label Reprise as President. He and Frank were tight. I told Jimmy what had happened with Phil. I was scared for my family and didn't make any effort to hide it from Bowen.

"Now calm down and tell me exactly what he said" Jimmy instructed in his calm southern Texas accent. I told him word for word what Phil had said.

"OK" said a very relaxed Jimmy Bowen. "Put Mary on the phone."

Jimmy calmed her down by assuring her that Phil was acting on his own and simply stoned out of his brain not realizing anything he was saying. He told Mary to not worry and that he would see to the whole matter and not to let anything Phil said have an effect on her and the baby's health. Mary gave the phone back to me obviously looking a hell of a lot more calmed down.

"John, let me make a couple calls and see what the hell is going on here. Don't worry about a fucking thing. Go to bed and I'll talk to you in the morning."

The very next day someone from the florist shop showed up at our front door with a bouquet of flowers. Inside was a note apologizing for "Phil's behavior" and praising my talent and professionalism, and it was signed "from Scotti Brothers Management". There's no doubt that Bowen made a few "calls" himself and the matter was quickly defused. I would love to have been a fly on the wall when the Scotti Brothers called Gerhardt in on the carpet that morning.

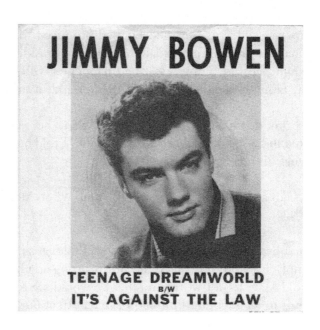

My mentor producer Jimmy Bowen

26 ELVIS AND KIM

One night while Mary and I were out Christmas shopping on Hollywood Blvd., I received a recorded phone message from none other than Joe Guercio. When we arrived home I listened to the message and was disturbed by the anger in his voice. "John, this is Joe. Where the hell are you for Christ sake? Do you want to work, or not?" and then he hung up.

"Where the hell does he get off leaving me a shitty message like that?" I asked Mary. I called him back. Joe answered and before I could say anything he said "Do want to work for E or not?" "E" meaning none other than Elvis. I thought he was joking until he explained. "Burton just turned in his notice and he's going to play for Emmylou Harris. The spots open if you want it"

James Burton had played guitar for Elvis since his comeback debut at the International Hotel in 1970. Prior to Elvis, he played guitar for another hero of mine, Ricky Nelson. His style on the Fender Telecaster was responsible in a big way for the hits that Ricky scored back in the late 50's and throughout the 60's. His solo on "Hello Marylou" and "Travelin Man" were iconic. I was a diehard James Burton student and ironically, my own style of playing mirrored his which is one of the reasons I was asked to take James's place. One of the other reasons I was offered the Presley gig was that I knew and worked with most of his band on various recording projects, including Guercio's.

"Hell yeah I want it!" came my answer.

"Alright" answered Joe. I'll get the albums out to you and you start rehearsing. Someone from the office will get to you on the other details. Welcome aboard. Next time stay close to your telephone."

Conductor, Joe Guercio and the King

I was ecstatic and shouted out the news to Mary. This was as big as it gets in Hollywood and now I was about to be catapulted to a much higher profile in town and that meant more money and more session work, not to mention the chance to play behind the king of rock & roll himself.

I called my mom up and told her the news and of course she was in the clouds. It was good to share some "good news" after the ordeal of losing dad. Word traveled quickly and soon everyone I knew seemed to have heard the news. It was a very exciting time, to say the least.

In the meantime, while I awaited word from the Elvis camp, I stayed busy with recording dates, playing on everything from pop sessions to television commercials. I even found time to fly up to Reno, Nevada to back up the popular Hager Twins, from the hit television show Hee Haw. Jon and Jim Hager were a ball to play behind. They had a great sense of humor and I enjoyed their brand of Bakersfield country music, which was not far removed from that of Buck Owens.

Jon and Jim were super friendly and treated myself and the band like true professionals. The audience loved them and although they weren't the greatest singers in country music, they were terrific entertainers who knew how to win over any audience. Sadly, both Jon and Jim are gone now. Ironically, they both passed away a year apart from each other, Jim on May 1st, 2008 and Jon on January 9th, 2009

At this time, I also started work on an album by singer/songwriter Kim Carnes, a new upcoming artist who was starting to gain a strong following in radio. Kim was a fantastic artist with a raspy voice not unlike Rod Stewart or Bonnie Tyler and a talent for writing the most beautiful songs imaginable. Kim got her start, like many others, as a member of the "The New Christy Minstrels" and it was there she met her future husband, songwriter Dave Ellingston. Both were a joy to work with, and the sessions for what would become one of her most critically acclaimed albums "St. Vincent's Court" would include a stellar line up of the "who's-who" of L.A session greats. Besides myself, the recording band featured Little Feat drummer Richie Hayward, Lee Sklar on bass, Bill Cuomo on keys, Matt and Danny Moore with Brian Cadd on vocals along with Bobby Cochran on additional guitars. I was honored to get the call to play mandolin as well as electric and acoustic guitars. It was evident from the very start that Kim would eventually become a super star. She was so talented and such a professional who knew exactly what she wanted in the studio. She was a sheer joy to have worked with.

Back at home the news wasn't as good. I received a call from a very upset Joe Guercio.

"Burton decided to come back, man." Straight to the point, in true Joe Guercio style.

"The fucker took a 50 cent raise and came back" he said sarcastically.

"Sorry man, I know this is a letdown for you. We'll work on some other stuff again soon."

And with that, I lost the Elvis gig. There was nothing to do but call friends and family and let them know what happened.

From what I had gathered, the guys in Elvis's band weren't that thrilled with Burton coming back after jumping ship. I knew all the guys so well that it was a real let down not to be able to work with them but it was a bigger let down not getting the chance to play for the King. In the years that followed, I worked with various members of his band and had heard about how difficult and agonizing it had been to work for Elvis during those final two years of his life. In a way, I'm glad I wasn't a part of it. I had been through the mill with Kristofferson and certainly didn't want to find myself in the same position with Elvis or anyone else. Things happen for a reason and I'm convinced to this day that losing the gig with the King of rock & roll in the final years of his life was a blessing in disguise. Still, it *was* Elvis Presley and it would have surely been a nice feather in my career hat. But life and career go on so, "that's alright, mama".

Losing the Elvis gig was disappointing, but as luck would have it I didn't have to wait long for another offer to come rolling in. My recording sessions with Kim Carnes had turned out so well that she offered me the lead guitar spot in her new band soon to be hitting the road as opening act for Neil Sedaka. Sedaka had been enjoying an enormous comeback after not only writing the hit song "Love Will Keep Us Together" for pop duo Captain & Tennille, but enjoying his first major top ten hit in years as a single artist with "Laughter In The Rain". He had signed with Elton John's new label and was riding high on the charts and now playing major concert halls throughout the country. Kim's band was fantastic with Bill Cuomo on keys, Jim Varley on drums, husband Dave on guitar along with ex-Kenny Rogers & The First Edition veteran, Mike Settle on acoustic guitar and vocals. All the guys were terrific to work with and total pro's onstage. This was going to be fun. To kick things off we appeared on the NBC rock show Midnight Special and performed two songs. Kim was great onstage and her powerful voice was spot-on perfect.

We hit the road with Neil Sedaka mostly playing classy concert halls. The audiences were usually in their mid-thirties and up and a lot more well behaved than the crowd I had played to with Ronstadt or Arlo.

In New Orleans Kim, Dave and Mike helped celebrate my 26th birthday by getting me drunk for the first time in my life at the hotel lounge following our concert. Upstairs in the club an Elvis impersonator named Elvis Wade was appearing and everyone thought it would be a hoot to watch him. The waiter sat us front row center at a table right at the front of the stage making it difficult for us to keep a straight face while Elvis Wade launched into his tribute show. I wasn't paying attention to the amount of beer I was drinking and was starting to get rather light headed as the show went on. Wade would keep looking our way, probably aware that he had some high-profile music people in his audience, he would sing "Love Me Tender" looking straight into Kim's eyes as beer would shoot out my nose from trying not to bust out laughing.

The funniest moment came when Wade sang the Presley classic "American Trilogy," the huge production number so famous in all of the real Presley performances. The trouble was that this particular Elvis didn't carry a 40-piece orchestra, just a five-man band, which featured the bass player playing two instruments at once, his bass guitar and a trumpet. It was hilarious. Then at the final crescendo, when it comes time for him to hit the last, dramatic high note at the end of "His truth goes marching…on" Wade dramatically sang the song with all the Elvis he had inside of him. That is, except for the final high note. Instead, as the drummer played a big roll, Wade bent down and sang "His truth goes marching….." and then tilted his head and pointed to his bass player, who casually walked up to the microphone and in a high squeaky voice sang out, "ON!"

That did it. We all collapsed at the table laughing hysterically as the band played the familiar Elvis parting theme song. Wade took his bow and disappeared back into obscurity as we tried to collect ourselves. Mike Settle got me back to my room. I fell on the bed and the room started spinning like a Coney Island ride.

"Hey this is cool" I shouted. "This is the greatest birthday of my life!"

Just then the ride stopped and I felt something not quite so good. "Oh no" I thought, and ran to the bathroom where I spent the next several hours. The next morning as we were boarding the airport limo I felt as if the weight of the world was sitting on my face. That would be the last time I would drink a beer for the next few years!

The tour ended in New York City where we played Avery Fisher Hall to a sold-out crowd. It was a fitting climax to a wonderful tour which I was sad to see come to an end. After the show I went to

Neil Sedaka's dressing room and asked him for an autographed photo as a memento of our touring together. He was a bit of a space cadet and hard to get a read on, but very pleasant even if he hadn't a clue who I was. He signed the picture and I tucked it quickly under my arm without reading it. I thanked him and expressed how much of an honor it was to have toured with him.

When I got back to my hotel room and looked at the picture, it simply read "To John, nice seeing you, Neil Sedaka." *"Nice seeing you?"* I thought. I had been touring for five weeks with the man and all he could come up with was *"Nice seeing you?"* Needless to say, the photo never made it to my wall.

I loved working with Kim and her husband Dave and the rest of the band. I would go on to record one more album with her called "Sailing" and remain good friends in the years to come. Our pianist Bill Cuomo would stay on with Kim and eventually produce her mammoth hit single "Betty Davis Eyes." I was so happy for her. It was always a joy to see someone so talented and grounded hit the bell, and Kim certainly did just that.

That same year I found myself back in the studio with none other than Joe Guercio and the Elvis band recording a national TV commercial for Hilton Hotels. Joe was close to Baron Hilton and was able to secure the advertising account for the ad. Joe and I co-wrote the jingle and I was hired to sing the theme song, backed by the Sweet Inspirations. It was a financial windfall for me for a couple of reasons. Having co-written the jingle, Joe and I received a flat fee of $10,000.00 each. But singing it was another story.

During the session Joe was a pile of nerves. As conductor for Presley, Joe commanded all authority and nobody dared to question his actions. Joe was used to calling the shots. But on a recording date he lacked control and confidence, especially when he found himself producing a high dollar ad campaign for Hilton Hotels. All the big shots from Hilton as well as the ad agency were in the booth while the session was on. It was total confusion in the control booth with everyone talking at once and each with his own idea on how things should be done. All of this added to Joe's frustration as he tried his best to maintain an element of calmness to the studio players.

Elvis's band, Ronnie Tutt, Jerry Scheff, Glen D Hardin and James Burton laid down the track as I sang lead in the vocal booth. Guercio worked everyone hard and put us through take after take until we were headed for over time. Two of the Sweet Inspirations had another session and much to their frustration had to leave, but Joe demanded that they stay and finish his date. Every take seemed perfect but for some reason Guercio wasn't pleased and kept pushing the musicians and singers to do more and more until finally two of the Sweet Inspirations threw their headphones off and walked off the date. Tempers were heated and now there was nobody left to add harmonies. No problem, I just overdubbed my own harmonies, much to the relief of Guercio. For that effort, I was paid 3 times more than I was originally supposed to make, and that meant thousands of extra dollars in residuals from AFTRA (American Federation of Television & Radio Artists). The commercial spots ran during the Nixon-Frost interviews, one of the most watched shows in television history.

27 MAC DAVIS AND PEACH TUXEDOS

My long-time buddy and partner in crime Thad Maxwell phoned me one day to say that he was leaving Mac Davis to join a new band made up of members from the legendary country rock group, the Flying Burrito Brothers. This left the guitar spot open in Mac's band and Thad suggested to Mac that I be the one to fill it. I liked Mac a lot, especially after all the kindness he showed to my father back when I shared the bill with him while playing with the Bellamy's. By now Mac had his own network variety show and was riding high on a string of pop hits such as "Stop and Smell the Roses", "I Believe in Music", "Baby Don't Get Hooked on Me", "Something's Burning" and a few others. He was also appearing all over television from the Tonight Show to Midnight Special as well as selling out Las Vegas shows at the MGM Grand Hotel.

Mac career's was as hot as hot gets. I also respected him as a songwriter and put him right up there with Kris Kristofferson. Mac wrote Elvis's most critically acclaimed hit "In the Ghetto" as well as "Sweet Memories". He also penned the hit "Watching Scotty Grow" for Bobby Goldsboro. Mac had the talent and the credibility, and I was more than happy to jump on board.

However, from the first day I rehearsed with Mac's band I felt a bit uneasy. The other musicians seemed to act as if they were the stars of the show and not Mac. A few of them had an arrogance as well as a sour attitude towards country music, fancying themselves as hard rockers in the same vein as Led Zeppelin or AC/DC. Furthermore, they seemed removed from any sensitivity towards Mac's music, just going through the motions and playing what was written down on their charts. They were a touring band and not a solid recording unit like the kind of bands I was used to working with in the studio.

Overseeing the rehearsals, which were held at Studio Instrument Rentals soundstage in Hollywood, was famed producer Mike Post whose credits included the music for TV shows like The Rockford Files and NYPD Blue. Mike also produced the big hit "Classical Gas" for Mason Williams. Post was big time and a very tough guy to work for. I had heard all about the way he chewed out road musicians for not reading charts correctly or for playing the wrong parts. He would call players out in front of everyone and humiliate them for their lack of professionalism. I wasn't about to let myself be subjected to that, so once again I phoned my old session boss Jimmy Bowen for help.

Mike Post's career would have never happened had it not been for Jimmy Bowen, whom Mike worked under for many years. They were tight friends and Post respected Bowen who was still one of the top record producers and label heads in the business. I explained to Jimmy about getting the gig with Mac and that I was worried about facing Mike Post, namely because I couldn't read music. I was given a great ear by the man upstairs and could play just about anything a producer or artist needed, but like Glen Campbell, I could not read written notes. I feared this would lead to a showdown with Post, and probably in front of the entire band. Bowen knew my worth. I was his main session guitarist at that time and not just your average road band musician. "Don't worry about a thing, man." Bowen said in that Texas drawl. "I'll speak to Mike about it."

When Mike Post entered the rehearsal hall on my first day as guitarist I was a bit nervous. All the band members had music stands and charts except for me. Mac's guitarist, a loud boisterous heavy-set character named Jefferson, was a bit of a self-ordained big shot in the band and told me in a loud voice so all would hear, "Hey Beland, wait until Post finds out you can't read his charts."

I didn't say anything. I just set up my gear and prepared to rehearse. Mike came into the hall and before we started up, asked to see me privately. I put my guitar down and walked out into the hall with him, to the snickers of Mac's band going on behind us. "Hi John" Mike said in a warm friendly tone as he shook my hand. "Listen, man. Jimmy called me last night and filled me in about you. He really had some great stuff to say and wanted to let me know that you're the real deal. I know you can't read charts but neither could another one of Bowen's guitarists, Glen Campbell. I know you're a serious session player and that you work for the biggest producer in town and that's good enough for me. Don't worry about a thing. These knot heads of Mac's like to screw around and not take this stuff seriously. That's why I jump down their asses. Don't worry about me. We're cool and it's good to have you on board." What a relief. Good ol' Bowen.

Onstage with Mac Davis 1977

The first gig I did with Mac was at the MGM Grand Hotel in Las Vegas. And I was a bit shocked at the kind of show Mac was doing. I expected it to be more about Mac Davis, the respected singer-songwriter. Instead, Mac's show reflected his weekly CBS variety show, with dancers and singers and other people's material including a 50's oldies medley with flashy lights and corny choreography. To top things off, the band had to wear these god-awful peach colored tuxedos and sit in an orchestra section with the horns and the violins led by a conductor who was also in a peach tuxedo, waving his baton and beating a tambourine adorned with fancy colored ribbons. I felt totally out of place watching all this unfold. This was nothing like the show Mac did a year before when my folks came to see us. I kept my mouth shut and did my gig, mostly playing 2nd guitar to Jefferson, the ringmaster and leader of Mac's rhythm section. The only decent part of the show came when Mac sang "In the Ghetto" accompanied on acoustic guitars by Jefferson and myself and a string section. It was powerful and showed Mac to be a sensitive, credible artist and not the plastic image he was projecting all through the rest of his performance.

Off stage things were just as strange. Mac's band, led by

Jefferson, seemed to jump on any musician who had other things going for them besides Mac Davis. Mike Boddicker was a skilled keyboardist, who was starting to be in high demand in the studio. Mac's band never seemed to let up on him, calling him names and ribbing him relentlessly all because of his recent studio success. I soon had learned that such was the way in the Mac Davis organization from the band all the way up to Mac, who was also very opinionated and seemingly jealous of any other artist's success. It was a "good ol' boys" club for sure. You either played along or you were an outcast. Boddicker eventually quit and went on to record with Michael Jackson leaving the Mac Davis band and their peach tuxedos behind in a cloud of smoke.

After Vegas we hit the road with Mac playing rodeos and fairs throughout the country. These shows were a bit more down to earth since we didn't carry horns or strings and didn't have to wear ridiculous peach tuxedos. It was a more honest show and Mac was very good onstage, and much more relaxed and believable than the MGM Grand fiasco. Mac was an interesting person. He could be a real down to earth guy until a skirt entered the room. Then he became another macho guy ... arrogant and smart ass and not much fun to be around. He was hard to get close to, unlike Kristofferson or Ronstadt. In fact, he rarely had a word to say to me other than an occasional word or two at rehearsals. Now and then he would hang with the band and join in the comradery. But for the most part he was aloof and not that easy to get to know.

Mac Davis was managed by one of the biggest managers in Hollywood, Sandy Gallin, whose roster included such celebrities as Michael Jackson, Neil Diamond, Barbara Streisand, Richard Gere, Joan Rivers and many more of the top names in the business. I believe that Mac simply got caught up in the celebrity of it all and in the process lost track of who he really was. He became a television celebrity and slowly drifted away from the credibility he had received as a respected hit song writer. As part of the Gallin stable of Hollywood celebs, Mac seemed to lose the audience that mattered the most, the same fan base that followed Kristofferson, Dylan, and Willie Nelson, etc. Instead he opted for TV and Las Vegas and occasional corny films roles ... becoming a hamster in a wheel, of sorts.

I came to resent the Mac Davis gigs. Now I became the brunt of the jokes when the band caught on that I was recording a new solo album with Jimmy Bowen, and that I was continuing to fly to Nashville and L.A for session work. All the cheap shots were aimed my way from playing "hillbilly music" to playing "that country shit." I felt trapped but didn't want to leave Mac because of the new baby and the fact that we needed a bigger place than what we had been living in back in Hollywood, so I reluctantly agreed for us to move to the suburbs ... to a house Mary had found, right down the street from the Maxwell's.

The touring seemed endless. The same old fairs and rodeos and the same old faces around me 24/7. I felt detached from everyone, even Mary. In my heart I knew I didn't belong in Mac's gig. My place was playing a more credible part in the music business than peach tuxedos and an endless parade of county fairs. I was unhappy and lost. As Mac's touring took us eastward we were joined in New England by our new opening act. Dolly Parton.

Dolly was something straight out of the wildest imagination possible. Onstage she wore pink chiffon gowns and huge blonde wigs with long finger nails and a shape that had been the brunt of jokes on every TV talk show in the country. Naturally, the guys in Mac's band were relentless in their wise cracks and bad jokes about Dolly and I'm certain she heard them, or at least knew what they were saying behind her back. They considered her a "hick" and a "hillbilly" while at the same time under the delusion that they were famous heavy rockers from Los Angeles. One day, between shows, I happened to spot Dolly sitting alone backstage and so I walked up to her and introduced myself.

"Hi Dolly" I said, "I'm John Beland, one of Mac's guitarists."

With possibly the warmest smile in show business, she looked up to me and said "Well, it's certainly good to see you too, John Beland."

Dolly and I in New England shortly after we first met. I was still with Mac, but not for long

"Sit down here and talk to me" she demanded with that devilish smile.

"You know Dolly, I met you years ago in the hallway at WSM after you had finished an interview with Ralph Emmory and I'm rather embarrassed about it."

"Wait a minute" she said as she squinted her eyes and studied mine.

"You were that naughty guy in Linda's band making fun about me and thinking I didn't see you. I remember you, John Beland."

Then Dolly laughed out loud and simply dismissed it with, "OH, boys will be boys"

From that moment on we became good friends. We chatted about everything and I felt as if I had known her my entire life and for the remainder of the tour we would become very close and share many thoughts and feelings between us.

Mac's band gave me hell for seeing Dolly. "Hey Beland, hanging out with your hillbilly girlfriend again?" Over the following weeks on tour Dolly knew I was unhappy with Mac. I told her that I detested the gig, especially his band. She reminded me of the insults and barbs she had to contend with when she first arrived in Nashville. It seems that such ignorance always comes from the smallest of people and in the case of the Mac Davis Band you couldn't find anything or anyone smaller. At the end of the tour I said goodbye to Dolly. I felt a strong bond between us as well as a tug at the heart too. I had a feeling we would see each other again. Talk about an understatement.

Summer found us back in Las Vegas playing yet another two-week run at the MGM Grand Hotel. Once again, we put on the peach tuxedos and played the same old boring show twice a night. By now Mac had fired Jefferson and the rest of his band except for keyboardist Rick Lipp and I. He had it with their juvenile pranks and lack of professionalism. The final straw came when the entire band, with the exception of myself and Rick, demanded a raise from Mac. Jefferson wanted us all to demand a raise from Mac's office. Mob rule. I wanted no part of it, much to their disdain. In an instant they were fired. They were replaced quickly by more competent musicians and for a while life with the Mac Davis show actually became tolerable. Jefferson and his cohorts faded away into obscurity never to be seriously heard from again.

One cool thing that happened to me at the MGM Grand Hotel was bumping into a very shy young singer backstage in the dressing room area. Like so many times before, I had arrived in Vegas a day early to get my clothes and guitars settled into the band dressing room. This also gave me a chance to catch the closing shows of the previous week's acts who were appearing there. This time, it was the incredible Jackson 5 who were closing out a week's run. Amazingly, the Jacksons weren't doing bang up business at the Grand and only playing to little more than a half-filled room. At this time in their careers the public had seemingly grown bored with them and their hits were now few and far between. But I was a huge fan of their front man, the amazing Michael and I couldn't wait to hear them. I was just coming out of the band dressing room when I spotted Michael in the empty hallway. There was nobody else around so I simply walked over to him and introduced myself.

"Hi, Michael" I said extending my hand. "I'm Mac Davis's guitarist, John Beland"

Michael was a handsome kid, tall skinny and no signs of any cosmetic work on his face, which was relatively still black. He was a very friendly guy and he shook my hand very gently, saying with a smile and a soft high-pitched voice

"Oh hi, John. So nice to meet you."

"It's a real honor to meet you, Michael" I replied. "I'm a big fan of yours."

He seemed embarrassed but smiled and said, "Thank you very much."

"You know, Michael, I grew up on the south side of Chicago and James Brown was a huge influence on the bands I started out with. I know he was a big influence with you from what I heard."

Michael lit right up when I mentioned James Brown.

"Oh my, yes of course. He had a huge impact on me. He still does!"

"Well, it's a real thrill to meet you, Michael. I'm sure you've heard that a million times. I'm really glad I came here a day early so I could watch your show."

"That's so nice of you, John. Good luck with Mack and have a great gig here. I better get downstairs for the last show."

"Well, I'll be watching from the wings. Knock 'em dead" I said as he headed down the stairs to the stage area, followed by his brothers.

They were all dressed in flashy outfits and seemed very tight with each other. From the side of the stage I watched their show. They carried a very big band complete with a killer horn section but they also played their own instruments too, and were damned good! When the show started up and the curtain rose I could not believe my eyes and ears. The Jackson 5 rocked the MGM. They were sensational. But the real magic was with Michael. I had never witnessed a performer with so much talent as Michael Jackson. He floated across the stage like magic and sang his heart out with the ease and conviction of a seasoned veteran. I stood there with my jaw dropped. It was almost like a religious experience watching that kid perform. The crowd, mostly black, went crazy as Michael and his brothers went through hit after hit with the energy of a comet. It was one of the greatest performances I have ever seen.

As they finished the final song and the curtain dropped Michael walked by me covered in sweat, and stopped and smiled "How was the show, John?"

"Man," I said in a state of shock "That was the most incredible show I had ever seen. You were brilliant, man."

Michael laughed out loud, smiled and said "Have a great gig, John. It was great meeting you" and with that he went up the steps to the dressing room. Michael Jackson would climb a hell of a lot higher than that in the months to follow! I was truly blessed to have met him and witness the incredible talent he possessed. He remains the greatest act I have ever seen on any stage.

On August 16, 1977 I woke from a long sleep to a startling telephone call from one of Mac's roadies. Elvis was dead. He had been found in his bathroom at Graceland and the news hit Las Vegas like an atom bomb. It was as if someone had thrown a bucket of cold water on me as I sat up and immediately tried to call Joe Guercio, who lived only a few miles away from my hotel.

Joe was too distraught to come to the phone but his wife Corky confirmed the news. The king of rock and roll had died. That night we had to do another show at the MGM Grand with Mac. It would be a strange evening, considering the news of Presley's death. Elvis was loved by all the stage hands and musicians along the strip and the news hit everyone hard.

Strangely enough, Mac showed up backstage calm and cool and

seemingly unaffected by the news. Weird when you consider that in a big way he owed his career to Elvis recording "In the Ghetto." During the past engagements Mac had been throwing out tasteless jokes about Elvis's weight gain to the Las Vegas audience. For example, just prior to us performing "In the Ghetto" Mac would say to the crowd, "I wonder what fat farm Elvis is at this week." The MGM stagehands were so tired of Mac's tasteless jokes about Elvis that once they even complained to Mac's conductor about it, threatening to walk off if Mac persisted in making fun of Presley's condition.

That night, we did the show with Mac. The room was packed. Then came the part we dreaded, the spot where we played the hit song Mac had written for Elvis, "In the Ghetto." I sat on the stool at the front of the stage alongside of Mac and began the opening riff on my acoustic guitar. Mac didn't say much at all about Elvis's passing. He just went straight into the song. It was quite emotional playing "In the Ghetto" that night, hearing the violins so sweet and yet so sad playing behind us. But what made it even harder was hearing the sobs and seeing the tears of those sitting in the front rows, all effected deeply by the events of the day. For his part, Mac sang the song and dedicated it to Elvis then proceeded with the rest of his show, smoke bombs, dance routines and all.

A few weeks later we were playing at a fair somewhere near Memphis, Tennessee. We were on an outdoor stage as always and there was a packed grandstand of fans there to see Mac. The show proceeded as usual until we got to "In the Ghetto." You could have heard a pin drop as we played. For three minutes, complete silence as Mac sang the tune that helped launch his own career. When we finished there was a momentary silence followed by applause and then heavier applause and then thunderous applause along with a long-standing ovation. Mac stood there frozen and obviously affected by the outpouring of emotion from the audience. Everyone onstage was moved and out in the audience the applause wouldn't stop. The show was cut short and Mac retired to his trailer dressing room. As I was putting my guitar away one of the roadies came up to me.

"Hey John. Don't go to Mac's dressing room. He's had a breakdown and crying his eyes out."

I thought "I'll be damned, he *is* human after all."

28 SOLO ALBUM IN NASHVILLE – 2 SHOWS A NIGHT IN VEGAS

Back in L.A, Jimmy Bowen had left a message with my answering service wanting to get together with me for a brief meeting. That night we met at Hollywood Sound Recorders on Selma Avenue where he produced most of his sessions. I found him in the control room, cool and calm as always. "Hey John" he said in that famous Texas drawl "Sit down. Let's talk."

Bowen leaned back in his producer's chair, smoking a joint and tipping back his trademark fisherman's cap. "How'd you like to do a solo album for Atlantic?" he said. I was shocked but this was classic Jimmy Bowen, always hitting you off guard with news.

"Well, I guess so, Jimmy. But I really haven't written anything for myself as an artist. In fact, I haven't given much thought to doing another solo project at all."

"Well start writing then because here's the deal. The future is in Nashville. Your future is in Nashville. Something big is happening there and I'm going to be part of it. I want you to be part of it as well. Music is changing and the tide is going to be shifting to country music. Not the shitty old style outdated redneck crap, but new writers, young intelligent artists as well as new recording technologies. It may not be evident this year, but mark my words when I say that it's going to be big and you need to focus on pulling up roots and heading to Tennessee. L.A is dying but the music isn't."

I listened intensely as Jimmy spoke of the future of pop/country music. I respected him more than any other person in town and didn't take a word he said lightly.

"Well, put me down for it." I answered. "I'll start writing now."

"Good boy" he said while taking another hit. "When you think you're ready, let me know. We'll be recording in Nashville at Glaser Brothers Studio where my new office will be. We're going to do some good stuff together, John."

I was thrilled but concerned. I didn't know if I was emotionally ready to tackle another solo run. I had been so busy as a session musician and playing with Mac Davis that I pretty much put any solo ambitions on the back burner. But I wasn't about to turn it down either. When opportunity knocks I'm the first one to open the door.

In the months that followed I flew back and forth between Nashville and Los Angeles recording my solo album with Jimmy Bowen. Atlantic Records flew me first class to and from Nashville and put me up at the famous Spence Manor hotel on Music Row. Money seemed to be no object.

At Glaser Brothers Studio I recorded my album with the help of the best musicians in town like Reggie Young on 2nd guitar and Jimmy Capps on acoustic guitar. On drums I used the great Larri Londin as well as Jerry Carrigan. On bass the one and only Joe Osborne, who had played on all the early Ricky Nelson records. On keys, the legendary David Briggs. It was a great band and all the guys were as nice as could be.

It was fun working with Jimmy Bowen as my producer and his engineer Ron Treat at the board. They were always open to any idea I had and not once was I ever vetoed on a suggestion.

For one particular song "True Love Never Runs Dry" I wanted some harmony parts, as the song was written with the Everly Brothers in mind.

"No problem" replied Bowen as he picked up the phone.

I sat next to Jimmy behind the board, curious on who he was calling.

"Donald, Bowen here. Listen, John Beland's doing a solo album and he's got this Everly style song and it needs harmonies. Can you do it? Great! We'll see ya tomorrow at Glaser Brothers at 10pm."

With that, Jimmy hung up the phone.

"Who did you call, Jimmy?" I asked.

"Well, if you're going to do a song like the Everly Brothers, you need an Everly Brother. Just talked to Don and he'll be here tomorrow."

I was frozen! "You mean to say that I'm singing with Don Everly tomorrow night?" I asked in amazement.

Bowen seemed unaffected. He and Don were the best of friends so it wasn't any stretch for him to call one half of the most famous vocal duo in rock and roll history on the phone and get him to sing on my project. Not only that, but the Everly Brothers were my biggest influence ever. Bigger than the Beatles. I couldn't wait for the session the following evening.

The next night, a terrible thunderstorm hit Nashville. Jimmy and I had arrived at the studio just before the heavens opened. Our engineer Ron Treat had the tape all set for the evenings vocal session with Don Everly and myself. I was like a kid on Christmas Eve and couldn't wait to work with one of my all-time heroes. But as the night progressed and the storm grew more intense, there was no sign of Don Everly. There was a closed-circuit camera by the back door of the studio that fed into the control room, but nobody resembling the famous Everly Brother showed up.

The only person who appeared at the back door was unrecognizable to any of us on the screen. It was most likely one of the many "colorful" characters who strolled Music Row, crashing in on sessions wherever possible. The man on the screen was a stocky guy with his coat pulled up over a cab driver's floppy hat. He kept banging on the door, but Ron Treat said to ignore him as he was most likely one of the weirdo's of the Row. Eventually, after getting nearly drowned in the huge rain storm, the stocky figure in the floppy hat disappeared.

Unfortunately for us, the rain must have kept our legendary vocal guest away too, because Don failed to show up for the session. "Well, shit" said Bowen. "Let's call it a night. John, here's Don's phone number. Give him a call in the morning and find out what the hell happened to him."

"OK, Jimmy" I replied, disappointed that I didn't get to sing with my hero that night.

In the morning I called the number Bowen had given me. The recognizable voice of Don Everly came over the phone.

"Hello?" he asked.

"Hello Don, this is John Beland calling."

Suddenly Don's voice became angry and he shouted back "Where the fuck where you guys last night?" I hadn't a clue what Don was talking about. "We were in the studio waiting for you," I responded.

"Well couldn't you hear me banging on the goddamned door?" he said in a pissed off tone.

"Man, we couldn't hear you or see you on the outside camera" I responded. "The only person we saw was….. And then it hit me. "Uh, hey Don, what were you wearing last night?" I asked, fearing I already knew the answer.

"I was wearing my old army coat and a floppy cap" he shot back.

"Oh, oh" I thought. That stocky little guy in the floppy hat who was banging on the door in the rain was Don!

I apologized up and down to Don, explaining what had happened. He settled down and said "Man, that's ok. I've been trying to lose a bit of weight lately. I guess I looked a bit different to you guys. I'll be down tonight. This time open the fucking door!"

That night Don showed up, along with two friends. To my delight Don had brought the legendary writer of "Peggy Sue" and "I Fought the Law" Sonny Curtis, and the one and only drummer for Buddy Holly, the original member of the Crickets, J.I Allison. I was in rock & roll heaven. We joked about the previous night's misunderstanding and then for the next hour Bowen, J.I, Sonny and Don shared some the greatest rock and roll stories I had ever heard. All these guys had grown up in Texas and had been friends from the very beginning. I sat in my chair silently, taking it all in and listening in wonder to their tales of adventures back in the Buddy Holly days.

What an experience.

After a while it was time to get to work. Don brought Sonny to add a third part to our harmonies, which was just fine with me since Sonny was a killer singer himself. I grabbed my guitar and played the guys the song. Don started singing along on the chorus with me and I thought I was going to lose my cool hearing that famous Everly vocal wrapped around mine. Then, on the third run through, Sonny added the third part and it sounded incredible.

"Damn" said Don, "We sound like those Crosby, Stills and Nash guys!"

Everybody busted out laughing. Then Don made me sing the tune again while he figured out the second harmony part.

"You'll have to be a little patient, John" he said to me. "After all, I wasn't the harmony singer of the act." The reference, of course, was to his brother Phil.

I thought it was a shame that they were still broken up. Nobody sounded as good as the Everlys. I really hoped they would get back together again, but at this time they were a long way from reuniting. Eventually Donald and Phillip would put their differences aside and reunite at London's Wembley Stadium for their historic come-back concert and would remain together for years to come. Meanwhile, Sonny would join up with his old friends The Crickets, taking over Buddy's spot and touring the world with the band for the next three decades. This was a moment in time I will always cherish, having had a chance to sing with the architects of rock and roll, the guys who wrote the book and paved the way. How lucky can one kid from Hometown, Illinois be?

29 "HERE YOU COME AGAIN - DOLLY"

After I finished the album with Bowen it was back to L.A and back into the peach tuxedo with Mac Davis again. I dreaded it. It was a real let down coming from Nashville where I had worked with these fantastic musicians and living legends only to return to the monotonous grind of playing two shows a night in Vegas with Mac. I didn't wish Mac any ill will and I still respected him for the talent he *was* but I didn't respect him for what he *did* with that talent, namely selling out and becoming just another forgettable pop personality with little substance and mostly smoke bombs and glitter. But then one day, much to my surprise and relief, I received a call from none other than Dolly Parton. By this time Dolly had exploded on the charts and all over the media with her number one pop hit "Here You Come Again." She was everywhere you turned, while Mac's spotlight dimmed to a flicker.

"This better be John Beland on the phone" came the unforgettable voice I had missed so much.

"Dolly! It's so great to hear from you!" I shouted back.

"John Beland how the heck are you?" She asked.

"The truth or fictional answer?" I asked sarcastically.

"Are you still unhappy with Mac?" she asked

"Yea, I am. I hate it. I feel so detached from the real world and sick of playing Las Vegas in a damned peach tuxedo" I explained.

"Come to work for me then" she said.

"Are you serious?" I asked.

"Yes, I am, and I promise you won't have to wear a peach tuxedo" she said giggling in that famous chuckle of hers.

"Of course, I will" I shot back. "I'm so happy for you, Dolly. You deserve all that's happening and I'm thrilled to play for you."

"OK" she said "Better tell Mac. Knowing him he's not going to like it."

"Well" I replied in a serious tone "The sad thing, Dolly, is that he's not going to like it because one of his musicians decided to leave him for another act" I explained. "It'll have nothing to do with losing me because of my talent. It's going to be about his jealousies, insecurities and ego. So, I don't feel guilty."

"Well, I'll let you handle it" she replied. "We start rehearsing in a few weeks and my music director, Greg Perry will be calling you to make all the arrangements."

"That's great, Dolly" I said. "I'm so looking forward to seeing you again."

"Well then you better hurry and get your butt over here" followed by that signature giggle. "See ya soon, John."

I had another Las Vegas run to do with Mac and held off telling him at first. He had just started to pay a little more attention to me and it was nice to be able to share more than just "Hi, Mac" with him. I wish he would have acted that way when I first came on board, but it wasn't to be. He was a hard guy to get close to, nice enough but in a distant way. I would have liked to have seen him dump the whole Las Vegas farce of a show in favor of one with integrity and substance, but it never happened. The pay was good and steady but the gig was tough to endure. Now, it was about to end.

One night, just before we were to do our second show at the MGM Grand I noticed something very strange happening backstage. One by one, the three girls who sang for Mac came up to me and gave me big hugs, all with what appeared to be tears in their eyes.

"What the hell?" I thought.

Then it struck me. Maybe Mac found out about my going over to Dolly and was getting ready to fire me. I guess I'd soon find out.

In the middle of the show, I moved to the center of the stage with my acoustic guitar to play "In the Ghetto" like always. But before we started the song Mac asked me to hold up. "This is my guitar player John Beland" he started out. I kept thinking "Shit, he's going to fire me on stage!"

Mac continued. "And I thought it might be a good idea to let him know that he's the new father of a beautiful little girl just born a few hours ago."

The MGM Grand crowd roared and stood up to give me a standing ovation. But it hadn't struck me yet. "What the hell's going on?" I thought. Mac looked at me and laughed and said "Hey, man. You're a daddy!" Then it dawned on me. Mary had the baby. We had a new daughter!

My body went limp and I dropped my expensive Gibson Everly Brothers guitar into the audience and sat on the stool dumbfounded. One of the audience members handed the guitar back to me and I resumed my position at the microphone. Mac laughed and asked me "John, are you ok to continue?" The audience laughed. "Yeah, I'm ok, Mac" I said with a huge smile on my face. In reality I couldn't think of a thing other than to see my lovely new daughter, Jessie.

Jessie

John Beland

I started the opening guitar riff to "In the Ghetto" and to my horror, my guitar was terribly out of tune from its fall into the crowd. Everyone and Mac roared with laughter.

"Get off this stage and go home and see that baby" Mac said, followed by another round of applause. I walked off the stage and waved goodbye to everyone. But there was more to my goodbye than just seeing my new daughter, Jessie. I was waving goodbye to the gig with Mac. It was over and time to move on. I never would put on that ugly peach tuxedo again. Mac would go on to have one or two chart singles again, but his big hit days and his network TV Show were over. He did manage to score a country hit with a self-written tune called, ironically, "It's Hard to be Humble." Say no more.

I started rehearsals with Dolly Parton soon afterwards, again back at Studio Instrument Rentals giant sound stage in Hollywood. Dolly had a big band complete with three great singers. The conductor and pianist was a strange kind of guy who never seemed to smile much. His name was Greg Perry and he was quite a case. Dolly and Greg were very close, although I found him to be quite the opposite of Dolly's personality. He was quiet and not very sociable where Dolly was a full-on tidal wave of charm. After meeting the band, I set my gear up and got ready to start rehearsals when Dolly came in the room. She looked fabulous, dressed in jeans with a bandana on her head and looking every bit the "country girl."

"Hi John Beland" she said out loud and came over and gave me a big hug.

"It's great to be here, Dolly" I replied with a big smile. "I'm really looking forward to playing with everyone."

"Well we're looking forward to playing with you too" she replied in a loud, giggling voice.

I felt great about coming to work for her. Everyone in her camp was as professional as could be and the band seemed 100% into her music, unlike the Mac Davis band whose only interest was collecting a weekly pay check and enjoying being treated like rock stars. Dolly was in control of everything. However, the fine-tuning chores belonged to her conductor Greg Perry, who was a hard driver when it came to making the band sound letter perfect. Looking back, I now realize how important a job like that was. It was a big responsibility handling the band for a mega hit artist like Dolly Parton. Some could handle that responsibility with ease while some buckled under the weight of it. Greg Perry would be caught somewhere in the middle.

One change I noticed when I came to work for Dolly was the difficulty it was to get close to her. She was now surrounded by an army of helpers, management, PR people and agents making it nearly impossible to get close to her as in the past. I understood the high visibility of her celebrity. I had seen it before with Kristofferson, but I did miss the easy access to her and the intimacy we shared when we toured together with Mac only a few months earlier. But that was then. Now she was Dolly Parton, the hottest personality in show business. Such is fame.

On tour with Dolly at O'Hare Airport. Sharing a joke between flights

I settled into my spot as lead guitarist, occasionally playing acoustic guitar and harmonica as well. Whenever she would introduce me it would be during a solo, as in the middle of her hit single "Here You Come Again" she would tell the audience. "And this is John Beland on guitar. He thinks he's pretty good. Well, I think so too!"

One of the first gigs I played with Dolly was at the 1978 Houston Livestock Rodeo at the Astrodome in Houston Texas. I had played the same venue a year prior with Mac but Dolly's appearance was a real experience. Once again, the band was taken to the center of the arena and Dolly made her entrance in a Roman Chariot. We played to 44,000 people that night and if there was any doubt that Dolly Parton was the biggest star in the entertainment industry, all doubts were blown away by her appearance at the Astrodome. It was a real rush to be sitting behind her playing acoustic guitar on "Jolene" and witnessing her ascension up to the super star stratosphere. She commanded the stage and held that stadium in the palms of her hands to thunderous applause. It was amazing.

We also played in San Francisco where my mom, sister and brothers all came out for the show. Dolly was so sweet to all of them and especially to my mother who was still suffering the loss of my dad. It was a much-needed escape for her and I was so grateful to Dolly for her compassion and kindness towards my family.

Clowning outside the studio with Dolly 1978

Between tours with Dolly I received a call from Jack Brumley, brother of steel guitar legend Tom Brumley who played for Rick Nelson and the Stone Canyon Band. Jack was managing Rick and wanted to know if I would be interested in playing lead guitar for him. Rick was forming a whole new Stone Canyon Band except for Tom and wanted my help in putting it together. Of course, I jumped at the chance. Rick was one of my biggest influences and I was an expert on all of his recordings, hands down! Also, my style of guitar was similar to that of his long-time guitarist, the great James Burton. This time, James wouldn't be beating me out of this gig!

Of course, I agreed to jump on board and thought about who to call to fill out the now empty musician spots. I called my old buddy Thad Maxwell for bass, who was also a Rick Nelson fanatic. I then called Mac Davis drummer Billy Thomas, one of the best singing drummers in Hollywood. On piano Jack picked the great Elmo Peeler, a terrific session piano player. On second lead guitar Jack had hired Don Preston, a hot telecaster player who worked with Leon Russell. This time out Rick would have two hot lead players. And to add to that great line-up, Rick hired Elvis's former backup vocalists, The Sweet Inspirations, Myrna, Pat and Sylvia. It was a great band and rehearsals would begin soon. Since Dolly was off for the month she gave me permission to play for Rick at his Las Vegas debut at the Aladdin Hotel.

We rehearsed with Rick at Studio Instrument Rentals in Hollywood. He had his own rehearsal hall there and although it was relatively small it was real comfortable, just like rehearsing in your living room. I got there early to set up, excited as could be to finally meet Ricky Nelson, my all-time rock and roll hero. Thad and the rest of the band had already set up with the help of Rick's fantastic road crew, Clark Russell and John Cardoza, two incredibly funny guys who made the gig even more exciting. They were almost like a comedy team but make no mistake, these two guys knew their gig inside and out and were the best road crew I had ever worked with. I had just plugged into my amp when the door opened and in he came, Rick Nelson. He looked exactly like he did on TV, young handsome and extremely warm and friendly.

"Hey guys" he said in a soft friendly tone.

"Hey Rick" we all answered back. I laughed because we sounded as if we were all reading a page of dialog from the "Ozzie & Harriet Show."

Rick looked great in a pair of faded jeans and a red western shirt. His hair was just above shoulder length and perfect. Not a hair out of place. From the minute he walked into the room I felt I had known Rick all of my life. We immediately hit it off as if we had been best friends forever. For a while we talked about his records. Thad and I told him how important those recordings had been to guys like us, who studied every one of James Burton's solos like a priest studies the Bible. Rick was rather surprised and quite shy about it all, which I found surprising.

He was very humble and almost apologetic about his rock and roll days. I came to understand why he felt that way after getting to know more about Rick's post "Garden Party" career. For the years that followed his last major hit, Rick had surrounded himself with younger band members and clueless managers who found his old rock and roll legacy outdated. It seemed as if every producer who recorded him tried to reinvent Rick Nelson, or "modernize" his material and style. In fact, Rick's prior band members would sometimes cringe and make obvious bored expressions on their faces while performing his hits. It was no surprise that Rick seemed to be an abused artist when our paths crossed that evening.

Rick was now handled by Greg McDonald, who previously worked as kind of a "yes man" for Colonel Tom Parker. Although Greg had never managed anyone prior to Rick, McDonald was a diehard fan and both connected. If there ever was a business problem Greg couldn't handle, he'd simply seek the Colonel's advice. The first sensible thing Greg did was to fire the previous band Rick had except for steel guitar legend Tom Brumley. McDonald and Rick wanted to put together a band of musicians who mirrored the style and dynamics of his old James Burton, Joe Osborne, Ritchie Frost group from the hit days. Furthermore, Greg convinced Rick to mercifully shed the Stone Canyon Band image once and for all, this time for something more reflective of his deep down true love, rock and roll. James Burton, whose legendary Telecaster playing had been a signature sound on most of Rick's hits, had been my biggest influence as a guitarist. My own style was a direct result of studying his amazing guitar technique by listening endlessly to every record of Rick's that featured James on it.

The reason for this major shakeup in Rick's camp was the fact that he was going to debut at the Aladdin Hotel in Las Vegas and, like Elvis, McDonald wanted it to be big. This would be Rick's first appearance in Las Vegas and if all went well it would assure him of big money and a higher visibility than he had with the Stone Canyon Band. To pull everything off McDonald had to remold Rick and convince him that his old hits weren't the out-of-style old records from a by-gone era that others would have had him believe. His fans were now in their 40's and still ready to fork over big money to see Ricky Nelson on that Vegas stage, looking fantastic and singing all the hits they remembered him for. It was smart thinking on McDonald's part and with John Beland he found a loyal ally and a diehard fan who also shared his vision for Rick.

The new band was terrific. We rehearsed for weeks at Studio Instrument Rentals in Hollywood, resurrecting forgotten hits of Rick's such as "It's Up To You" and "Poor Little Fool" and this time staying true to the original arrangements instead of the diluted versions played by the prior Stone Canyon Bands. Each tune now had fire and rocked as if they were reborn. In fact, they were! We still did Stone Canyon Band favorites like "Garden Party" and "She Belongs To Me" but for the most part it was a much different Rick Nelson show than people had seen in the past 15 years. He was back!

For Rick's part, he looked fantastic. He hadn't aged at all! Gone was the shoulder length long hair and the fringe jackets from the 70's... now he dressed sharp and looked tremendous. He was excited. You could see it in his eyes. We, the band, supported him 500% and Rick felt his old confidence come back with every rehearsal.

Opening night in Las Vegas was electrifying. The first show was sold out, standing room only. When the lights dimmed a screen came down from the ceiling and a 5-minute film montage of Rick growing up on the Ozzie & Harriet delighted the crowd. While the film played, the band took their positions behind the screen. The film ended with a 16-year-old Ricky Nelson singing "I'm Walkin" on his parents show. When it came to the chorus the screen suddenly raised and there we were finishing the song, live with Rick center stage playing his famous Martin guitar with the leather case around it that spelled out the words Rick Nelson. Screams and yells filled the room as we rocked out the rest of "I'm Walkin". It was riveting.   Rick was terrific. He joked with the crowd and sang flawlessly through 90 minutes of hits. It was a smashing debut. Backstage everyone celebrated and guests came by with tons of congratulations, including Rick's mom Harriet and brother Dave. At times I felt like I was actually in one of the Ozzie & Harriet episodes!

Everyone was riding on a cloud and nobody wanted the night to end. I had to hand it to Greg McDonald. He delivered. We all delivered. It was a thrill to have played a part in the comeback of an artist whose influence on me was enormous, an artist who I grew up watching every week on the family television back in Hometown. As a kid I fantasized about being in Hollywood and playing guitar behind him, like my hero James Burton. But it was only a kid's fantasy, a farfetched silly dream that replayed in my mind each time Ozzie Nelson introduced his rock and roll son on TV. How surreal to now be living that very dream, and there was a lot more to come.

30 "I WILL ALWAYS LOVE YOU". GOODBYE DOLLY, HELLO RICKY.

Back in LA rehearsals resumed with Dolly. By now her rise to the top of the entertainment ladder had skyrocketed more and more each week as her single "Here You Come Again" shot up to number one. It seemed as if she was everywhere on TV as well as print. But with her new-found success came a whole new entourage of staff, agents and publicists. When I walked into the soundstage at Studio Instrument Rentals (S.I.R as commonly called by all the musicians) my first day back since working with Ricky, the scene around Dolly had changed. Now she seemed harder to approach on a personal level. Someone was always running interference claiming Dolly was "too busy to be bothered right now" or "Dolly's not feeling good, or I'll pass your message along" and mostly, "Now isn't a good time."

Furthermore, her musical conductor and pianist, Greg Perry, had turned Dolly's once fun and family oriented rehearsals into a boot camp where he rode herd over most of the musicians in her band. Many times, he would embarrass not only the musician he was scolding but the rest of the band as we had to sit by silently while one of our own got chewed out, including the top brass management now attending the rehearsals. It was simply a power play, obvious to us all. Perry was an unlikeable character to begin with. His nerd-like looks and his total lack of humor made him distant and impossible to get close to. He and Dolly were very close … why, I have never figured out to this day. They were completely opposite personalities, yet Dolly totally relied on his talent.

One day, we were rehearsing the show for the top brass at Dolly's management company and for this rehearsal they brought in producer Mike Post to oversee the music. I had a good history with Mike and respected him tremendously. With Mike in the room we could finally get through rehearsals without a temper fit by Perry. At least this is what I thought. We ran down the show but somewhere in the very beginning Perry called out for everyone to stop. We all came to a grinding halt as Perry, speaking into a microphone, laid into the drummer, chastising him for missing a beat. The soundstage was silent as he went on and on trashing the poor guy for making a simple mistake, totally humiliating him in front of the big guns seated before

263

us.

That did it. I had it with this ego maniac and dropped my guitar into the stand, with the volume still on causing it to feedback, and stormed off the stage, not before calling Greg Perry an "asshole". I was red with anger and walked out to the hallway where I was met by Mike Post.

"Before you say anything, Mike" I fumed, "that guy is a total fucking asshole."
Mike calmed me down and with a grin agreed with me but suggested I cool down I get back on stage and finish rehearsing.

"No Mike" I answered. "I'm going home." And that's what I did.

Later that night Perry called me.

"John, it seems to both Dolly and I that you're unhappy working with us and…"

I interrupted. "Not "us" Greg, you. You were an asshole today and I don't work under those conditions for anyone."

Perry continued "Dolly says that you seem to be much happier working with Rick Nelson and perhaps that would be a better place for you."

I cut him off again. "Greg, we both know what's going on here. Yeah, I do have a much better time working with Rick. So much so that I quit. And you can tell Dolly that I am hurt that she didn't call me herself." With that I hung up. My next call was to Greg McDonald, Rick's manager.

"Greg, is that guitar spot for Rick still open?"

In a matter of two minutes after hanging up from Greg Perry I was now lead guitarist for Ricky Nelson. I couldn't have been happier. Before I went to bed that night, I wrote Dolly a highly personal letter explaining how hurt I was that she didn't call me herself. I had considered our relationship more than just employer/employee. But I wished her all the best and signed it with love. I sent it to her assistant Judy, knowing it would reach her. I felt a bit sad that it was over with Dolly and me. We were very close and I had confided in her as she did me ever since the first day we spoke to each other when she was just an opening act for Mac Davis. I knew she truly cared for me and it would have been so easy to fall in love with her if I wasn't so familiar with the business we were in. But I did feel deeply for her and knew I would miss our relationship both professionally and personally. A few weeks later a letter arrived in the mail. It was from Dolly.

"Dear John, I am in a plane between Nashville and Canada _ "alone" and I was thinking of you. First of all, I wanted to tell you that you were right about it being hard to accept Greg calling you instead of me. I would have felt the same way. I should have called. I know it must be hard to be the leader of a band and make all the right decisions. It's not easy to do the right thing either - all the time. Someday, when you have your own band you will understand it more. John, if you could find it in yourself to forgive me I ask your apology and I hope you can love me again as a friend. I only ask for the chance to make it up to you someway in time to come. I don't know why I have always felt so close to you or why I have such an interest in your career but I think you are someone special and I believe very strongly in your talent. And in all honesty, I think that you are too good to be just another musician in just another band. So maybe it was meant to be.
I hope I have touched your life in some way. You have mine. I still love you and will watch your career very close and be proud of all you achieve. I'm sorry John. Please look over me. It would mean a lot to me to know you still think of me. As a friend it really would.

With Love
Dolly
I care."

I immediately went back to work with Rick ... this time as his permanent lead guitarist. From the very start Rick and I connected. I felt it was because of my deep respect and knowledge of his recording legacy. In fact, in many ways, I knew more about his records than he did. I was convinced that Rick was embarrassed about his rock and roll past. Since the early 70's he had been passed around from producer to producer all trying to reinvent him into something he wasn't. His very own musicians even downplayed his old hits to the point of mockingly performing throw away country versions of them live. This treatment had gone on so long that by the time I got with him he was hesitant and embarrassed to do more than a few of his past hits, believing they were old and corny and not relevant to today's music scene. He couldn't have been further from the truth.

I found an ally in his new manager Greg McDonald who, like me, was a true fan of Rick's past as well as present. Greg wanted bigger and better things for Rick and he sensed that I was the real deal and wanted the same thing. Together we worked to regain Rick's confidence in his past history and the more Greg, myself and the band assured Rick how great those records of the past were, the more Rick came out of his shell. We started working up old chestnuts of his like "It's Up To You" and "Poor Little Fool" and other great rock and roll classics. You could see him light up every time we worked up a new one from the past. Rehearsals were as fun as anything I had ever experienced before.

Onstage at the Palomino Club with my idol and best friend Rick Nelson 1979

From where I stood, Rick's country rock direction, although commendable, was totally wrong. He wasn't a country act in the slightest, even though he had one of the greatest steel guitarists, Tom Brumley, playing in the band. A lot of his material from the post-hit decade was commercially average except for an occasional standout such as "Garden Party". But for the most part his Stone Canyon Band product failed on radio as well as at the record stores.

At the time I joined Rick, McDonald had secured him a new deal with Epic Records. They had hired legendary sideman and producer Al Kooper to produce the next album which would be recorded at the Record Plant in Hollywood.

Al came to a few of our Vegas shows and we hit it off fine. I liked him. He was a real character with an impressive history. It was Al's signature organ riff that graced the Dylan classic "Like a Rolling Stone" and he was a founding member of the famed horn band Blood, Sweat and Tears. He had the credentials alright. However, when I heard the demos of the songs Al had selected for Rick's album I couldn't believe it. They were boring and totally "not" Rick Nelson songs and though Al had hired the who's-who of studio musicians to play on the record, not even the Beatles could have made these songs any better than what they were ... boring. As I was still relatively new to the scene I didn't speak up or voice my opinion regarding the material, but I could tell by McDonald's lack of excitement that he too had doubts about the selection of Al Kooper as Rick Nelson's producer.

I was booked on the dates along with some heavy hitters such as Doobie Brothers, Michael McDonald, Don Preston on guitar and Tom Brumley on steel. It was a weird setting, I had never recorded in the famed Record Plant but had certainly heard all the stories of drugs and groupies abundant. And the stories were spot on. However, in the studio things were more subdued although a bit disorganized. That is, nobody seemed to have any definitive direction and the band seemed more like a ship without a rudder. Kooper would chime in occasionally, but nobody seemed to take the reins. For his part, Rick stayed in the vocal booth and barely ever came out. He offered little input and seemed as if the entire session had swallowed him up. There were a few notable creative bursts such as the Dylan classic "Mama You've Been on My Mind" which came off very good. But in the end, all the greatest players in Hollywood couldn't compensate for the fact that the material and production plunged far below everyone's expectations. And to me, the most notable thing of all was Rick's voice. It sounded weak and tired and strained. Certainly not the same clear crisp quality he had when he recorded in the 60's and part of the early 70's. The entire project seemed doomed for disaster.

If the recording sessions in Hollywood seemed gloomy and stale, life on the road with Rick Nelson was anything but. From one club to another, fair dates, television, the crowds still showed up in full capacity to see him. Each performance played to high energy enthusiastic fans both young and old. Rick still "had it" and the audience couldn't get enough of him. In strong contrast to Dolly's stuffy band environment, Rick's musicians and crew got along like a fraternity party. There was never a bad word or flared temper exchanged between anyone despite the grueling tour schedule. Life on the road with the Rick Nelson band was simply a blast.

Perks were always waiting for us no matter what town we played in. The once poodle skirt teeny bopper 60's fans of Ricky Nelson's had now grown up into beautiful middle-aged bombshells, all ready and willing to make themselves available to their idol and his band regardless of where we played. We were kids in a sexual candy store and every one of us had a sweet tooth!

Not only were beautiful women always available but so was cocaine. There always seemed to be fans and guests stopping by the dressing rooms or back at the hotel happy to share their stash of blow with Rick and the band. Coke was pretty much the only drug we indulged in on the road. It gave us a much-needed lift after hard traveling and keeping up with such a crazy schedule.

It wasn't just us. In 1979, the year of disco and Studio 54, it seemed the entire entertainment industry was running on the flaky white powder. It was everywhere you went and not only done by rock and roll musicians but by some of the most conservative names in the business of entertainment, politics and sports. We were no exception. But as fun as it was, we never let anything get in the way of a show. Rick and the band always hit the stage straight arrow and never failed to deliver a killer performance. We never had a bad show. Rick was always a total professional and he always gave 500% on that stage. Fans were never disappointed after a Rick Nelson show.

Onstage with Rick at the LA County Fair 1979

We performed close to 200 shows that year and were seldom home. Amazingly, we never once did a bad show. Each one was full of energy and the fans ate it up. Rick gave his all to the delight of screaming fans, both male and female.

One of the funniest gigs we did with Rick was at the legendary night club "Gilley's" in Pasadena, Texas. Gilley's had recently become world famous since being used as the backdrop in the smash hit film Urban Cowboy starring John Travolta. The club was owned by country star Mickey Gilley and it was huge, all except the stage that is. For some reason the stage was tiny and it was everything we could do to not fall over ourselves. Furthermore, the dressing room was just a big old empty room filled with giant tractor tires. There was no security and all through the night fans kept trying to break down the door to get to Rick. We all took turns putting our backs against the door to keep them out. The famous bull riding machines were there, as in the film, throwing off throngs of drunken patrons every which way up in the air and on their asses. They were a wild crowd, noisy and rip roaring and eager to see Ricky Nelson. When the show started everyone crammed up along the front of the stage, hoisting their beer mugs and whooping it up like a scene from Gunsmoke. We came to the part in the show where Rick sings his big hit "Lonesome Town", with just himself accompanied on his acoustic guitar. In most cases audiences were so quiet you could hear a pin drop as Rick strummed and sang the classic lyrics: *"There's a place where lovers go to cry their troubles away. And they call it Lonesome Town, where the broken hearts stay..."*

In most cases this was the most tender, heartfelt song of the night, but not on this evening. All through the tune loud banging and ringing bells kept erupting from the back of the room. Every ten seconds a flurry of loud pounding would nearly drown out Rick's performance. Somehow, he managed to get through the song and afterwards, in the dressing room he asked one of the club's managers what the noise was during "Lonesome Town." About as proud as a father bragging about his new born son, the guy said "Shit, Mr. Nelson, those are our punching machines. If you hit it hard enough with your fist you get a free beer!" Only in Texas!

Tearing it up onstage anywhere USA with Rick 1979

Another time in Hot Springs, Arkansas following a performance at a club called The Vapors, the funniest thing I can ever remember during my career happened. A drunk, very attractive middle-aged woman waited for us as we returned to our hotel. She ran up to our roadie John Cardoza and begged to see Rick and wouldn't let go of him then followed us up five flights where our rooms were. We decided to pull a joke on her! In my room I had recording gear with me as I did a lot of songwriting on the road. We took one of the microphones and ran it into the next room where it was concealed under a hat. I happened to do a spot-on impersonation of Rick and so Cardoza decided to tell the girl that she could see Rick, providing she follows some rules. John explained to her that Rick was in the middle of a divorce and that the press was all over the place trying to catch a photo of him with another woman. Discretion HAD to be a MUST! She nodded her head and said that she understood. Then came the fun. Cardoza told her that she could meet Rick but that Rick would be wearing a pillow case over his head so that the press wouldn't catch him in any compromising situation. Meanwhile, in the very next room I had drawn a ridiculous cartoon of Rick's face on the pillow case and placed it over my head, pretending to be Rick. The band and Rick were in the next room listening in on monitor speakers. "This is ridiculous" the woman said. "Are you sure this is the only way I can meet him?" "Absolutely" replied a serious John Cardoza. "I'm on strict orders to follow procedures. That's the way it has to be." How Cardoza said all this without cracking up still baffles me. Cardoza escorted her into my dimly lit room where I was waiting, wearing only a towel around me and a white pillow case with the ridiculous cartoon drawing of Rick's face on the front.

"Are you really Ricky Nelson?" the woman asked in a very suspicious tone. Meanwhile Cardoza closed the door behind her leaving us alone. In my best Rick Nelson impersonation, I answered "Uh, hi. Yes, it's me. Uh, thanks for uh, understanding the situation."

"Well, this is the craziest….Whatever" and with that she turned off the light and started kissing me like there was no tomorrow. Suddenly she stopped. "Wait a minute, I REALLY have to see your face before we go any further. This is very weird!"

"Uh, ok then. Can you do me a favor then and get me a drink of water from the bathroom?" I asked. "Sure Ricky" and with that she headed for the bathroom while the REAL Rick Nelson, wearing exactly what I wore, including the pillow sheet with the cartoon image on it, switched places with me at the door. When she came out there was Rick standing by the door with the same exact cartoon pillow case on. "I can only do this once" Rick told her. And with that he removed the pillow case revealing the real him.

The girl was in shock and simply said "Oh my God, it IS you!"

"Uh, yep. It's me" Rick said while drinking the water. "But I have to put this back on now. Can you get me another glass of water please?"

"Well, alright. But this is the weirdest....and her voice trailed off as she went back in the bathroom. When she did, Rick and I made the switch again. The guys in the next room were monitoring everything and I could hear their muffled laughs through the wall. Here's what they heard then.

"Oh Ricky, I've loved you forever. I can't believe we're finally together" Mind you, all the lights were now off in the room. "I've written to you over and over and …….. Suddenly her hands managed to slip under the pillow case I was wearing. "Wait a minute! RICKY NELSON DOESN'T HAVE A FUCKING BEARD!"

Howls of laughter shook from behind the wall as she tore off the pillow case from my head revealing a bearded me, then proceeded to throw furniture and anything else she could get her hands on. "YOU GODDAMN BASTARDS!" she screamed as a lamp flew across the room. Fortunately, John Cardoza was at the door and pulled me back into the safety of the band's room while our drunken fan screamed and cursed the world from out in the hallway where security soon came and led her back to her car. Rick and the rest of us laughed so hard that we nearly passed out. I have to admit. It was fun being Ricky Nelson, if only for a few minutes.

One day I received a call from Greg McDonald. He informed me that Epic Records had shelved the Al Kooper sessions on Rick and had replaced Kooper with a new producer named Larry Rodgers, who had his own 16 track studio in Memphis. Larry had impressed the brass at Epic / Nashville by producing a few significant country hits for the label. Since Rick detested Nashville, Epic suggested Rodgers, his studio and rhythm section as a compromise. McDonald liked the idea of getting Rick out of Hollywood, away from the hangers-on as well as the marital dramas he was going through at home with Kris. Since Rick had never recorded outside the confines of Hollywood, this might new deal might offer a welcome change from his past recording failures.

Behind the board with Rick Nelson 1979

McDonald asked if I would accompany Rick and work with him on this new project. I was flattered to say the least. I desperately wanted to have a hand in Rick's recording career knowing that I could bring a lot to the table. I knew just about everything regarding his old hits. I studied those records as if they were the bible. I was also a proven hit songwriter and arranger with a strong studio track record myself. Finally, I was a friend who sincerely cared for Rick and wanted only the best for him. He and I had a close connection and McDonald felt that the two of us together could come up with an album that reflected the real Rick Nelson without the interference of some hip west coast producer who's answer to Rick's fall from radio was to re-invent him like so many others in the past. I jumped at the chance and soon plans were made for Rick and me to head to Memphis. This would be a turning point in Rick's career and I was thrilled to be in on the ground floor.

31 THE MEMPHIS SESSIONS 1979

Besides being Rick's personal manager, Greg McDonald had a connection to none other than the infamous Colonel Tom Parker, legendary manager of Elvis Presley. Prior to coming on board with Rick, McDonald worked with the Colonel for many years. This connection proved to be invaluable to the relatively inexperienced young manager now handling another huge name in rock and roll. Though not generally known to the public, from the sidelines the Colonel advised and counseled Greg on any and all matters relating to Rick. When it was announced that Rick and I would head to Memphis, amazingly the Colonel offered to let us stay at none other than the King's own home, Graceland, during the entire time we were recording. Rick, however, thought this was a creepy idea and passed. It had only been a couple of years since Elvis died and Rick didn't want to wake up to the sound of a ghost making peanut butter and banana sandwiches in the kitchen at 3 in the morning! Furthermore, staying at the King's house meant "no women" and THAT was a deal breaker. Instead, we stayed in two hotel suites at a posh hotel in downtown Memphis.

Lynn Lou Studio was in a funky part of Memphis. In fact, the studio was no more than an old house converted into a 16 track studio with offices. On our first day there, Rick and I met Larry Rodgers who was a real easy going, laid back guy whom we immediately liked. He had a cool sense of humor and a sharp mind when it came to recording. Larry took us on a tour of the place. The rooms were small and the bathroom was the size of a closet. But the main studio was very cool, although small in size it had a feeling of home about it. There was an antique barber's chair in the middle of the room as well as other rustic antiques. Both Rick and I loved it! The control booth was also small but all the top of the line gear was there for us to make a smash hit album.

Larry played us a few songs he had selected for Rick's approval, and they were terrific. All very commercial and very much in the style of Rick Nelson. There was a great John Fogerty song called "It's Almost Saturday Night" that really rocked. Also, a beautiful ballad called "Sleep Tight Goodnight Man." Another powerful song was called "Laid back In the Arms of Someone" which was a real killer tune. I was knocked out. For once, I thought here's a producer that truly *gets* what Rick Nelson is all about. Furthermore, Larry was a fan, like myself and Greg McDonald and wanted to score a hit with Rick, not just make another 12-song throw away LA album. We wanted blood. We wanted a hit!

Larry left it to Rick and I to come up with other songs when we got back to the hotel. This was a great approach because we both worked terrific under the pressure of having to come up with songs only hours before the session. We would sit around the table in Rick's suite with a couple of guitars and trade off ideas, just the two of us so there were no distractions, nobody to tell what to do or run interference. It was intimate and the best way to work with Rick Nelson. We kicked around a few old rock and roll chestnuts until we found the ones that fit Rick like a glove. One was the old Bobby Womack classic "It's All Over Now" recorded years earlier by the Rolling Stones. We added a rockabilly feel to it and presto, it sounded like one of Rick's old hits! I could tell he was getting more and more excited with every new song we picked. You could see it in his eyes. He was a true rocker and not the soft sounding folkie country rock singer others tried to make him. His heart was in rock and roll and that was evident from the direction this album was now headed.

On October 27, 1978 recording began at Lyn-Lou Studio in Memphis. The rhythm section included myself on electric guitar joined by members of Larry's house band, Shilo, Perry "Dumpy" York on drums, Danny Hogan on bass guitar and their hot guitarist Bobby Neal on acoustic guitar. The guys were all fans of Rick's and went out of their way to make the tracks as tight as possible. They were also a terrific bunch of guys making the session more fun than Rick could remember ever having on his LA sessions. These guys were all down to earth southern boys who treated Rick with the respect and comradery he hadn't felt in a long time.

We started out with a song I came up with in the hotel room the night before. It was an arrangement I had for an old favorite Bobby Darin tune called, "Dream Lover." The song was originally a fast rocker but I slowed it down to a James Taylor style along with a signature acoustic guitar hook. The new version we worked on gave the once teeny bobbing lyric a whole new dimension. The song took on a sad, lonely adult perspective of a man hungry to find that perfect someone who only existed in his dreams. I had originally arranged it for Australian country singer Lee Conway for his next album I was booked to do. However, his album was cancelled and so I played the arrangement for Rick. He nailed it as if he had written it. Furthermore, the band and I tried to incorporate shades of Rick's "Stone Canyon Band" era but with a more commercial top 40 approach. Another thing we agreed to do was not to use keyboards or steel guitar. This was to be a "guitar" album, simple and true.

Before we started the next number, Rick began fooling around at the microphone with his guitar joking about Elvis and singing bits of the King's classic, "That's Alright Mama." It was done as a joke between sessions but it sounded damn good. "Rick" I shouted from my spot on the floor "Man, we should cut it! It rocks!" "You think so?" he replied in embarrassment. The guys all shouted out their approval, as well as Larry Rodgers who had been listening from the booth.

"Give it a shot, Rick. It sounds great" Larry replied on the talk back.

I launched into a James Burton style Telecaster riff as Dumpy let loose on a smashing rockabilly drum pattern. Bobby Neal laid down a strong solid rhythm acoustic and we let loose on it. I'll be damned if it didn't sound like one of Rick's early 60's rockers. He sang his ass off and we nailed the song in only a few takes. It smoked and all of us were blown away when we heard the playback. These first tracks set the pace for one of the most fun, creative albums I had ever been involved in and it was clear Rick was having a field day. I had never seen him as animated in the studio as he was during the recording of this album. The next day we were all sitting around our positions in the room getting ready to cut the next track when the conversation turned to the "Buddy Holly Story" movie. Rick shared some stories about himself and Buddy and all of us were glued to each word. When he finished we worked up an arrangement of the Holly classic "Rave On" and the more we ran it down the more it came to life. Again, we rolled the tape and cut it right then and there and again, Rick made it his own in that classic style of his.

All the sessions followed the same formula and the whole experience was something we never expected. Everyone involved was 100% behind Rick and that had a deep effect on his input. He rattled off suggestions for every track and we ran with each one. Rick confided in me later that the Memphis sessions reminded him of the old days when he was making those great hit records with his old band. It was evident from the album that Rick had decided to get back to his roots and dissolve the country rock Stone Canyon Band direction. This included letting his good friend and steel guitar legend Tom Brumley go. Tom's playing had slowed down a bit lately and the time on the road was starting to show. Besides, Rick's decision to go back to rock and roll left little to no room for the steel any longer. It was a tough decision for Rick, and I could tell it was excruciating for him to make the call to Tom. They had been together for many years as far back as 1969. But the times had changed and Rick wanted to set a new course for his career. One of the few times I saw Rick really emotional was the night he called Tom from the studio in Memphis. It tore him up to let Tom go, but Tom would go on to work with many other top artists in the years that followed.

Rick, Greg and I also talked about bringing in Bobby Neal who had been in the studio band Shilo. We needed a strong 2nd guitarist to fill the sound onstage. Rick basically banged away on the guitar while performing and quite often our soundman Clark would simply pull him from the mix during the rocking songs. One time in Lake Tahoe we recorded a live album. Rick's guitar was so out of tune on the recording that after the show I had to go into the sound truck and overdub his playing myself. Bobby was a die-hard Ricky Nelson fan like myself and I really wanted him in the group. He was a fantastic guitarist and a terrific guy with a real love for rockabilly music like both Rick and I. After the album was finished we spoke to Bobby to see if he might be interested in joining the band. He jumped at the chance and we were thrilled to have him aboard.

There would be no "easing" into the band for Bobby. His first gig with us would be about the biggest gig imaginable in pop music at the time. Rick would be the host of a little show out of New York and we would be performing his old hits for the first time in decades on national TV. The show was called Saturday Night Live. Welcome aboard, Bobby!

32 LIVE FROM NEW YORK, IT'S SATURDAY NIGHT LIVE!!!

By far the biggest show on television in 1979 was Saturday Night Live. Hands down it was the show of shows for any music act to do. This would be the last year of the original cast, Bill Murray, John Belushi, Gilda Radner, Jane Curtain, Garrett Morris and Dan Aykroyd. Rick was set to host the show which would feature folk singer Judy Collins as special guest. We would be spending a full week in the Big Apple rehearsing for the show and everyone in Rick's camp was pumped, including Epic Records who planned to release Rick's "Dream Lover" as his next single to coincide with his appearance on SNL. Our band was as tight as any band around. On drums the great Billy Thomas, on bass guitar the multi instrumental John Davis, on piano the talented arranger Elmo Peeler, on rhythm guitar fresh from Memphis Bobby Neal and myself on lead guitar. You just couldn't beat this group. We wanted viewers to be blown away when Rick hit that stage and for people to hear those classic hits just as they sounded on the record, and not some cheap throwaway version of them.

Rick looked sensational, every bit the star he was. He was slim and trim and sexy and ready for prime time. He even brought along his old acoustic guitar with the white leather case around the body that read "Rick," the same one he played on Ozzie & Harriet. All the elements were there for a killer show. The Saturday Night Live offices at 30 Rockefeller were a combination of a M.A.S.H unit and a Keystone Cops silent movie. I recall a glass door that led to the writers' rooms. In the middle of the door was the outline of a person who had run through it. The first member of the cast I met was Garrett Morris, a very friendly gentle kind of man. He told me that the cast and crew were very excited about Rick hosting the show. He felt that this was going to be a stand out episode.

Meanwhile, Rick met with the writers and together they worked up a number of funny skits. The most memorable one would be where Rick is trying to find his way home, but ending up in the kitchens of Leave It To Beaver, Father Knows Best, Danny Thomas Show and I Love Lucy. It was side splitting and remains one of the classic skits from SNL to this day. One thing Rick was crystal clear about was that there would be no making fun of his parents or their TV show. The Nelsons were a tight knit devoted family and Rick told the writers that as far as any satirical reference made to his folks would be off limits. The writers agreed.

Prior to SNL I had played before thousands of people and appeared on numerous national television shows from the Tonight Show to American Bandstand and never bothered with being nervous in the slightest. In fact, whenever I appeared on a TV show I always focused more on the camera crew and those in the studio than getting lost in the notion that millions of people across the country were watching me. But SNL was different. This was the biggest show on TV and many of my hip LA musician friends would be watching it as well as those I grew up with back in Hometown, Illinois. On top of that, I would be getting close up shots on all four songs every time I played one of those iconic guitar solos. I confess that I was *quite* nervous! The way they do the show is that two complete shows are run back to back, the first being a dress rehearsal and a chance for the writers to tweak up skits or eliminate gags that didn't work. Two separate audiences are brought in: one for the rehearsal and one for the actual live to air. This also gave the performers a chance to get comfortable with the material before the red light went on. As airtime approached, I took my position onstage as Rick would be opening the show following an introduction skit by Bill Murray, Danny and John. Once their skit was over the familiar theme music struck up, the red lights went on as announcer Don Pardo said those famous seven words "LIVE FROM NEW YORK, *IT'S SATURDAY NIGHT!*" The studio audience roared as Pardo read the credits and guest announcements and then he said "*LADIES AND GENTLEMEN, RICK NELSON!!* I couldn't see the audience because of the lights and cameras but I heard them scream and roar as Rick hit the stage. He told the TV audience that if they wanted to see the "old Ricky" they should turn down the color control on their TV set, and it would be "just like old times". That was my cue to kick off Rick's classic hit "Hello Marylou." When the solo came up I suddenly had two cameras right on me. I kept my focus on Rick who was smiling right at me as I played the solo without a hitch. Whew! Then we went into another huge hit of Rick's, "Traveling man". Once again cameras swiftly moved right to me when the solo came up. I played it spot on thanks to Rick making things seem comfortable onstage. He was such a pro. Finally, we ended with the classic "Fools Rush In". This was the first time in decades that Rick performed these hits true to the original records and the studio audience went crazy when it was over.

While the applause continued and Rick took his bows I couldn't help but think that *this was it, the comeback*. There was no way this wasn't going to be the resurgence of his career. Elvis was long gone, but Rick Nelson was still there, and better than ever before. The show went on and Rick was terrific in the skits. Our last musical number was "Dream Lover" and for that Bobby Neal and I played acoustic guitars. The set was dark and shadow-like and it was a bit difficult to see my guitar, but we pulled it off beautifully. Rick sang it flawlessly and I'll be damned if it didn't sound like a smash hit. Again, the audience ate it up. At the very end, the rest of the band and I joined Rick and the cast onstage to wave goodnight as the credits rolled and the closing theme played us off. I stood next to Danny and Gilda and wondered what everyone thought of the show back in Hometown or Napa where my mother watched along with my grandmother, brothers and sister, or back in Hollywood where my fellow session musicians and friends were. I also thought that it had been a long road to get to this stage, with this artist. I was sitting on top of the highest mountain that night. When the cameras were off and the studio audience had filed out I ran into Danny Aykrod who put his arm around me and simply said "This was one of the good ones."

A funny side note. Just before air time the producers and writers were panicked because they couldn't find Belushi. The word went out and everyone was in a panic, especially considering that he was in the opening skit! I was by the elevator backstage when it opened and out poured a very wasted John Belushi being held up by two friends. They disappeared into a room and slammed the door. I thought "Oh, oh, he'll never make the show." But to my amazement, when show time came there he was looking fabulous and completely together. To this day I haven't a clue what they gave him in that room, but whatever it was I would love to get my hands on it!

The excitement and optimism that we felt doing Saturday Night Live followed us for the next few weeks on the road. Audiences and gigs multiplied. At some venues fans rushed the stage just like in Rick's teenage years. Women screamed and fans went wild. We all felt as if nothing could go wrong, but we were wrong.

In their blunder, Epic held back the release of "Dream Lover" in order to add a conga drum on the final mix, one of the A&R guy's brilliant ideas. With the single release now being held up, we lost the potential radio momentum and when it was finally released, "Dream Lover" only made it as far as the 60's in Billboard. It was a terrible letdown. The opportunity for the label to promote that record on SNL was so obvious and yet they blew it.

We continued to do an endless parade of gigs hopping from one town to another all across the country, traveling in a small Lear Jet once owned by African dictator/tyrant Idi Amin, who had recently been deposed. Wherever we went the shows were sold out and the reaction was incredible, yet with all that excitement on tour, Rick's record company just wouldn't put their promotional muscle behind him. The album we did at Larry Rogers was in Limbo with no set release date. I couldn't understand Greg McDonald's passive response to Rick's recording dilemma. Greg was good for booking Ricky but hell, *anybody* could book Rick Nelson. Where McDonald showed his weakness and lack of knowledge was in all matters relating to the record business. He didn't have a clue and thus never took the bull by the horns with regard to Epic Records. Little by little I started seeing the light fading at the end of the tunnel. Rick would never get a shot like SNL again and I felt as if the comeback like we had hoped for would now be just a lost opportunity. Rick had come so close, but unfortunately not close enough thanks to his record label. A new act would host SNL the next Saturday. As for Rick and the rest of us, we continued performing on the road, the endless road.

33 TAKING FLIGHT WITH THE FLYING BURRITO BROTHERS

On the few days when we were off the road with Rick, I wrote and demoed my songs for Criterion Music in Hollywood. I had signed a staff writing deal for $600.00 a month with the company and started spending much of my time laying down demos in their 16 track recording studio just below their office on Selma Avenue. Criterion Music was a family-owned publishing company started back in the 1940's by Mickey Golsen, one of the early west coast publishing pioneers. One of the songs the company published was the classic 40's hit "Moonlight in Vermont." But now the company was run by Mickey's son Bo, a great guy and true visionary. Bo brought in new blood to the company by way of hot young writers such as Jackson Browne and Rodney Crowell. Under Bo's watchful eye, Criterion had scored hits by Dean Martin, Dino, Desi & Billy, Jackson Browne, The Trash Men and many more. The first song I wrote for the company was a tune called "Rodeo Eyes" and as luck would have it we scored a top 20 country hit when it was recorded by singer Zella Lear on RCA. Because I now had an open door, I practically lived in Criterion's studio, constantly recording demos on new songs.

It was at this time I started using some members from the country rock band The Flying Burrito Brothers as musicians on my songs, namely steel guitar wiz Sneaky Pete Kleinow, and my old Swampwater bandmate Gib Guilbeau who was now fronting the Burritos as lead singer and fiddle. With the exception of their debut album on A&M Records, I wasn't a fan of the Flying Burrito Brothers by any stretch, especially the latest incarnation of the group which also featured former Byrds bassist Skip Batten. But Pete and Gib were monster musicians on their own and I used them to play on my songs whenever I could.

One day while recording with the guys I was approached by Gib, Pete and the Burritos manager Martyn Smith about possibly joining the Flying Burrito Brothers. At first, I thought they were joking, but soon I could tell they were serious. By 1980 the Burritos were dead in the water. The once pioneering country rock band founded by the late Gram Parsons had recently lost their record deal at CBS and were now playing small clubs and occasional overseas gigs for very little money. They certainly had strayed far from the original course set by the founding members Gram Parsons and Chris Hillman. I went to see the band live at the Roxy Theater on Sunset Strip and thought they were very uninspiring. The Flying Burrito Brothers desperately needed a creative blood transfusion as well as a record deal. I didn't give them an answer right away because I wanted to talk it over with Bo Golsen, whose opinion I valued.

Although I made a healthy paycheck and was now the band leader, I knew that things with Rick Nelson would never surpass the heights of Saturday Night Live. It was obvious to me that his current manager Greg McDonald, although very good with regard to booking Rick, was totally inexperienced in the record business, as evident in the inexcusable blunders with Rick's last single, "Dream Lover." If I remained with Rick I'd only be a hamster on a wheel, another sideman playing hundreds of dates over and over again and without any chance of another comeback on the horizon for Rick. What I really wanted to do more than anything was produce records. The studio was my true home, not the road.

Bo explained to me that if I joined the Burritos I could not only get a crack at producing but I would have a great opportunity to have the band record my songs and maybe land a hit for the act. Mind you, up till that point the Flying Burrito Brothers had never scored a single hit. Bo went on to say that he had connections with Curb Records president Dick Whitehouse, general manager of Curb Records and that if I joined the band he could get our demo tapes directly to Dick and very possibly land the Burritos a new record deal.

I had just written a new song inspired by a recent heartbreak, called "Damned If I'll Be Lonely Tonight" and used the Burritos for the demo with Gib singing the lead and myself adding the harmonies. The demo was strong and sounded like a smash country hit and Bo wanted to take it to Curb, provided I was interested in joining the band. It was a very hard decision as Rick had treated me terrific and we had a very close working relationship. Furthermore, we traveled in style and stayed at the best hotels; furthermore, he used me on all of his recordings and television appearances. It was a tough call.

I sat down with Rick and explained the situation. It was an opportunity for me to move ahead of just being somebody else's guitarist, and Rick knew that. As expected, Rick was fully supportive of my grabbing the offer from the Flying Burrito Brothers and wished me all the best. Rick was more than an employer, he was a close friend and didn't think twice about allowing me to pursue an opportunity. He surely was one of a kind.

The lead guitar chores would now be turned over to the great Bobby Neal , who was one of the finest rockabilly guitar players ever. Not only was his playing excellent but he was a warm likeable personality with a great sense of humor and also a huge fan of Rick's. Rick would be in great hands with Bobby, that was for certain. With great reluctance I said goodbye to Rick and the band and joined the raggedy, worn-out former pioneering band The Flying Burrito Brothers. From the very start I felt as if I had made a huge mistake by leaving Rick for this outfit but time would prove me wrong, in a big way.

1979 Playing the Napa County Fair with Rick. My mom, brothers and sister came to the show. Unforgettable time

My first gig with the FBB would be in Sienna, Italy, at a massive outdoor concert. The Burritos were still popular abroad and could still draw crowds, in spite of themselves. The band was very loose and played a strange variety of songs ranging from Texas swing to old, tired country chestnuts. They were a far cry from the innovative original line-up of Gram Parson and Chris Hillman's band. In fact, they were no more than another west coast country bar band when I came aboard. The lineup consisted of some very notable players such as steel guitar legend and original founding member Sneaky Pete Kleinow, ex-Byrds bassist Skip Batten, Gib Guilbeau on fiddle and guitar and drummer John Messery. As players they were all more than competent. In fact, Sneaky Pete was a living legend on the session scene having played on albums by John Lennon, Joe Cocker and the Bee Gees.

Gib Guilbeau was a much-accomplished songwriter whose tunes had been recorded by everyone from the Byrds to Rod Stewart and he was a killer singer and fiddle player. In fact, it was Gib and I who creatively led the pioneering band Swampwater only 9 years earlier. Skip Batten, however, was a very weak player and a terrible songwriter, in my opinion. Although he once played with the once iconic group The Byrds, his style of singing, playing and songwriting never added to the group's identifiable trademark sound. Batten may have been in the Byrds, but unfortunately, he was part of the final lineup of the band which, arguably, was the worst lineup in the group's history with the exception of the great guitarist Clarence White. That final lineup bore no resemblance to the beautiful sound of the original Byrds. Furthermore, that particular final lineup of Roger McGuinn, Gene Parsons, Skip Batten and Clarence White scored little to no commercial success, a sad ending to the stellar legacy of the once ground-breaking band.

In many ways, the situation with the 1980 Flying Burrito's Brothers mirrored that of the final Byrds lineup. Both historic bands had once been led by visionaries but over time eventually wound up pale reminders of their glorious past. The Burritos had just lost their last major record deal due to lack of sales. They had recently released a "Live in Japan" album on a small independent label to an uninterested public and although they continued to tour, doing small clubs and occasional festivals, for all intent and purpose the 1981 Flying Burrito Brothers were grounded. The FBB were now managed by Martyn

Smith, a likable Welshman who was very knowledgeable about the record business and very committed to the band. Martyn had been a close associate of Eddie Tickner, manager of Emmylou Harris & the Hot Band who was one smart manager and had plenty of experience handling Emmy, Gram and the Byrds. Martyn was a great choice for the Burritos because he was also a dedicated and a hard, no-nonsense worker, like Eddie. He saw the potential for a Flying Burrito Brothers commercial success, but at the time I joined he didn't know how or where it would come from.

From the beginning I instantly hit it off with Pete and Gib. I had known them for years. Pete had played on my first solo album and Gib was my bandmate during the Ronstadt/Swampwater years. Both had a terrific sense of humor and were a lot of fun to be around. Batten had an arrogance that made him a bit distant and hard to really get close to. I don't believe he was all that supportive about my joining the band. Rehearsals were strange. Pete and Skip were lazy and didn't particularly enjoy rehearsing. Their standard way of rehearsing was to run a song down for a few times and then say, "that's good enough." This was in sharp contrast to my background. Every rehearsal I attended with the many acts I had worked with was meticulous and intense. The FBB rehearsals were a joke. I didn't care for half the material we were doing either in that the guys played all of the songs well, however, the material wasn't anything like I had imagined the Flying Burrito Brothers to be. It wasn't country rock as I knew it. There were no sweet harmonies or beautiful songs with standout powerful arrangements like the kind you would hear from Poco, Pure Prairie League or the Eagles. It all sounded like bar band shit to me, forgetful and loud.

After the first day of rehearsals I thought I had made a dreadful mistake by leaving Rick. This band was hopeless and nothing like the Flying Burrito Brothers I thought I would be joining. However, I had committed to the tour of Italy and had rehearsed with the band so I agreed to continue on. What was I getting myself into? This group had about as much chance on getting a hit record as I did joining NASA. But as fate would have it, things were about to change. Amazingly enough that change would come from a little film that would soon shake up the country music industry. In fact, Pete had just returned from playing steel on one of the film's songs called "Looking for Love" by Johnny Lee. I asked Pete the name of the film and he said, "I think it's called Urban Cowboy."

John Beland

34 RHINESTONES, SPANDEX, COWBOYS AND COCAINE. URBAN COUNTRY ARRIVES.

The gigs in Italy went surprisingly good. Much to my amazement, the crowds ate it up at every show. We played for thousands in ancient outdoor courtyards in towns like Sienna, Milano and Pisa, and at every show the fans would not let us off the stage, chanting "Booooreeeeetos" over and over until we returned to the stage. At one particular show we played in front of a massive sign that had a cartoon of then President Carter strangling Italy with his bare hands and on each side of the stage communist flags were waving. Towards the end of our performance I noticed the military surrounding the front of the stage, all brandishing guns and riot helmets. All of us were starting to get a little concerned when suddenly a big fight broke out right by the front of the stage. Everyone started running and smoke and dust filled the air. We were quickly escorted off the stage into a guarded trailer while the army tried to break up the fight between two political factions. No encore that night.

At another show we received so many encores we simply ran out of songs! I suggested we do Mr. Tambourine Man, since Skip had been a "Byrd". We strolled back to the stage to thunderous applause and Gib thanked everyone for attending. I hit the classic intro that Roger McGuinn had made so famous and before we could even start singing, the crowd erupted waving cigarette lighters and swaying to and fro as we sang "Hey Mr. Tambourine Man". It was an electric moment for sure.

I really didn't get it. The Italian audiences really didn't give a damn whether we resembled the original Flying Burrito Brothers or not! Even the songs that I cringed to while playing were eaten up by the crowds. It was all very gratifying, I'll grant you, but beyond the crowds and the applause, I still felt as if the music we played was sloppy and meaningless.

We returned to the USA and I went to work writing songs aimed for The Burritos. I practically lived in Criterion's little studio, demoing nonstop and using the band as often as possible. After a while we wound up with an impressive collection of solid country songs and damn good demos, good enough for Bo Goldsen and Martyn Smith to take to Curb Record's president, Dick Whitehouse.

I had now moved to Napa California following the breakup of my second marriage to my wife Mary.

Hollywood had taken a toll on me. Drugs, namely cocaine, were everywhere. Like everyone else in Hollywood I was doing it too, using it as a boost in the studio and as an emotional crutch of sorts. But eventually cocaine no longer became "fun." I started seeing fellow musicians I had known and respected start to deteriorate and I was beginning to head that way too. I decided it was best to get away from it all and headed up to the beautiful wine country. I would commute from Napa to Hollywood frequently and with the help of my mother I found a great condo by the Napa River where my daughter and I moved into. While I was away on the road mom took care of Sarah with all the love and kindness you would have expected from her. She was a saint.

Back in Hollywood John Travolta's "Urban Cowboy" had exploded on the scene. Everybody started sporting cowboy hats and wearing boots. A number of country western night clubs started appearing all over town. But the biggest club remained the Palomino Club in North Hollywood. It had always been popular but now, with the advent of Urban Cowboy, you couldn't get in the place! Suddenly, country music was "cool" and selling like hotcakes. For the first time ever country albums were selling platinum and the market shot up like Jack's fictional beanstalk.

It was during this madness that the Flying Burrito Brothers landed an album deal with Curb Records. Label head Dick Whitehouse liked the demos I had recorded on the band and offered us a deal. But there was a hitch. Whitehouse wanted one of his staff to produce us. This came as a real blow because my sole interest in joining the band was to eventually produce the act myself. It was put to us that if we refused their choice of staff producers the deal was off. I was ready to quit. I didn't want to be just another member in any band. It was my demo production that landed the deal offer in the first place and after 11 years of studio session credits under my belt I certainly had the qualifications and experience to produce the Burritos for a major label. My production skills were good enough for the Beatles to sign me 8 years earlier. Why weren't they good enough for Curb records? I was furious.

Bo and Martyn sat me down at Criterion's office one day to try and sway me into relinquishing the production in order to save the deal. Bo argued that if I "played ball" with Curb right now and we landed some hits later, I would be in a much stronger position to lobby for the production gig. Reluctantly, I caved in. Whitehouse knew I was angry about giving up production so he allowed us the final say with regard to whom would actually produce us. Instantly I recommended my old boss Jimmy Bowen and was turned down with no explanation. I then brought up producer Ken Mansfield with whom I worked on many dates over the years. Curb refused again. Amazingly, Whitehouse suggested former Bellamy Brothers producer, and my old arch enemy, Phil Gerhardt, the same one who threatened to blow my car up 5 years earlier. Gerhardt was now working for Curb and actually expressed great interest in producing us. This time I refused in no uncertain terms. Finally, Whitehouse strongly suggested their "golden boy" producer Michael Lloyd, who was currently producing country hits on none other than the Bellamy Brothers. Lloyd had impressive credentials mostly with milk toast acts, pop acts like Barry Manilow. Even the Bellamy's newer hits sounded soft and bland with no edge whatsoever. Nevertheless, he was producing big hits and that's all that mattered to Whitehouse and Curb.

Lloyd had a state of the art studio behind his million-dollar home right next to the Beverly Hills Hotel. It was there we had our first meeting with Curb's boy wonder. Michael's home was something out of the pages of Architectural Digest. It was immaculate with fine artwork and expensive furniture fit for someone like Liberace. It certainly wasn't the kind of place you would expect to find country rock music being recorded. Lloyd, a thin elf-like little guy, took Gib and I on a tour of his studio which was quite impressive and immediately tried to warm up to me by hinting that he could use me on some of his many recording projects. I went along with his flattering my ego although I did detect an arrogance when he started playing us some tracks he had produced on other artists. He was label owner Mike Curb's favorite at the label, so Lloyd was used to getting his own way. I had heard from other musicians that he could sometimes act like a spoiled kid and a bit full of himself, which proved to be true.

At the end of the meeting and after listening to some of his past work we agreed to have him produce us. Away from Gib and Pete's ears, Lloyd assured me that I would be the main guy he would depend on when the recording started which I gathered was a compliment of sorts.

On the day of the first session things went sour when Lloyd announced that he didn't like our drummer, Mickey McGee who was one of the best drummers in town and who formally had played for Linda Ronstadt and Ricky Nelson. Michael kept riding Mickey during the run through of the first song and I could tell that Lloyd was gunning him. Michael had already replaced bass player Skip Batten with session musician Dennis Belfield, much to my delight. But Mickey was certainly more than capable of playing the sessions. It was here that I got a taste of Lloyd's coldness when he announced on the floor that Mickey could "go home" because his drumming wasn't "working out." It was a bitter pill for Mickey to take and he was very humiliated. This left me, the only band member, playing on the tracking sessions. Batten and McGee had been axed from the floor. Pete was absent and Gib was relegated to the vocal booth. Lloyd chose to stay in the safety of the control booth while a humiliated Mickey packed up his drums and left the room. Michael then picked up the phone and booked session drummer Ron Krasinski who proved very capable. Still, it was a heartless thing to do as well as having to witness.

Like Lennon and McCartney, Gib and I gave each other equal writing credit for the songs we delivered, regardless of who wrote what. For the most part, I wrote "Damned If I'll Be Lonely Tonight" and "She Belongs to Everyone but Me" both after my fizzled affair with Jean Anne Chapman. Together, Gib and I wrote the Buck Owens inspired "She's a Friend of a Friend."

Although Michael turned down our suggestion to do two Bob McDill songs called "Song of the South" and "Louisiana Saturday Night" (later to be number one hits by Alabama and Mel McDaniel) he did come up with a solid one written by Johnny Cymbal and Austin Roberts called "I'm Drinking Canada Dry". We had a very impressive song roster and a good shot for getting on the charts. If we did pull off a hit record it would be the first time in the band's 13 year history that they scored a significant chart hit. Our fingers were crossed.

It was now evident to Gib and Martyn that my suggestion about getting rid of Skip Batten was the right move. Batten expressed his displeasure over the direction we were headed, namely because we had passed on his not so "inspiring" songs. Earning his management percentage, Martyn fired Skip which left Gib, Pete and I as a trio. Although it was too late to remove Batten from the album cover which had already been shot, he never appeared on the album or was mentioned in any way in the liner notes. Years later in an interview Skip said he had "quit" because he didn't like the direction I had taken the band. I commented back that the only direction I wanted to pursue was having commercial hit records, plain and simple and that Skip, as evident by his failed run with the Byrds, didn't fit into those kinds of plans for the Flying Burrito Brothers either.

Secretly, I wanted to change our name as well. I felt uneasy about calling ourselves the "Flying Burrito Brothers". That original band had broken up years ago and whatever fan base they had won was all due in part by the vision of Gram Parsons and Chris Hillman. By keeping the name we were setting ourselves up for harsh criticism from the hip rock and underground press. Had we simply changed to name to The Guilbeau / Beland Band, or Golden West, as I suggested, I'm certain that we would have still landed the hits and at the same time retained our integrity. Besides, country radio at that time hadn't a clue about who the Flying Burrito Brothers ever were. But the rock and roll press did. So why keep the name and risk all that hassle? But Martyn, Gib and Curb wouldn't hear of it. They had struggled for years under that name and weren't about to let go of it just when it appeared that commercial success was finally right around the corner.

In 1980 our debut album HEARTS ON THE LINE was released. Our first single, written by Gib and I, "She's a Friend of a Friend" received considerable airplay and to all our amazement broke into the top 50 national country music charts! The following single, written by Rickard Leah, "Does She Wish She Was Single Again" made top 20. And finally, our 3rd single written by myself and Gib, "She Belongs to Everyone but Me" broke into the charts. We had done it! This was the first time in 12 years since the group's inception that the Flying Burrito Brothers had scored a commercial hit record. As a result, the flood gates had opened and we were now a legit top country hit act with tours and TV offers rolling in. It seemed as if nothing could go wrong until one day I received a phone call from my sister, Sue. Something was wrong with mom, seriously wrong.

35 GAINS, LOSSES AND A MILLION MILES IN BETWEEN

When I returned home to Napa off our latest tour, my sister got me alone and shared some major concerns about mom. Sue had recently discovered bandages with blood stains in mom's bedroom.

We both had noticed a change in mood swings from her in the past few months as well. I decided to confront her when the kids weren't around the house. She was in the kitchen preparing lunch for the kids when I told her that I wanted her to sit down and talk to me. I could tell she was nervous and could see her face turn pale as she sat down with me in the living room. I told her what Sue had discovered in her bedroom and she broke down and cried. She confessed that she was afraid to go to the doctor, especially after all she had endured during Dad's fight with cancer. I told her that she needed to get to the doctor's as soon as possible and that I would see her through it. An appointment was made to see the doctor the very next day and mom was examined as my sister and I waited in the reception room, nervously waiting. We didn't have to wait long. The doctor came out and escorted us back into his office where I found mom sitting in a chair, ash white and crying.

"Your mother has breast cancer and I'm afraid it's advanced beyond anything we can do" he said.

"What do you mean, Doc?" I shot back. "Surely there's something you can do for her."

The doctor explained that mom had simply waited too long to do something about it. Now it was too late. My sister held my mother in her arms as I asked the doctor for the answers I wanted to hear. They didn't come.

"How long does she have, Doc?" I said in a low almost inaudible voice.

"A month. Maybe two."

There would be no surgery, no magic bullet, just unanswered prayers. All that remained for us was the ticking of the clock and the fear of each sunrise. Mom, Sue and I walked out of the doctor's office and sat in my car beneath the shade of a tree. At first there was silence for what seemed an eternity until mom said "Jack, I'm sorry, don't be angry." With that we all fell apart.

I dropped Mom and Sue off back at Mom's apartment and then I sped off to the nearby Catholic Church. I had to speak to someone before I exploded. I knocked on the rectory door and Father Flemming, the pastor answered. I broke down in front of him with the horrible news and he kindly took me inside.

"How am I supposed to believe in God when he lets something like this happen?" I cried? "I could understand his anger at me, Father. I know I've led a wild life. But this woman has been a saint and has never done a single thing to hurt anyone, including God himself."

I kept asking Father Flemming "why" over and over. There were no answers, of course. Such was life and like Johnny Tillotson once told me "John Edward, the older you get the more difficult life becomes."

In the days that followed mom and I went for walks downtown in Napa. At times there would be long minutes of silence between us and then at times she opened up to me.

"Sometimes when I walk down the street" she said one day "I look into the eyes of men passing me and wonder if one of them is Dad trying to find his way back home." She missed him beyond words, but soon her longing for him would be over.

I had to get back to work. Bills needed to be paid and food needed to be on the table, as Mom could no longer work. I rejoined the Burritos for more shows across the country, trying my best to get through each one knowing what mom was going through back in Napa. My sister took care of mom and the kids while I was away, trying her best to maintain some sense of normalcy to their lives. As for me, the road seemed endless, a blur of faces coupled with the redundancy of the same old songs night after night. Sometimes after the shows I would go back to the room and numb myself with cocaine, but it was just a temporary band aid. Still, I needed any kind of comfort I could find. The music helped as well as minor distractions like women or going to clubs with the guys after the concert. But at the end of the day, I was still hurting and still fearing her loss more and more as the end inched its way closer and closer. I was scared.

In the weeks that followed I shuttled back and forth between shows with the Burritos and Napa where mom had now been moved to Keiser Memorial Hospital. I felt like a tennis ball being battered back and forth. One minute I would be at mom's side in her hospital room and the next minute I would be standing onstage playing to a wild screaming audience. Everything seemed to me moving in slow motion, everything except the clock. One evening I was driving through the countryside in Napa, wanting simply to be alone with my thoughts under a beautiful star filled sky. I drove through the vineyards and up thru the surrounding hills trying to clear my mind of the turmoil and anxiety that kept racing through it. I stopped at the edge of steep hill overlooking the valley. It was a beautiful serene setting, the stars twinkling just above me and the lights from the valley twinkling below. I got out and sat on the hood of my car gazing into the sky wishing that all of this was just a dream and I would wake up to the smell of my mom cooking breakfast and the clatter and laughter of my daughter Sarah and my younger brothers and sister gathered around the table. Suddenly, a bright shooting star shot across the sky and I felt a strange sensation like something or someone was calling for me. Mom.

I hopped into my car and raced back to the hospital. My heart was pounding as I floored the gas pedal without a thought of my own safety or being pulled over by the police. When I arrived I quickly made it to her room where I was met by my Aunt Delphine and Uncle Tony, my favorite aunt and uncle who had flown in from Chicago to be with mom. The room was very dark except for the lights on the machines monitoring her heart. Aunt Delphine held my hand and whispered to me "Honey, it's time." She led me to Mom's bedside. She was drifting in and out of conciousness. I took her hand and stroked it. Delphine and Tony took the other. Then mom looked up at me and smiled and in a faint whisper said, "My golden boy." The beeps from the machine grew slower and slower until they became one continuous tone. She was gone.

I walked out of the room and leaned against the cold brick wall and crumbled to the ground. From mom's room I could hear the mournful cries of my aunt and uncle, calling mom's name over and over. The nurses rushed in followed by a doctor. That was it.

I had to get out of the hospital, or explode. I got back in my car and sped off into the night. Through the vineyards at great speed, racing my car with no sense of any direction until I reached the end of a tall ledge where I came to a screeching halt. I wanted to drive over the ledge, off into the air where I could find peace and stop the pain from tearing at my heavy heart. I revved up the engine. "Do it" echoed in my head. I revved it up again and again. "Do it, just do it!" But I couldn't. I switched off the key and silence quickly fell all around me, only the sound of crickets and a distant dog howling at the crescent moon. Dawn was breaking through the darkness as I rested my head against the steering wheel and fell apart. She was only 50.

Mom and dad were my sole reason for running away and getting into the music business. They weathered the slings, arrows and taunts from my grandmother, my Aunt Elaine and Uncle John who forecast ruin and doom for me. We had been through so much together and now they were both gone. Life would never be the same for me again and success would never taste as sweet as before.

We buried mom on a beautiful hillside next to dad. They were together again. My Aunt Elaine and Uncle John attended the funeral. Afterwards, my aunt tried to reconcile with me by attempting to show that had it not been for their phony job offer to my dad we would have never left Hometown, Illinois and thus I would never have had the opportunity to get into the music business. "Fuck you" I thought as I turned and walked away. I would never see, or have anything to do with them again.

When the funeral was over and everyone had left for a reception back at the house I stood by the grave, reminded of a song that always reminded me of my parents devotion to each other.

> "Then one day they died.
> And their graves grew side by side
> On a hill where robins sing
> And they say violets grow there the whole year round
> For their hearts were full of Spring."

Mom and Dad together forever

36 NASHVILLE OR BUST

I continued to divide my time between Napa and the road. I got rid of my condo on the river and moved into Mom's apartment where I could take care of Sarah and my brothers Joe and Tom. Mom's death had shattered the family and eventually my brothers and sister splintered off in various directions with their individual friends. While I was away on tour our dear neighbor and good friend to mom, Veda, helped take care of the kids while I was away. Everyone was hard hit over mom's death, but Veda helped out as much as possible during those difficult days following mom's passing. We couldn't have made it without her.

Back in Hollywood the calendar was starting to look like a war map. The first major tour for us as a hit country act was opening for none other than Gram Parson's former partner Emmylou Harris. This was a great shot for us, visibility-wise. However, we would be facing a crowd that was very familiar with the history of the Flying Burrito Brothers, many of them diehard Gram Parson fans as well. Would they accept this new incarnation of the band?

We still had a few local gigs around southern California to attend to, one in particular was at a country western club called The Crazy Horse Saloon in Pomona, California, where we would be opening for a new band just signed to RCA Records called, Alabama. Alabama was still relatively unknown when we opened for them. Their entire merchandising was set up on one small card table. There had been a lot of hype going around L.A about this band. Somebody in their camp even went so far as to announce that Alabama would be taking up where the now disbanded Eagles had left off. This drew a pretty negative response from the LA music community who were all diehard Eagles fans. Who were these country clowns to waltz right into the Eagles' home turf and announce that they would take their place? I was curious and looking forward to hearing about a band that seemed to have the country music industry buzzing.

When they hit the stage, I was shocked by how average they sounded. They sang decent enough, but instrumentally they were no better than your average corner tavern house band. The guitar player Jeff, was very weak. He played with absolutely no fire or stand out style. Their arrangements were just as boring as their song selections which, for the most part, were all covers. They were a far cry from the Eagles. That was for certain!

I couldn't understand what the hype was all about. A year later Alabama would be selling millions of records and filling up auditoriums nationwide. Their merchandising would soon be transported in two semi-trucks. Just goes to show "you can't judge a book by looking at the cover."

On that same night we played with Alabama I spotted a knock-out waitress working the tables. She was slim and trim with long, light brown hair cascading down her back. She was wearing a thin T-shirt and blue satin shorts and every guy in the house wanted to get their hands on her. As it happened, our roadie Bill had a date after the show with this girl's roommate and asked if I wanted to join the three of them for a few drinks afterwards. I jumped the chance. Janice Smith was her name and she was quite the catch. It seemed obvious to me that she felt the same because no sooner did we reach their house than the beautiful waitress from the Lone Star Tavern was rolling and tumbling in her water bed with the newest member of the Flying Burrito Brothers. She was beautiful with a body to die for and I couldn't get enough of her. The next morning found us locked in each other's arms sleeping like babies when suddenly there was a loud knock on the front door.

"Oh, shit!" Janice whispered.

"Who's at the door" I asked rubbing my tired eyes.

Then came the words no guy likes to hear. "It's my boyfriend! Quick get in my roommate's room fast!"

Grabbing my clothes and completely naked I found myself ushered to another bedroom into the same bed as Janice's roommate, who was naked and passed out. I heard a muffled conversation through the wall followed by the slamming of the front door. The bedroom door opened and Janice simply said "He's gone. C'mon back." I didn't ask what happened. I was too focused on jumping her bones again, which I did. All through the morning we made love and chatted away the hours. I really liked this girl and wanted to see more of her. And once again, she felt the same.

The band was set to pick me up at Janice's house on our way out of town en route to join up with Emmylou's tour, and this time we would be doing it in style. Gib and Pete had told me that their friend "Jimbo" had rebuilt an old touring bus and now it was as sharp as a brand-new Silver Eagle, the 'creme de la creme" of country music touring coaches. Naturally, I boasted all about this to Janice, trying to score even more points with her. After all, I was now a true-blue country music star. How else would one of such notoriety travel? I promised to keep in touch with Janice as we walked out the front door to the curb where the bus would pick me up. There was no doubt in my mind that I would come back to see her as soon as possible. This one was a keeper! We chatted a bit and waited for our new custom built touring bus to come rolling down the street. Suddenly I heard the sound of an old car backfiring.

"Did you hear that?" I asked Janice.

"Yeah. Sounds like somebody's car dying" she answered.

Just then our eyes opened wide and our jaws dropped as an old beat-up white bus rattled down the street and made its way right to us. As it came to a halt I noticed that the small bus had been covered over with a single coat of white paint, so thin that beneath the paint you could make out the following words above the windshield: *CHURCH BUS*. At first I thought it was a joke but when I saw the whole band squeezed inside I knew it was for real. Gib and Pete stepped out to greet me as if totally oblivious to the hideous monstrosity before us.

"This is our new tour bus?" I asked.

Gib answered "Well, it didn't come out exactly as Jimbo said it would but it'll get us there."

"You're fucking kidding, right?" I chimed back. "It's a goddamn church bus!"

At this moment a smiling Martyn came bounding out of the bus with a beer in hand as jovial as could be. He slapped me on the back and said in his thick Welsh accent,

"Hey JB. How do you like the new bus?"

I looked at Janice who was doing all she could to not faint from laughter. I peeked in the door and saw the band packed in tightly with our luggage and gear. There was one metal table attached to the floor, similar to the kind of table one would find in a jail cell but funniest of all was the seat next to the driver … it was a metal folding chair! Everyone was in a festive mood as I kissed Janice a sad goodbye, picked up my bags and slowly entered the bus as if I was headed up the steps to the guillotine. Jimbo the roadie, a huge biker-like presence, was perched on the driver's seat as I slowly passed him by. "Hey John" said Jimbo with all the cheer of a Santa Clause, "How do you like the bus?" I seriously thought I had fallen into a criminal mental institution. I just squeezed into my seat and peered out the window at Janice as we slowly moved forward an inch at a time. Surely I still had Rick Nelson's phone number somewhere in my pocket!

We inched our way all over the southwest part of America huddled together in the tiny church bus that Gib's friend Jimbo had built. It held 100 miles to the gallon and had no air conditioning nor heating. It was embarrassing, but as Gib said "It'll get us there." We were now playing major arenas as the opening act for Emmylou, who traveled with her band in a beautiful shiny new Silver Eagle touring bus. It was quite a sight to see … our tiny, white church bus parked right next to the huge Silver Eagle of Emmylou's at the artists' entrances of the auditoriums and concert halls we played. Onstage I joked to the crowd that we desperately needed a hit record so that we could afford to get rid of our little white church bus. The crowd thought I was making a joke until they filed out of the arenas after the show! From the bus I could hear them talking as they passed by, saying things like "He wasn't kidding! Look at that thing!" or "They really do ride in a shitty church bus!"

The reception to our shows was positive for the most part. Emmylou's band and crew were terrific. A few of them like drummer John Ware, were old friends of mine. John had played on my solo sessions for Apple records. Emmylou, however, was distant and not very approachable. Perhaps it was because of her closeness to the late Gram Parsons and the fact that we were now using the Flying Burrito Brothers name. In any case she never spoke to us and kept an icy distance. I envied her band. They were sensational and rightly dubbed "The Hot Band." Unlike us, they were tight and well-rehearsed and played their asses off, while we played good but not "great." I missed the caliber of Rick Nelson's band and wished the Burritos would put as much effort into the show as Rick's band did. It was a constant source of frustration within me.

The reviews of our debut album "Hearts on the Line" were mixed. In the rock and alternative press, we were slammed as phonies and accused of living off the past glories of the founding group. However, in the country music press we received much more favorable reviews without the mention of Gram Parsons. In fact, country radio jumped on our records and we received solid national airplay. Country fans didn't give a shit about the original band. To most country fans we were a brand-new act, with a funny name.

It didn't matter to the hip rock press that our individual credentials certainly proved that we were anything but phonies. Pete, a founding member, had worked with everyone including the Bee Gees, John Lennon, Joe Cocker and many more. Gib had worked with Neil Young, The New Riders of the Purple Sage, Arlo, Ronstadt as well as having his own compositions recorded by Rod Stewart, Ron Wood, The Dillards, The Byrds etc. Mine included Ronstadt, Arlo, signing to the Beatles label, Joan Baez as well as writing national country hits for other artists. Not bad for three "phonies."

Although our records were receiving serious airplay and chart action, I was not satisfied with Michael Lloyd's production. Our records sounded lightweight like the Bellamy Brothers and Lloyd himself was too far removed from the kind of style and background of country rock we were used to. He was a wealthy, pop music, Beverly Hills guy while we were the hard-core Palomino Club set.

One big blunder he made was shockingly unforgivable. I had written a ballad called "Why Must the Ending Be So Sad?" and for the recording I wanted Dolly to duet with me on it. I called her and she told me to send a demo of the song over to her at the Beverly Wilshire Hotel where she was staying. I gladly followed up on it and rushed the demo over. She loved it and agreed to do the guest appearance. I told Michael and the session was set for the following week. The day of the session Dolly showed up in fine form, joking and laughing and being, well…Dolly. We ran the song down and she rehearsed for about a half hour to my pre-recorded vocal and it sounded incredible. Our voices blended like brother and sister. After the session Dolly informed Lloyd that it was important he received a clearance from her label RCA as soon as possible, because she would soon be leaving the label and when that happened RCA would not approve her guesting on our album. So, time was of the essence. A week or two later I received a test pressing of our album and instantly listened to my track with Dolly. I was horrified when I heard this high whiney voice singing harmony to mine. Where was Dolly?

As it was explained to me, Michael waited too long and could not get the clearance from RCA for Dolly's performance. Instead, without consulting myself or Gib, he shockingly recorded his own thin, falsetto voice in Dolly's place. It was absolutely horrible and to make matters worse it was too late to do anything about it. The album was already on its way to manufacturing. I was livid. What was once a beautiful duet track with Dolly Parton was now reduced to 3 minutes of pure shit, thanks to Curb's brilliant choice as our producer. To this day I still can't listen to it.

Whenever I discussed my dissatisfaction over the choice of producers I would always get the same response. "Well, we're getting hit records so what's the problem?" I wanted our records to have some punch to them, starting with hard hitting drums as in the recordings on CBS act Foster & Lloyd, another duo making great records under the production of Steve Buckingham. Our recordings sounded as if they were recorded under a blanket. The drums sounded like cardboard boxes making everything sound like a Perry Como record. We desperately needed a change but Curb would have nothing to do with it. The more hits we logged up the more Curb embraced Michael Lloyd. So, we (namely "I") were stuck with him for another album.

From Los Angeles to Manhattan the Flying Burrito Brothers crisscrossed across the country in our little white church bus, like a politician running for president. We played country clubs, fairs, concerts as well as television appearances. It was a miracle that the bus held out. In Colorado we had to climb through the Rocky Mountains in the middle of winter and the bus had no heating system so we were all huddled together dressed in big coats and hats. Many times, we nearly ran out of gas and as always Martyn had to knock on the door of the homes of the service station owners pleading to let us fill up our dry tank. It was a rough ride that year.

The more ground we covered the higher our singles rose in the charts. We started getting tighter onstage and the crowds responded. We still had to answer the same old question when interviewed "What do you think Gram would say about the Burritos being a hit country act." I'd reply with some polite response, but inside my head I was thinking "How the hell should we know? Why don't you dig him up and ask him"? It was great to hear our records on the radio, even though I hated the way they were recorded. We did what no previous Flying Burrito Brothers lineup had ever accomplished in the ten years prior to my joining the band … landing hits. Say what you will about the genius of Gram Parsons. Gib, Pete and I proved that we were no light weight phonies.

Back in Los Angeles I continued dating Janice Smith and soon we decided that she move in with me up in Napa. I guess in hindsight I rushed into the decision way too soon, but in 1981 all my decisions seemed rushed. At first, the brother Joe and daughter Sarah liked Janice. She could be sweet and loving and a joy to be around. But as time went on she would start bossing the kids around, laying down rules and even putting a padlock on our bedroom door, "mom's" bedroom door! She acted as if the kids were potential thieves. Things soured fast. Meanwhile, it was around this time that Martyn, Gib and I had a meeting concerning our location. Martyn suggested we move to Nashville and become part of the country music community 100%. It made sense. For the past year we had been flying in and out of Nashville on promotional trips for Epic / Curb and every time we did we were treated terrific by the powers that be. It was suggested to us that politically it would be the "smart thing" to do. Radio would embrace us more if they knew we were a serious Nashville act and our label Epic / Curb Nashville would certainly take us a bit more seriously knowing we made such a commitment. In 1981 we decided to make the move from California to Nashville and set up an office just off of 16th Avenue on famed Music Row. But first there was another album to do with Michael Lloyd and before THAT, another decision, Sneaky Pete.

Besides being a famous steel guitarist, Pete Kleinow was also a well-respected film animator whose credits included working on Star Wars, Caveman (with Ringo Starr) the Pillsbury Dough Boy and surprisingly enough, GUMBY! Dividing his time between both occupations was becoming nearly impossible for Pete, especially since we now had hit records and a demanding schedule. It wasn't uncommon for Pete to cancel a tour at the last minute due to a film schedule change and we would always be left to scramble for a last-minute replacement. Many times, promoters would cancel our gigs when they found out that founding member Sneaky Pate would not be there. It was a dilemma for us and now, with the plans for relocating on the table, we had to confront Pete about a commitment, one way or the other. Since Pete couldn't commit to the band, the decision was made to continue as the Burrito Brothers, now a duo featuring Gib and myself. I was against it. Why the hell would we want to have a band name as a duo, especially THAT name? But once again, Curb Records made the call. Thus, we were now The Burrito Brothers. I cringed every time we were introduced onstage. I wanted us to be called Guilbeau & Beland but the argument was that the label had already put in a lot of money promoting the Flying Burrito Brothers and that the name was still fresh in the ears of radio. We would virtually be starting from scratch if we used our own names. "So, what?" I thought. Our records were still commercially strong and with a little press we could make the name transition with little to no problems. But the subject was closed.

Gib and I now called, The Burrito Brothers

In 1982 we went back into the Beverly Hills studio again with Michael and recorded our second album for Epic / Curb called "THE BURRITO BROTHERS -SUNSET SUNDOWN". For this album we continued to use Sneaky Pete on steel, but this time only as a sideman. We had written some pretty strong songs on this new album and Michael Lloyd seemed to be a bit more flexible towards our production ideas than on the last album. On banjo we used the great Larry McNeely, saxophone legend Tom Scott and former Rick Nelson bandmate Billy Thomas for harmonies.

Michael had come up with a great song penned by hit writers Johnny Cymbal and Austin Roberts called "I'M DRINKING CANADA DRY. Gib and I wrote two other strong singles CLOSER TO YOU and IF SOMETHING SHOULD COME BETWEEN US (LET IT BE LOVE). These tracks packed a little more punch than our previous album which came as a relief to me. We worked very hard on the project and the result was a pretty damned good album.

Norman Seefe color pic from the Burrito Bros "Sunset – Sundown" album

The famed rock and roll photographer Norman Seef took the album cover of Gib and I standing on a hill above the Sunset Strip exactly at sundown. I wore my best country clothes and hat while Gib wore our dear friend, the late Clarence White's old leather fringe Nudie outfit. It was a great photo. On the inside cover Norman took a classic black and white shot of Gib and I playing our brand new jumbo Guild F-50 acoustic guitars which arrived from the Guild factory in New Jersey the very same day as the shoot. I still have mine today as a matter of fact. The photo was reminiscent of the old Everly Brothers pictures. Norman, who was my choice, was brilliant.

With the album in the can I flew to Nashville with Gib and Martyn on Epic / Curb related business while our road crew helped pack and move Janice and Sarah to our new house just outside Nashville in Fairview, Tennessee. Behind us in Napa, my brother Joey moved in with my sister Susan while my brother Tom moved in with his best friend's family. Mom's apartment was empty. With both her and dad now gone there was no reason to stay. Napa would always be a bittersweet memory but now it was only an image in a rearview mirror. Ahead lay Nashville Tennessee, a new life and a new chapter to an already long and strange career.

The Burrito Bros on the Grand Ol Opry

37 16TH AVENUE & BEYOND

SUNSET SUNDOWN delivered more hits for us in 1982. First came a tune I had written along with Gib called CLOSER TO YOU. We had written it with Larry Gatlin and his brothers in mind. It was a solid vocal harmony song with a big chorus, perfect for country radio who jumped on it instantly. We were now settled firmly in Nashville as well. Martyn found us an old house on 19th Avenue which served as our new office. We were right in the center of everything.

Meanwhile, Janice, Sarah and I moved into a beautiful home on the outskirts of Nashville in a rural farm community called Fairview. Martyn and his wife Taylor also bought a house in Fairview, right behind ours. Janice got along fine with Sarah and things seemed to be working out perfectly. So good in fact that we decided to make it official and get married. Again, I had only lived with Janice a short while and though there were a few "flags up" with her, I ignored them and went ahead and tied the knot.

The service was held at a non-denominational church in Franklin, Tennessee. Gib served as my best man and Martyn gave the bride away, since Janice's father had recently died. The reception was held at the famed Music Row bistro and bar called Close Quarters and everyone who was anyone showed up. In fact, a lot of uninvited guests, mostly struggling song writers and singers I barely knew started showing up and cleaning us out of champagne. Still, everyone including Janice and I and Sarah had a lovely time, although I did find it a bit uncomfortable when a drunk Rick Blackburn, head of CBS / Nashville, kissed the bride, a little longer than I cared for. One of the neat things that happened after we cut the cake was getting a special gift from Martyn and Gib. It was a small box with something moving inside of it and when we opened the top and looked inside there was the cutest Springer Spaniel puppy we had ever seen. We instantly fell in love with him and named him Arthur. He would go on to be a big part of our family for the next 17 years.

The hits kept coming. After CLOSER TO YOU, written primarily by me, came IF SOMETHING SHOULD COME BETWEEN US (LET IT BE LOVE), a song mostly written by Gib which I helped him out on musically. The latter was a pure country rocker ala The Eagles style with big harmonies and even a hot banjo appearing in the final chorus, courtesy of the 5-string virtuoso, Larry McNeely. It was a great record, one of the few of ours that I was 100% happy with. But now we were a duo, no more band dramas. It was just Gib and I along with our faithful manager Martyn and publisher Bo Golsen and the gigs came rolling in. First off and soon after our arrival in Nashville, we hit the road as opening act for the legendary George Jones.

Jones was a living legend for his music as well as his personal life. As a singer, he influenced everybody, from up and coming country hit makers to the Rolling Stones. His ability to twist and bend melody lines was unmatched. Along with producer Billy Sherrill, George turned out some of the greatest records in country music history such as THE GRAND TOUR, THE RACE IS ON and, arguably, one of the greatest country songs of all time, HE STOPPED LOVING HER TODAY. However, fueled on cocaine, pills and booze, old "Possum" as he was nicknamed, could be a dark, sad story much like the late Hank Williams Sr.

Most of the gigs we did with George were terrific. He was great onstage when he was sober, singing hit after hit along with a funny sense of humor. The fans were as loyal as church goers, even when George walked out stoned, forgot words and stumbled through the show.

Then there was the time we played in George's hometown in Saratoga, Texas. After Gib and I finished our 45-minute set George's band set up for the main event. A banner hung above the stage that read "Welcome Home George". I noticed that a few of the musicians looked a bit nervous and not happy in the slightest. They began the show featuring various band members singing standards to the waiting crowd. One of the band members was a very young beautiful Lorie Morgan, who was married to George's bass player at the time. Lorie was an unbelievable singer and a real crowd pleaser, but she was now singing well beyond her usual allotted time and the crowd starting getting restless waiting to see their hometown boy, the legendary George Jones. The more Lorie sang the more people would yell out, "Where's George?" Each time Lorie would start yet another song the crowd grew more intense, booing her and demanding George show up. I noticed Lorie crying while she was singing. The booing grew louder and the crowd now sounded like a lynch mob. Then, the announcement came.

"Ladies and gentlemen due to an illness tonight's George Jones Show is cancelled and refunds can be made at the ticket office. We apologize"

The audience knew better. The booing now erupted into jeers and shouting as the auditorium houselights went back up and pre-recorded music was played. Backstage I noticed everyone scrambling back and forth talking about George not showing up. He was too fucked up to come out of the bus. It was a terrible but common occurrence at George Jones' shows. In fact, his new nickname became "No Show Jones." It was obvious to Gib, Martyn and I that cocaine was George's Achilles Heel. We noticed how god awful thin he had become and how his eyes seem to always be wide open without blinking. He was a wreck and soon his substance abuse became more famous than his music.

One night in Nashville Martyn, Gib and I were heading to the Hall of Fame Hotel on 16th Avenue where anyone who was anything would stop by, hang out and listen to the house band, made up of the best session musicians in town. It was always a great scene at the Hall Of Fame bar. Anyway, we were walking through the parking lot when we heard the sound of someone's car horn continuously beeping. We trailed it down to a white automobile and could see that the driver had passed out with his head leaning on the wheel of the car, setting off the horn. Then, on closer look, we were shocked to see that the unconscious driver was none other than George Jones. Martyn and Gib checked the doors but they were all locked. We had to act fast because we knew George was holding drugs and that the cops would soon arrive. Martyn broke the window on the driver's side and opened the door and then like clockwork, Martyn pulled George out and took him into the hotel where he bought "ol Possum" a room. Martyn left him on the bed to sleep it off. We never heard a word back from George but presumed that someone took him back home the following morning.

Our latest single, and last one with Michael Lloyd, "I'm Drinking Canada Dry" was starting to move high on the charts so we hit the road again this time with the one and only Hank Williams Jr. I loved Hank's records and so did the rest of the country. He was hotter than a pistol with number one hit singles, produced by my old mentor Jimmy Bowen, as well as album sales busting into the pop charts, a rarity for a country act. Hank, the only son of the great late Hank Williams, Sr., started out being managed by his mother Audrey who put the boy on the road at an early age singing his daddy's songs backed by Hank Sr.'s old band The Drifting Cowboys. When Hollywood made a movie about his famous father, Hank Jr.'s voice was used instead of actor George Hamilton's. As the years went by and Hank grew up he wanted to record his own songs and break away from singing his father's hits but Audrey and MGM Records wouldn't have it. On August 8, 1975, while on a hunting trip in Montana, he fell off Alax Peak and was nearly killed. Most of the bones in his face were crushed and after numerous surgeries had drastically altered his appearance he started wearing hats, sunglasses and sporting a beard to cover up the many scars he received from the fall. When he recovered from his accident, Hank stopped singing his father's songs in favor of a more southern rock, bluesy style of country music. He teamed up with Bowen and began a long string of number one hit singles and albums that showcased his new songwriting and hard ass vocal style. He was no longer standing in the shadows of his dad. He was now the number one country act in the business.

Hank liked Gib and I. He was a Flying Burrito Brothers fan and he and his staff treated us terrific. Opening for Hank was a challenge because his fans were a very rowdy crowd. Furthermore, Hank's own road band were not only ear splitting loud but were stoned out of their heads most of the time onstage. The Burrito Brothers carried little gear onstage, a few amps and keyboards etc. but Hank's band had more gear onstage than Led Zeppelin. To make matters worse, his band lacked the playing skills of the musicians who played on his records. They were not a good band, loud but not very good.

At one gig Gib and I were sitting in our trailer dressing room following our opening set when hank's roadie burst into the room. "Hey John, Hank wants to know if you can play with the band right now." I looked at him puzzled. "Man, I just finished playing. And he already has a guitarist." I answered. "Well, the thing is" he continued "Hank's guitar player was climbing up on top his amp to do a guitar solo and lost his footing. He's knocked out!"

I could hear the rumble and roar from the hall and felt that my addition to Hanks band wouldn't have made a bit of difference to his show. The fans were going crazy and Hank was tearing it up onstage. "Man, I'm gonna pass" I said. "Hank's doing just fine without me."

38 LEFTY FRIZZELL AND A FEW CHANGES

One of our biggest influences was the late great country legend Lefty Frizzell. Orville "Lefty" Frizzell was second in popularity only to Hank Williams back in the early 1950's. His vocal style influenced such modern-day country singers such as Merle Haggard, Randy Travis and John Anderson. Lefty came on the scene in the early 50's with such monster hits as "I Love You A Thousand ways" "If You've Got the Money (I've Got The Time)", "Saginaw Michigan" "Always Late" "Mom & Dad Waltz" "Long Black Veil" and many more. He was flamboyant onstage as well, being one of the first country performers to wear rhinestone fringe cowboy clothes onstage. His influence on generations of country stars to come can never be measured.

In early 1981 Gib and I flew to Nashville to meet the staff at CBS Records and to record promotional ID's for the radio stations around the country that were playing our records. "Hi, this is John and Gib and we're The Burrito Brothers, and we want to say that you're listening to KWHL in Moline Illinois, the best country station ever!" "Hi, this is John and Gib and we're the Burrito Brothers wishing everyone at KWHL in Moline Illinois a very merry Christmas." etc. etc. CBS put us up at the Hall of Fame hotel right in the heart of Nashville's legendary Music Row. During the afternoons there wasn't much for us to do so one day I decided to go right next door and visit the Country Music Hall of Fame. It was the middle of the week and there were only few tourists there so I figured I could kill a little time and check out all the historic exhibits. After all, it only cost a few dollars.

Once inside I walked around the beautiful building checking out all the old stage costumes and memorabilia of my favorite country stars from the past. There were Web Peirce and Hank Williams custom suits and guitars with their names inlayed right across the guitar necks. Boots, hats, sheet music, everything historic in country music was there. It was fascinating. Then I came across the one exhibit I had been hoping to find, Lefty Frizzell's stage outfit and his famous Gibson guitar. There was a little card on the window explaining who Lefty was and his importance in country music. I stared at the big old Gibson J-200 acoustic guitar, imagining Lefty onstage strumming it while singing his hits night after night in the early 1950's. The stories that guitar could tell.

I wanted to find the actual Hall of Fame plaques and see Lefty's award for myself. It was a short walk over to the room where all who have been inducted into the Country Music Hall of Fame were honored. There was Hank Williams, Loretta Lynn, Faron Young, Roy Accuff, Jim Reeves, one by one in a long line of the most famous names in country music, all but one. Lefty Frizzell. I was shocked to not find Lefty amongst his contemporaries. Perhaps they were repairing his plaque. I figured I'd ask one of the tour guides what the deal was.

"Excuse me, miss" I said "I was looking for Lefty Frizell's Hall of Fame plaque on the wall and couldn't find it. Can you tell me where it is?" The girl gave me a confused, weird look and simply said "Well, he isn't a member of the Hall of Fame."
"Are you kidding me" I replied? "You guys feature his outfit and his guitar along with a detailed card profiling his importance in country music. You mean to tell me he was never inducted into the Hall of Fame?"

"That's correct, sir" came the cold reply.

I couldn't believe it. Next to Hank Williams, the most influential stylist in country music whose costumes and guitar are displayed in the Hall of Fame Museum had never been inducted into the Hall Of Fame. This would be the equivalent of the Rolling Stones being omitted from the Rock & Roll Hall of Fame. What was the reason? How could Lefty been passed over?

I went back to our hotel and told Gib what I had discovered and like me, he was shocked. We asked around town and found out that there had been a political issue that had something to do personally between Lefty and one of the Hall of Fame board members. What wrong could Lefty possibly have done to cause him to be ignored by the CMA Hall Of Fame? Surely, other recipients had darker personal baggage than Lefty. Hank Williams was certainly no choirboy and yet he has been all but canonized in the eyes of the Hall of Fame. Did Lefty murder someone? Was he a communist?

I dug deeper. Lefty had a drinking problem, as did 70% of the biggest names in the business, and he had burned some bridges as his career spotlight started dimming in the 60's. By the 70's he was long past his prime and playing gigs around the country using pick-up bands. In his final years he recorded two terrific albums. One yielded a sure-fire hit song penned by Lefty and his friend Whitey Schaffer called "That's The Way Love Goes". His recording of the song could melt the polar ice caps. The sadness and warmth of his aged vocal gave the song one of the most emotional readings I had ever heard. Lefty, already a broken man, had hoped the song would be his comeback record. However, the label decided to give it to a new younger artist on their label named Johnny Rodriguez, who scored a number one hit with it. Lefty was heartbroken and died shortly after, broke and relatively forgotten.

Since Gib and I were hot with a few hits under our belts we were able to be heard by a lot of people. We also weren't intimidated by the powers that be in Nashville at the time. Other artists tip toed around what they said on radio and TV. Gib and I didn't give a damn what we said or how we acted. We were our own act and not manipulated by any record company or management. Nobody pulled our career strings. We made a deal to only do interviews if the reporter would add that the Burrito Brothers request that country music fans everywhere write to the Hall of Fame and demand that Lefty Frizzell be inducted.

Letters started pouring into the Hall of Fame, each one demanding that Lefty be inducted. Other artists heard about our campaign and hopped onboard like Jon Anderson and David Allen Coe and even Lefty's widow Alice and daughter Lois embraced our cause. Our manager Martyn was told, through sources, that we were stepping on important toes and advised us to stop. When we heard about it we only stepped things up. On our live shows, radio and television across the country we asked fans to write in. Then on the evening of October 11, 1982, while driving home from a recording session in Muscle Sholes, Alabama I picked up the CMA Awards Show on my radio. The signal was very weak, but I turned it up loud as not to miss the Hall Of Fame Inductee awards segment. Finally, I pulled over to the side of the road and listened with my breath held.

"And this year's Hall Of Fame inductees are..... Roy Horton, Marty Robbins and, Lefty Frizzell." Through the crackle and the hiss of the fading radio signal I could hear the crowd cheering. I hit the steering wheel and shouted "YES!" I drove all the way home with smile on my face and a bit misty in the eyes as well.

A few weeks later I met with Lefty's widow, Alice. She was a warm, friendly lady and was most grateful about what we and everyone else did to see that Lefty received his due. In return she gave me his original leather guitar strap with the name Lefty Frizzell across it. Alice died shortly afterwards. Many young and up and coming artists today seem to imagine that having a hit record is the top of the mountain. For Gib and I the top of the mountain was righting a wrong for a man we never personally knew but who inspired ourselves and so many others. In Lefty's words "that's the way love goes."

Hall of Famer Lefty Frizzell

Gib and I continued to log up the miles in 1982. The more success we achieved the longer the tours became. We did countless gigs, interviews and local radio appearances throughout the country promoting our latest single. At times I barely could remember what town we were in. We had a great band and a tight show and shared the stage with many of the top acts of the day. One particular act we shared the bill with was none other than my old boss and dear friend Rick Nelson. We were booked as Rick's opening act at Billy Bob's Texas in Fort Worth, Texas and I was thrilled to see not only Rick, but the rest of the guys in the band as well. It was a bit of a strange feeling not joining them onstage when Rick came on. But it was fabulous seeing them all again and reminiscing backstage. I managed to find Rick alone in his dressing room and poked my head in.

"Hey, Rick. Are you busy?"

Rick smiled and in that familiar soft voice of his said "Hey John, wow come on in."

"Man, Rick, it's so cool seeing all of you again. I sure miss playing with you guys" I said.

Rick replied "We miss you too, man. Seems funny that you guys are opening for us."

"I know" I replied. "Maybe I'll jump ship and leave with you guys after the show tonight." Although it was meant as a joke, it wasn't. As cool as it was to now be a hit country artist on my own, I missed the comradery and professionalism of Rick's camp. I still felt out of place with the name The Burrito Brothers hanging over my head.

"Hey Rick" I said "I'm still playing my old 56 Telecaster. I was wondering if you could sign it for me. I'm kind of collecting signatures of the acts I've worked with and of course yours would really be appreciated." Rick smiled and answered "Sure, no problem." I grabbed my Tele from my dressing room and brought it back for Rick to sign. It was an unusual moment because we had been so close, that my asking for his autograph almost seemed like a joke. Rick seemed to struggle for the right words and took quite a long time before he actually signed it. But when he did, he wrote the perfect words. "To John – Thanks for everything."

I knew he meant that. We had worked so closely together and had such a tight bond between us that I'm sure it was hard for him to find the appropriate words to write down. But when I read it, I was moved. I never saw Rick Nelson again. In a few years he, Bobby Neal and roadie Clark Russell would be dead from the crash of Rick's plane, ironically in Texas just weeks before I was to rejoin him again. Of all the acts I had ever worked with, Rick was at the top of the list, ahead of all others by a country mile. To this day I still miss our time together. What a time it was.

Once Gib and I settled in Nashville we demanded a change of producers. I had finally had it with Michael Lloyd after he had recently produced Gib and I singing on the soundtrack for a lightweight movie called "Dream Chaser." The film was produced by the folks who did "The Wilderness Family" a Disney style film geared for kids. The music we sang was written by LA songwriters Al Kasha and Joel Hirschhorn, two old Beverly Hills pop writers whose credits included the music to "Pete's Dragon." I detested the songs but since they were just for a low budget movie we agreed to sing them for the soundtrack, but only on the promise that our label would not release this to radio as a Burrito Brothers single record. The theme song was a terrible "Rain Drops Falling on My Head" rip off called "My Kind Of lady." It was awful and certainly the last song you would ever have expected to be recorded by the California country rock act The Burrito Brothers. Michael Lloyd and Curb Records head Dick Whitehouse assured us that the song would not be released as our single so we flew out to L.A and recorded it for the film.

A few weeks later while on the road Gib and I were sitting in a radio station being interviewed when the disc jockey said, "Your new single is quite a departure from your usual brand of country rock isn't it?"

"I'm not sure I understand the question" I replied.

The disc Jockey handed me a 45 single. The label read "The

Burrito Brothers – My Kind Of Lady."

I almost threw up. For weeks afterward "My Kind of Lady" kept showing up at our radio interviews like a bad penny.

To add insult to injury, the theme song was from a movie that hadn't even been released yet so those listening to our record would only gather that this crap song was our choice to record. I was white with anger and wanted no more of Michael Lloyd as a producer.

We got our wish. The Nashville division of CBS agreed that we needed a production change. Once again, I threw my name in the hat and once again I was shot down. CBS wanted one of their own and it was decided that Randy Scruggs, son of the great banjo legend Earl Scruggs, would be the guy for us. Randy had his own studio just outside of Nashville and he was the new "wonder boy" for CBS. Both Gib and I had known Randy from our days with Linda Ronstadt and we really liked him. However, as soon as we started working together I could feel a clash between Randy and me. Randy booked himself to play guitar on the tracks without even asking us. Furthermore, he even hired a Nashville session fiddler to play instead of Gib!

I also felt that his choice of tunes was lightweight for my taste but we soon found out that we had little say as far as material went. Gib and I had a couple great songs we had written but they didn't seem to excite Randy. It was a very uncomfortable experience but at least we had someone in the producer's chair that was more suited for our style than Michael Lloyd.

We recorded a full album with Randy that yielded one hit single "Blue and Broken Hearted Me" which turned out to be a very good record thanks to the great playing of Dobro ace Jerry Douglas. Because Randy was our producer we were able to get his legendary dad Earl to play banjo on the opening track. We were also invited to guest on Earl's new solo album "Sitting On top Of the World" which yielded another hit single "Would You Love Me One More Time?"" this time under the title "Earl Scruggs and the Burrito Brothers". The relationship with Randy as producer certainly was a lot better than the one we had with Michael Lloyd but it still wasn't the direction I had hoped we would find in Nashville. Although we had two more hit singles with Randy, the actual completed album we recorded with Randy never saw the light of day. In fact, it remains unreleased to this day.

Around this time, we were also having internal problems, with our manager and dear friend Martyn Smith. Martyn's drinking and cocaine use had gotten out of control since we moved to Nashville. He had personal issues with his wife as well. He was starting to become an embarrassment to us at social functions and was becoming increasingly harder and harder to work with. It broke our hearts because Martyn, Gib and I had been the Three Musketeers of sorts, having resurrected the forgotten tattered and weathered Flying Burrito Brothers and landed the act the first hit records they had ever had prior to us joining the band. Gib and I had discussed firing Martyn but we didn't have the courage. We loved him like a brother and just couldn't find it in our hearts to let him go. He had worked so hard for us and had been there for us during some very hard times. Now he was out of control and we had to do something about it.

Martyn and his wife Taylor lived right behind our house in Fairview, Tennessee just outside of Nashville.

Often, we would have BBQ's and hang out together in the backyard sharing many happy times together. But now Martyn and Taylor were barely speaking let alone sharing any kind of intimacy. Martyn's drug use kept growing and often there would be major fights between them.

One night, Martyn showed up at our back porch, carrying a full case of beer under his arm. He was obviously drunk and feeling good and wanted to hang out with us at our place. We invited him in and for the next few hours we reminisced about years past and all we had achieved together. I found Martyn in a very happy but odd mood. I brushed it off as him just being drunk. Finally, he said goodbye and gave me an unusually long hug before stumbled back through our yard and home.

The next morning Gib and I headed into Nashville for an early morning radio interview with the Armed Forces Network. As we took our seats in the studio and started putting our headphones on, the interviewer said, "Gee guys, sorry to hear about your manager." Gib and I looked at each other. "Why, what happened"? I asked.

"Oh, you haven't heard?" he responded in an embarrassing tone.

"No. What happened?" I repeated.

He handed us a copy of the morning's Nashville Tennessean newspaper. Our eyes hit the headline. "Burrito Brothers manager found dead in Fairview. Suspected suicide."

We were stunned and before we knew it we were on the air being interviewed by Armed Forces Radio. I can't remember a word of what we said. We just stammered through our answers and somehow got through it and then raced back to my house to find out what had happened.

Martyn had been found in his garage with the car running. On the front seat the police found a large bag of cocaine. There was no note left behind. Martyn just decided it was time to leave.

In the days that followed, Gib and I had to get back on the road for a few dates with country star Lacy J Dalton. We were still in a haze. We couldn't believe Martyn was gone. We felt like a ship without a rudder. Now, without a manager we were floating aimlessly without any representation. It was a scary time.

Meanwhile, a ray of sunshine broke through the gray skies when I learned that my song "Forever You" would be the next single record for the hit group The Whites. I was very happy when I heard the news because I had written the song exclusively for them. In writing a song for an act like the Whites you were taking a gamble. At that time in country music the radio playlists were dominated by crossover country artists who, for the most part, had abandoned traditional country instruments in favor of pop sounding guitars and keyboards. Crossover acts like Kenny Rogers, Ann Murray, TG Sheppard, The Bellamy Brothers and Alabama were turning out records that leaned more towards pop than country. Then, in the middle of this crossover country / pop domination came this little three-piece trio called the Whites, which featured Ricky Skaggs wife Sharon, her sister Cheryl and their father Buck. They also featured the incredible sound of a new kid in town who was re-inventing the traditional sound of the Dobro. His name was Jerry Douglas. With lush three part harmonies and Jerry's signature Dobro playing the Whites were literally inventing commercial bluegrass. They were a breath of fresh air in a cluttered arena of crossover wannabe artists. I was a huge fan of their music and had set out to write a song for them. I had found a greeting card in my desk at home that read "Forever Yours." I thought about it and changed the wording around to "Forever You."

"Though we're apart and time is stilled
Deep in my heart one vow holds true.
I swore it then and I'll swear it now
Now and for always Forever You.
Amazing love. The flame burns true
Forever you Forever you
We'll count the nights like lovers do
Forever You Forever You."

I recorded the demo in Nashville and hired the White's road band, including Jerry Douglas for the track. For vocals I used singers Rick and Janice Carnes, who had written two of the Whites previous hits. It was a one shot or nothing risk because if the Whites had passed on "Forever You" there wouldn't have been another artist who could remotely record a traditional sounding song like it. When the session was over Jerry Douglas asked if he could take the song to Ricky Skaggs, who was producing the Whites and of course I happily agreed. As it happened, they fell in love with the song and not only released it as a single but even titled the album, "Forever You." When I heard their version I almost burst out crying. It was so beautiful and captured everything I had put into the song. It would become a big hit for the Whites and bring in some very much needed income for me and my family.

Forever You album by The Whites

After Martyn's death Janice, Sarah, our dog Arthur and I moved into a beautiful old log cabin in Madison Tennessee just north of Nashville. It was a magical place and I loved living there, but Janice didn't. She preferred something more modern but gave into my love for the place. And to add to our recent good fortunes from "Forever You" we were now expecting our first child.

Gib and I still had no management. We were courted by a few firms but nothing felt right. It seemed that nobody could replace Martyn. Meanwhile we had tour obligations to fill, so back on the road we went. In December of 1983 Gib and I had a concert date in Michigan with our old friend and former member of Paul Revere & The Raiders, Freddy Weller who was now a country star in his own right. I was a little nervous about going because I had taken classes with Janice so I could assist in our child's birth. However, we needed the money and the trip was only for a couple days. I would be back in plenty of time for the birth with some much-needed money in my pocket as well. Gib and I drove up to Michigan where we did a show with Freddy and Hee Haw TV star Gunilla Hutton. When we arrived to do the show, a horrible blizzard had slammed down all across the state. Roads were out as well as electricity in many small rural towns, but the show went on. Just before show time I received a call backstage. Janice had given birth to our new daughter Jennifer. I was in the clouds when I found out but also a little disappointed that I missed the birth. The audience gave me a standing ovation when I announced it during our show. Jen would be the 3rd child of mine born while I was on stage!

The next day the storm got worse but Gib and I drove through it to get back to Nashville and see the baby. Half way there we hit a white out and our car ran into a ditch. We managed to pull out and slowly but surely made it home. By the time we finally arrived back at the cabin Janice and the baby were already home. Our new baby girl Jennifer was as cute as a button with a little red curl of hair on the top of her head. What a ray of light she cast on such a dark time in our career. She came into our lives at the perfect time. I was so happy that a few days later I wrote a song about Jennifer. I wrote about how that special someone who comes into your life can turn things around in a positive way. Like an answer to a prayer.

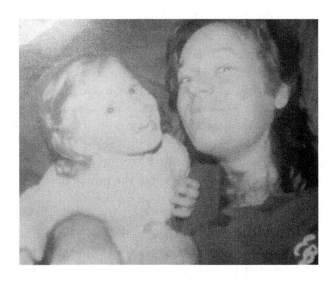

Jennifer

The song was called "Isn't It Amazing" and in time would become a major Gospel hit in 1987 for former Grand Funk Railroad lead singer Mark Farner.

> "Isn't it amazing what a prayer can do?
> When it all seems hopeless it will pull you thru
> Isn't it amazing how a broken heart grows strong
> When every now and then that special someone comes along."

Gib and I continued to talk to various management companies without success. In a way we felt as if we had been abandoned. With nobody at the helm we were helpless about dealing with the record labels and booking agents. Things were getting desperate. During all the confusion and uncertainty, Gib and I flew to London where we joined up with the annual International Country Festival promoted by Mervyn Conn. This was a huge package tour featuring many top country artists of the day such as George Jones, Ricky Skaggs, George Hamilton, Jerry Lee Lewis, Tammy Wynette, Box Car Willie, Little Jimmy Dickens and, the Burrito Brothers. We all traveled together performing in Germany, Denmark, Norway and ending at Wembley Stadium in London. It was tremendous exposure for us, at a time when we needed it badly. The UK country fans were a sight to see. Many came to the shows dressed up like Wyatt Earp, Bat Masterson or Davy Crockett. Some even sported six guns on their hips! We were even interviewed by an English journalist dressed in a loin cloth, Indian head dress and a spear! It was a great tour and the crowds were incredibly receptive, and for a while it took our minds off the problems we were facing back in Nashville. At Wembley, the show was broadcast live on BBC Television throughout the UK. It was a great shot for Gib and I and helped solidify us with country fans throughout Europe.

Touring with such a big line up of country stars gives you a real good look at the various personalities that the public never gets to see. For instance, at the time we did this tour throughout Europe, Boxcar Willie was known throughout North America not for any hit, but for his TV info telemarketing commercials. In the ads he came across as a jolly train hobo who sang fair versions of old Jimmy Rodgers train songs. He sold a ton of records and was one of the early pioneers of telemarketing for record albums. However, in Europe the country fans knew little about him. His act went over well but most audiences were confused over who this guy was and what he was doing on a tour with all these hit country artists.

After one particular show we did in Essen, Germany all the cast retired to the hotel bar where everyone could let their hair down and relax. Boxcar was there knocking drinks down like he was going to the gallows in the morning. He was quite funny and pleasant to be around when he was a bit tipsy, but in the morning well, that was another story and here's how it went.

Everyone was up very early because of the flight schedule. Each of us paid our additional hotel expenses such as phone, food etc. The lobby was full of acts paying their hotel bills and scrambling for a good seat on the bus to the airport. Suddenly there's a commotion at the front desk.

"Hell, what are all these goddamned extra charges?" bellowed out the familiar voice of the jolly telemarketing king Boxcar Willie.

The hotel receptionist was explaining the additional charges to Boxcar's room.

"I didn't take anything from the mini bar" he blurts out. "And I didn't watch any adult movies either!"

Everyone snickered under their breath because we knew damn well that nearly all of the musicians hit their mini bar and watched porn movies when they stumbled back to their rooms after a long night of getting hammered at the hotel bar! Furthermore, everyone knew that items in the room mini bars were marked up at least 90% more than the average item prices. A small bottle of cola from the mini bar could cost you as much as a bottle of wine at the hotel lounge. Most musicians tried to avoid going anywhere near the little refrigerator mini bar in their rooms. The clerk tried to be pleasant and understanding as an embarrassed Boxcar ranted and raved in his face. "I aint paying for no fucking movies I didn't watch! And I'm not paying for these room service bills either. I never ordered any goddamned room service!" The clerk calmly handed over a piece of paper to Boxcar.

"Sir, is this your signature on the room service receipt?"

More muffled laughter from the tour group. After a momentary silence Boxcar angrily dug through his pants and pulled out his wallet and then blurted out for all to hear. "I don't know how we fucking missed this building when we bombed your goddamned country." The muffled laughter now turned to silent disgust as everyone kept their distance from this redneck for the remainder of the tour.

Also on the tour was Gilley's house singer Johnny Lee whose record "Looking for Love" was a big hit in the USA thanks to it being featured in the smash hit movie starring John Travolta "Urban Cowboy." Gilley was an average country singer at best and though he was hot on US radio he was known more in Europe for being married to Dallas star Charlene Tilton. Dallas was a huge show abroad and fans followed each cast members career like religion. Night after night the fans in Europe would shout out to Johnny Lee "Where's Charlene?" and Lee would get very annoyed. Furthermore, his entourage of unknown musicians and singers from back at Gilley's were also obnoxious as hell when they got drunk, always trying to start a physical fight with someone in the hotel lounge after the show.

Lee and his buddies would stay up all night drinking and when we all settled into the bus the next morning he would go from seat to seat waking each cast member up saying "Hey Pard, are you asleep?" Nobody thought it was funny except Johnny Lee and his gang of Texas rednecks.

One morning someone on the bus gave Johnny a sleeping pill to shut him up. He ended up falling asleep in the bus aisle. When we arrived at the concert hall everyone on the bus walked over him. About a half an hour later Lee comes strutting in to the hall for a sound check.

"Man, I slept like a baby. Feel like a million bucks" he boasted. We all laughed because when he walked by we could see footprints all over his white satin Gilley's jacket.

As fun as the tour was, we knew what was waiting for us when we came home, still no management and mounting bills. We were also without a record deal. Our last single for Curb was a John Fogerty song called "It's Almost Saturday Night" and it was a great record, produced by my old friend and engineer from my 1973 solo album, Brent Maher. Brent was now a hot producer in Nashville with a new act he had just discovered consisting of a registered nurse and her daughter. They called themselves the Judds. I loved working with Brent, who I thought was the best producer we had ever had. He gave me total freedom in the studio and we made a great record together. Out of the box "It's Almost Saturday Night" started getting significant airplay, but eventually died. Curb records just didn't want to support the Burrito Brothers any longer and it was evident by the failure of our final single. Fortunately, we got our release from the label and went shopping for a new home.

Just when things were at an all-time low, luck finally turned our way when Leon Russell's manager Bobby Roberts called us about taking us on as clients. Leon had a new label called Paradise Records in Hendersonville, Tennessee just outside of Nashville. They had built a big complex of offices, video studios and a top flight recording studio. We met with Bobby and instantly liked him. Like Martyn, he was very personable and seemed to be a big fan of our music. We explained our dilemma. Bobby had read about Martyn's death and knew the spot we were now in. He offered us a management deal along with a record deal with Paradise and to make matters even better we could produce ourselves with no label interference. Finally!

Furthermore, Bobby signed me to a writer's deal with Leon's publishing company for a monthly cash draw which certainly eased some pressure on my home situation.

Leon Russell was an incredible talent who got his start as a session musician / songwriter like myself. His work with Joe Cocker, George Harrison, Bob Dylan, Eric Clapton still stands as some of the best rock and roll music ever made. I was a huge fan of his. That said, he was also extremely eccentric and that was a big handful for Bobby Roberts as far as "managing" an artist goes. Cash flow seemed to always be a problem for Bobby since when Leon would return from his tours he would immediately spend much of his road income for his farm before he would turn it over to the company, making it nearly impossible for Bobby to keep Paradise records functioning. Leon was a character. By this time, he barely resembled the thin long haired rocker with the top hat and American flag pants made so identifiable from his appearance at George Harrison's Concert For Bangladesh in the early 70's. By now, Leon appeared to be a tired short stocky old man, completely covered in long white hair and a long white beard. He could still belt out his trademark vocals and keyboard playing, but beyond that he seemed out of touch with the world around him. Nevertheless, his company was up and running and Gib and I began to make plans for yet another Burrito Brothers album with Bobby Roberts now onboard as our new manager.

I could sense that things were never going to be the same as they were when Martyn was alive as we had a solid team with him, Gib, myself and publisher Bo Golsen navigating the Burrito Brothers. Now it was just Gib and I and a lot of "trusting" involved. Furthermore, Gib and I were creatively drifting apart. The writing was on the wall but we were doing our best to not read it.

39 FOLLOWING THE ROAD AHEAD

For over two decades Gib and I had worked well together, creatively. We were also the best of friends. However, all the miles, concerts, recording and television had taken its toll on our working relationship. While Gib's musical tastes favored a more traditional style of country music, I was influenced by a more commercial country rock direction. I liked everything from Cheap Trick to Buck Owens and had recently been listening to artists like Marshal Crenshaw and Tom Petty. I felt a gap growing between Gib and I. I disagreed with his vision for the Burrito Brothers which seemed to favor bringing in outside songwriters such as his friend Max D Barnes or bringing his son Ronnie, now a young singer guitarist, into the act. We were a duo but now I felt others infiltrating our act and didn't like it.

For our Paradise debut album Gib turned up with a bunch of tunes co-written with his son and Max D Barnes. Max was a tremendous country hit songwriter but not for the Burritos in my opinion. We needed to get back to our southern California roots, not become another hack Nashville country act. We needed to write our own material. We each were hit writers and it made no sense to me that we should have to co-write with anyone other than ourselves. We were losing our identity. I felt that the legacy of the Burrito Brothers was that of a ground-breaking California country rock act and not as diluted mainstream fluff country artists. I had watched and listened to bands like the Nitty Gritty Dirt Band, Poco and Southern Pacific and admired how they made the transition from rock to mainstream country without sacrificing their integrity. I wanted that for us. However, Gib now had his new circle of established country writers and musicians around him, all filling his head with suggestions on what we should do to elevate our career. He even signed with Charlie Pride's publishing company as a staff writer. We had lost our way as an act.

Gib and I flew to Europe where we did some solo shows in Germany and Holland. We used outside musicians instead of bringing our band. This proved to be very hard. In fact, I felt like I was back with Johnny Tillotson jumping from one house band to another. Back home we did the same. Out on the road we went using a series of house bands and it was disaster. Although the crowds were still relatively good, we sounded like shit. Gib would forget words onstage while I tried my best to keep the local band behind us on track. I was starting to feel bitter and fed up with the Burrito Brothers. For me it was over but I held out a little longer in order to see what developed for us at Paradise Records and the new album.

We recorded at Paradise's new studio just upstairs from the business offices in Hendersonville. It was a great studio with state of the art gear and top-flight engineers. For the sessions I handled most of the organizing and hired legendary drummer Roger Hawkins, top bassist Glen Worf, session ace Fred Newell on 2nd guitar. For background harmonies I was able to get the famed Jordanairs, Elvis's legendary vocal group, to guest on one of the songs. I wasn't thrilled by the material we had to work with, and that included some of my own songs. However, we managed to make a good album despite ourselves.

But trouble kept finding us. After I had produced a full on-string session for three of our songs I was told that there was no money to pay the players. Furthermore, it looked as if Paradise Records would fold. So much for our association with the legendary Leon Russell. Sadly, once again another Burrito Brothers album would never see the light of day. Before anything began it ended. Once more we were on the street without a deal. Bobby Roberts gave us a release and again we were without management.

While Gib and I decided on what to do next I took a gig playing guitar for LA singer Nicolette Larson who scored a national hit with the Neil Young song "Gonna take A Lot Of Love." She reminded me of Linda Ronstadt, sexy, great vocal chops and had an edge to her personality. And I loved her new country album which just came out. The songs were solid and Tony Brown's production was excellent. Nicolette was good friends with Linda and the rest of the LA crowd. She was another pop singer also making the transition into country and it looked to me as if she might just have a shot doing it. Onstage she was terrific in the same way Linda was. She could belt out a song and drive the boys wild with her sexy floor length curly brown hair and beautiful looks. She put together a terrific band consisting of myself and monster Telecaster player Ray Flack, formally with Ricky Skaggs. On drums was Harry Stinson, a fabulous player / vocalist and on harmonies session singer Jim Photoglow. The band smoked.

We did a series of shows up and down the east coast. The best was in Miami where former Byrd Roger McGuinn got onstage for a rocking version of "So You Want To Be A Rock and Roll Star?" Another fun time was at a gig we did in Myrtle Beach, South Carolina when Nicolette announced to the crowd that I had sung the theme for the Brady Bunch TV series. I was totally embarrassed and the crowd just went crazy stomping on the floor and chanting "sing it, sing it."

When I actually went up to the mic and sang the first line in the song the place erupted. Everyone had a big laugh except a mortified me.

I had a ball playing with Nicolette, more fun than I had with the Burrito Brothers and a lot more musically fulfilling as well. It was reminiscent of my days with Ricky, a great band, terrific guys and rocking shows. Unfortunately, Nicolette never connected with country radio. In a way I understood why. She was a bit threatening to the female audience with her sex appeal and attitude. I loved her music but personality wise she failed to be accepted by country fans. I was sad to learn of her death years later. She was a sweet girl and as talented as they come. I was proud to have worked with her.

Back in Nashville Gib and I were approached by the publishers Alan Jones and Butch Johnson whose publishing company and recording studio were based out of Muscle Shoals Alabama. Al and Butch were quite a pair. Al was a very heavy guy, weight wise, with a long black beard and a deep Darth Vader kind of voice. He was a former bass player who teamed up with his good friend and engineer, Butch Johnson, for Pink Flamingo Music. Al wanted to sign me as a staff writer and in return finance yet another album with Gib and I. "Big" Al and Butch were terrific guys and were also big fans of ours. We decided to give them a shot since we had little to lose.

The result was a a double album in Muscle Shoals called "Back To The Sweethearts Of The Rodeo" a concept I had come up with in hopes of bringing us back to our roots. We leaned more towards a country rock album in the tradition of the Byrds landmark LP "Sweethearts Of The Rodeo." For this one we recorded some old chestnuts like the Everly Brothers "Take A Message to Mary" and "Should We Tell Him." We also did songs by the Louvin Brothers and Buck Owens, as well as some newer material written by Gib and I. The concept was admirable but when we received the test pressing of the album I was shocked. It sounded like it had been recorded in a tin can. The final mastering job was shocking. The album was released on an Italian label called Appaloosa Records and received favorable reviews overseas. Here in the States we couldn't get a deal for it. It was time to pull the plug once and for all.

Back home in Nashville I made the call to Gib and told him I wanted out. Surprisingly, he felt the same way. I had given up so much for the Burrito Brothers both financially and creatively. Now I wanted to reclaim my career as a top session guitarist / songwriter. Gib and I parted as friends. I loved Gib like a brother and together we had traveled on an incredible musical journey but now the road had ended and we were free to pursue other directions without the curse of the Flying Burrito Brothers hanging over our heads like the Sword of Damocles. We performed one last time and that was an appearance on Ralph Emmory's Nashville Network show "Nashville Now." We were booked with Lynn Anderson and sang our last hit "I'm Drinking Canada Dry" but before we played, Ralph told the TV audience "This is a historic day because the Burrito Brothers will be no more after tonight's appearance as they are splitting up. Ladies and gentlemen for one last time please welcome John and Gib, the Burrito Brothers!"

Backed by the Nashville Now band, many of them our good friends, we sang our last number. When we finished singing the studio audience rose up and gave us a standing ovation. It was a nice way to go out. As it turned out, only one of us was leaving the Burrito Brothers. When we sat at the panel and Ralph asked what our separate plans for the future would be I answered that I would pursue a producing career along with songwriting and session work. But to my amazement, Gib blurted out that he was resuming the Flying Burrito Brothers but with a different line up! Ralph did a double take as I did, since the show was all about the Burrito Brothers calling it quits. Another reason why I was glad to get on with my own career.

In the weeks that followed I continued doing sessions but I was getting bored with the entire country music scene. I felt like I was far away from home and needed to get back to where I used to be. But one recording session I did will forever stand out.

My old writing mentor and dear friend Dewayne Blackwell had recently moved to Nashville from Los Angeles and was now the head writer at Motown's country division Jobete Music. Dewayne was one of the most successful writers in the business. His hits included "I'm Mr. Blue" for the Fleetwoods and "I'm Gonna Hire Me A Wino" for David Frizell. Dewayne's songs had been covered by everyone from the Everly Brothers to Andy Williams. He was my first paid session client when I was 18 years old and from that point on I had played on all of his song demos.

I was ecstatic he was now in town and we wasted no time in hooking up at his office on Music Row. When I arrived at Jobete Music I was warmly greeted by the round, jovial Dewayne Blackwell who was holding court with his demo singers. They were all very talented and could sing incredibly. Dewayne told me that he had just written a new song that he thought had hit potential. He picked up a guitar and proceeded to play it.

"Blame it all on my roots.
I showed up in boots and ruined your black-tie affair"
I thought this was going to be good as he proceeded to the smash chorus.
"Well I've got friends in low places
Where the whisky flows and the beer erases my blues away. And I feel ok"

Dewayne was right. This sounded like a smash.

We set up a demo session at a studio in Goodlettesville, Tennesse just outside of town called Wind Walker Studio. It was a simple 16 track demo studio with low rates.

For the date Dewayne hired myself on guitar as band leader, drummer Steve Turner and bassist Larry Paxton. But it was Dewayne's choice for vocalist I objected to. I liked the guy and he sang very well, but for this song, I felt he needed a much stronger singer to carry the demo.

Garth Brooks hadn't been in town long. He was new to the community but was starting to get some work as a demo singer around town. Dewayne loved him, but I felt he was ok. I liked Garth tremendously and had already recorded quite a few demos with he and his friend Trisha Yearwood. But I urged Dewayne to find someone else, someone stronger.

Dewayne kept saying "Garth is going to be a star, John. I'm telling you right here and now."

I caved in and the session, including Garth was booked. It was a terrible winter's night and the city was hit with a major snow storm when we started rehearsing an arrangement for "Friends In Low Places."

We needed a catchy intro and I tried a number of things, but in the end, I just started the song very simply strumming the first 4 chords myself, to paint a picture of this good ol' boy strumming away in his truck. I must admit that Garth sang the hell out of it and surprised me!

A few months later Garth got a record deal with Capital Records. We were all excited and congratulated him up and down. He was so humble and embarrassed which was so typical of this great guy. But inside I felt that he had a rough road to walk down. I even confided in Dewayne that I didn't think radio would play a country record by a guy named "Garth." Dewayne always answered with the same response. "Just wait, John."

Then a few months later I was watching the live telecast of the Grand Ol' Opry from my home when Roy Accuff introduced this "new kid" as a special guest. Garth walked out with his signature hat and shy looks and took to the mic. He stood there alone for what seemed like an eternity. I was glued to the screen. He then went into his new record "If Tomorrow Never Comes" and the place went insane. Suddenly, like a religious experience, a light went off in my brain and I yelled out "Dewayne was fucking right!"

I quickly ran to my office and fired off a fax to Garth that said: "Garth, caught you on the Opry. Man, you're gonna do it, hoss! Congratulations! Beland"

A week later a letter arrived at my home. It said:

"Dear Garth Brooks fan,
As Mr Brooks is extremely busy and can't get to every fan letter personally, we invite you to join the Garth Brooks fan Club for a $10.00 membership.
Garth.
Thanks you for your support"
And bla bla.

I was livid and fired another fax off to Garth's manager Bob Doyle telling him what I just received in the mail. A few days later a package arrived, It was in a long tube. I opened it and pulled out the contents. It was a large poster of Garth holding his guitar.....and it was signed:

"To John
Here's to the good old days when only you would play my songs.
Love ya, Garth."

That framed poster hangs in my studio today. Garth would become a massive star and "Friends in Low Places" would go on to become the biggest selling country record of all time.

One day in 1984 from out of the blue I received a call from none other than my old Rick Nelson bandmate Bobby Neal , who had faithfully been handling the lead guitar gig with Rick ever since I left in 1980.

"Hey John" came the unforgettable, jolly voice I had sorely missed. "Bobby Neal here. How the hell are ya?"

"Wow, Bobby" I answered "Man, how great to hear from you, bud. How's everyone, Rick, Clark, the gang"?

"We're all doing good JB" Bobby replied. "Listen, what are you doing these days?"

"Well, Bobby, not much. The Burrito Brothers split up and I'm looking around for something exciting. Might just move back to LA. Why"?
"Well, I'm leaving Rick. My dad's sick and my wife Phyllis wants me off the road and back home to Memphis. So, I told Rick I needed to quit. Right away you were mentioned and Rick asked me to call you. Want to come back?"

I was stunned. "Are you kidding? Of course, I want to! Tell Rick I'm in!"

"Great" Bobby shot back. "I know he's missed you and who better to take my place than you. Here's the deal. I'm on the road with Rick right now. We're going to finish off these Christmas Texas gigs. After New Year the band flies home and I'll be leaving. Can you start at the first of the year?"

"You bet I can!" I said.

"OK, JB" Bobby replied. "Somebody from the office will call you right after the New Year. Glad you can do it. Rick will be happy about it, that's for sure. Take care and I'll talk to you soon"

"OK Bobby" I replied. "Thanks, and take care out there, bud."

I jumped for joy and immediately told my wife Janice. We were thrilled! It meant we were moving back to California where we had longed to be for the past decade. I had missed playing for Rick and couldn't wait to rejoin him and the band once again. In the days that followed we called our friends and had them scout for houses for us in LA. I started boxing things up and felt as if the weight of the world had been lifted from my shoulders. We were going home.

It was early in the morning on New Year's Eve 1985 when the phone rang. "Who the hell is calling this early in the morning?" I said to my wife. I took the phone call in the living room.

"Hello?" I said, in a groggy voice.

"John, this is Ronnie Guilbeau" came the reply from Gib's son.

"Hey Ronnie, what's up?"

"Are you watching TV?" Ronnie asked in a serious tone.

"No, I was still asleep when you called" I answered.

"Turn on CNN" came his quick reply.

The crash that took Rick and the band

I turned on the TV and instantly saw the image of a plane crash, flames and smoke billowing out of the wreckage. Then I heard the news reporters explaining what had happened. At first, I didn't understand what they were talking about. Then it hit me. My legs gave out and I sunk to my knees as I watched in horror the reports coming in from Texas. Rick and the band were all dead when their plane crashed in a field somewhere northeast of Dallas in place called De Kalb, Texas. There were two survivors, the pilots. I was numb. My wife was crying and trying to console me but I didn't shed a tear. It was as if I had been dreaming. I knew that I would wake up soon.

The phone started ringing off the hook. Everyone was calling. The news called wanting to know my reaction. Family relations called wondering if I had been on the plane. I refused to speak to anyone. I couldn't cry. I couldn't do anything but sit there watching the film of the burning airplane being repeatedly shown over and over again every

10 minutes. There it was lying in a field on fire, and inside the bodies of some of my dearest friends, including Rick.

In the weeks that followed, I read the news reports, some with outlandish accusations on what caused the crash. Some blamed Rick and the band for freebasing onboard and that it caused a fire in the cabin. I knew that was bullshit. I never once saw Rick freebase, and I never once saw Rick ever do anything that would cause him to put those around him in danger or even do anything that would jeopardize a gig he was booked for that night. In time it would be proven that drugs had nothing to do with the fatal crash. A faulty heater ended up being the sole cause. I had handled Rick and Bobby's deaths pretty well for the first few weeks. Then one day I was alone at the house listening to the radio and one of the stations did a tribute to Rick, ending with Rick's last hit, the one I had worked so hard on with him back in 1979 "Dream Lover." When I heard it on the radio I fell apart and all the grief and sadness seemed to wash over me like a tidal wave. They were gone.

I never stopped to think about how I could have ended up on that same plane only a few weeks after the New Year. I probably would have done everything I could to convince Rick and his manager Greg McDonald to buy a couple custom tour buses and get rid of that damned plane. Why Greg allowed Rick to fly in that old aircraft I'll never know. Was it because he wanted it to appear that Rick was a big star like Elvis with his own personal plane? Or did he think that traveling in a bus was too country western for a rock and roll legend like Ricky Nelson? It turned out that the plane had a history of trouble so why did he allow Rick and the band to put their lives in jeopardy like that? It certainly was a poor management decision, a fatal one at that.

Since the gig with Rick was obviously not going to happen, I made the decision to stay in Nashville instead of returning to California. I took it as kind of a sign that my place was still in Music City and that there was more for me here than back in Hollywood. Hollywood as I remembered it was now long since over. The once familiar faces and the music we shared together had faded away with the passing trends. The studio scene I had once been part of had also changed, many of the old studios had closed and venues like the Troubadour were now catering to a heavier metal, punk audience. As much as I missed LA, I discovered that what I was really missing was the past, the memories. I now had a strong reputation in Nashville as a musician and as a songwriter and so I chose to stay and see what new horizons awaited me in country music. It was a wise choice because more adventures did await me in the years to come, but that's a whole other book.

The trains still roar through Hometown daily like they did when I stood there as a 13-year-old dreamer, borrowed guitar in hand, wondering what exotic destinations they were headed for. Now the world is so much smaller and access to anywhere and anything in the world is much more easily obtainable than it was in 1963. Do kids today still marvel in wonder when they look down those tracks like I did? Is there another kid like myself standing there with guitar in hand imagining what lies at the end of those rails?

When I look back at the amazing journey I've traveled on, I'm amazed at how fast the years have flown by. Names once so dominant in my career have since have faded with time, except for a handful.

But the echoes remain, reverberating over and over again, each time a familiar song plays on the radio whisking my memory away, back to another place, another time.

We were all so beautifully young, full of passion, courage and seemingly, bullet proof. Thoroughbreds at the starting gate. We were all aiming at the stars, a lasso in one hand a guitar in the other.

From a naive crazy dream conceived on a cheap Silvertone transistor radio beneath the covers of my bed back in our little house in Hometown, Illinois to center stage at Carnegie Hall or the Grand Ol' Opry, it's been a surreal journey. And though the price of that journey was costly at times, I could never complain. Because hell, after all is said in done, I always had the BEST SEAT IN THE HOUSE.

The End.

EPILOGUE

In 1989 my son Tyler John Beland was born. After having three girls I was pleasantly surprised when the doctor announced that this baby had "outdoor plumbing." Tyler has been a sheer joy in my life. Gentle, kind with a huge heart and an abundance of musical talent to match. I could never want more in life than his love.

Tyler Beland

But then there's more. In 2012, I found out that I had another son who was living in Bend, Oregon. He was a well-known local singer songwriter guitarist with a few CDs to his credit who had recently discovered that the guy he had been listening to on the radio while growing up was, in fact, his real dad. Ironically, he had been playing a Clarence White Martin guitar for most of his career and ironically, he looked exactly like my father at a young age. His name is Chris and like his brother Tyler has a huge heart and a wealth of talent. We hit it off immediately when we first met in person and musically we learned that we have the same tastes and abilities on the guitar as well as singing. It was amazing. Chris and his wonderful family, lovely wife Annie, my incredible grandkids Eli, Harmony and Jude are now part of my family. What an incredible blessing that fell from above. But hey, that's the story of my life, isn't it?

Chris Beland

GRATITUDE

A huge "thank you" to my dear Pauline who never stopped believing in me and sacrificed her own personal happiness so I could devote all the attention needed to seeing this project through. Took a lifetime to find you, but I did. I love you, Pauline.

To my road manager Doug Kelder for keeping me on track and looking out for me during the completion of this book.

Many people are responsible for my success. Here are the some of the most important.

Robert DeMars
Dexter Coughlin
Lois Fletcher
Dan Dalton
Larry Murray
Johnny Tillotson
Jimmy Bowen
Dewayne Blackwell
Bo Golsen
Linda Ronstadt
Dolly Parton
Brian Cadd
Kris Kristofferson
Kim Carnes
Arlo Guthrie
Rick Nelson
David & Howard Bellamy
Gib Guilbeau
Thad Maxwell
Martyn Smith
Dr. Simon Mills

A very special thanks to Bob Davant for keeping this book project alive.

> "Time it was and what a time it was.
> A time for innocence a time for confidences"
> Paul Simon "Old Friends".

ABOUT THE AUTHOR

John Edward Beland (born July 24, 1949) is an American songwriter, session guitarist, recording artist, producer and author. Beland's career as guitarist started out in Los Angeles in the late 1960's, playing sessions and local live gigs with Kris Kristofferson, as well as future Eagles members, Glenn Frey and Bernie Leadon. Beland's first major break came in 1970, playing lead guitar for a young Linda Ronstadt, and helping Ronstadt put together her first serious solo band, Swampwater. Along with fellow bandmates Gib Guilbeau, Thad Maxwell and Stan Pratt, Swampwater toured the country with Ronstadt, appearing with her on such notable television shows as The Johnny Cash Show. Swampwater recorded two landmark country rock albums for Starday King and RCA Records. The group was one of the first Los Angeles bands to record in Nashville, known for their smooth harmonies and Cajun rock style.

After working with Ronstadt, Beland became a much in-demand guitarist, engaged by such high-profile artists as Arlo Guthrie, Johnny Tillotson, Kris Kristofferson, The Bellamy Brothers, Mac Davis, Dolly Parton and The Flying Burrito Brothers. As a solo artist, Beland recorded for Ranwood Records, scoring a chart hit in 1969 called "Baby You Come Rolling Cross My Mind". Beland also became the last artist to sign with The Beatles' record company Apple Records in 1973. As a session guitarist, Beland recorded with many music business legends in the United States and internationally. For over twenty years, he was the creative force behind the pioneering country rock band from California, The Flying Burrito Brothers. Through his leadership, the group achieved nine hit country singles for Curb Records in the early 1980's. Beland was also instrumental in the comeback of rock and roll legend Rick Nelson in the late 1970's, arranging and playing on Nelson's last hit single "Dream Lover", as well as Nelson's much acclaimed album The Memphis Sessions. He also toured and appeared with him on Saturday Night Live in 1979.

Beland is an American Society of Composers, Authors and Publishers (ASCAP) award-winning songwriter, his tunes have been recorded by a wide variety of artists from pop, folk, gospel to country music.

John Beland

Enigami & Rednow Publishers, New York
ISBN: 1945674167
ISBN-13: 978-1945674167

Made in the USA
Monee, IL
19 December 2020

54365290R00193